Optimization of Variability in Software Product Lines

A Semi-Automatic Method for Visualization, Analysis, and Restructuring of Variability in Software Product Lines

Von der Fakultät
Informatik, Elektrotechnik und Informationstechnik
der Universität Stuttgart zur Erlangung der Würde eines
Doktors der Naturwissenschaften (Dr. rer. nat.)
genehmigte Abhandlung

Vorgelegt von

Dipl.-Inf. Felix Lösch

aus Stuttgart

Hauptberichter:	Prof. Dr. rer. nat. Erhard Plödereder
Mitberichter:	Prof. Dr. rer. nat. Rainer Koschke

Tag der mündlichen Prüfung: 17. Juli 2008

Institut für Softwaretechnologie der Universität Stuttgart

2008

Bibliografische Information der Deutschen Nationalbibliothek

Die Deutsche Nationalbibliothek verzeichnet diese Publikation in der
Deutschen Nationalbibliografie; detaillierte bibliografische Daten sind
im Internet über http://dnb.d-nb.de abrufbar.

ISBN 978-3-8325-2105-9

Logos Verlag Berlin GmbH
Comeniushof, Gubener Str. 47,
10243 Berlin
Tel.: +49 030 42 85 10 90
Fax: +49 030 42 85 10 92
INTERNET: http://www.logos-verlag.de

To Jie

Acknowledgments

This thesis is the result of my three year work as a doctoral researcher in the corporate research division of Robert Bosch GmbH in Schwieberdingen.

First of all, I would like to express my sincere gratitude to Prof. Dr. rer. nat. Erhard Plödereder, head of the programming languages and compilers department of the University of Stuttgart, for the supervision of this work. He provided me with valuable guidance, encouragement, and sound advice during the last three years. I am very grateful to Prof. Plödereder for taking his time for regular and extensive meetings despite his tight schedule. The insightful conversations with him were a great help during the development of the ideas in this thesis. Without his continual interest in my research and without many useful comments and suggestions about my work this thesis would not have been possible.

I also wish to express my appreciation to Prof. Dr. rer. nat. Rainer Koschke, head of the software engineering department of the University of Bremen, who assumed co-supervision of this work. I would like to thank him for the assessment of my thesis. His suggestions have helped to improve its quality.

I am very grateful to Robert Bosch GmbH for offering me the opportunity to work on my Ph.D. thesis. I would like to thank my colleagues of the systems engineering and software engineering departments for their support and numerous discussions.

My special thanks go to Dr. Dieter Lienert who provided valuable guidance and suggestions for planning and organizing my work. He always helped me to balance the industrial and academic interests in my work.

Several business units of Robert Bosch GmbH have contributed to this thesis by providing development data on their systems for case studies. I would especially like to thank Martin Herrmann, Helmut Wilhelm, Mirjam Steger, Dr. Lars Geyer, Georg Grütter, Sebastian Bovigny, Christoph Hammel, Dr. Wolfgang Fleisch, Dr. Uwe Biegert, Werner Aberle, Christian Tischer, Dr. Birgit Boss, Dr. Bernhard Feuchter, Diethard Löhr, and Markus König for their time, support, and feedback.

I would also like to thank Sa Li and Jelena Perunicic for their support in implementing the ideas of this thesis in practical tools.

Finally, I would like to thank my parents for all their encouragement and understanding throughout the three years. Without their enduring support the completion of this thesis would not have been possible. My personal gratitude goes to Jie for her patience, love, and understanding.

Abstract

The widespread use of the product line approach by companies developing software for a large customer base is motivated by significant improvements in time-to-market, productivity, and quality. However, these companies very often face the challenge of increasing degrees of complexity caused by the variability that needs to be provided by their product lines. At Bosch this complexity is the result of a large number of features and variants, e.g., modern Electronic Control Unit (ECU) software product lines provide more than 1.000 features. In theory more than several million variants can be configured from these software product lines. This huge amount of variability makes variability management and product derivation tasks extremely difficult.

One of the reasons for this high complexity is that due to continuous evolution of the product line a large number of new variable features and configuration parameters are introduced but at the same time obsolete variability is not removed. For example, from a product line component offering only 16 features it is theoretically possible to derive $2^{16} = 65.536$ variants. This example shows that even a small number of features results in a combinatorial explosion of variants. Clearly, methods are needed that ensure the minimum number of variable features needed to derive existing and future products from the product line.

In order to address this problem, we developed a semi-automatic method and process for variability optimization which is presented in this thesis. The overall goal of variability optimization is to document, to analyze and to simplify the provided variability of software product lines without affecting the configurability of the product line for existing and future products. The presented method consists of four main phases: variability documentation, prediction, analysis, and restructuring.

Core elements of the method are the usage of a mathematical method, called Formal Concept Analysis (FCA), for deriving a visual representation of the provided variability in software product lines as a basis for analysis and a set of restructuring strategies that can be used to minimize the number of variable features required to derive existing and planned future products. Furthermore, the powerful visual representation of variability can be used for a number of important tasks that are related to variability management and product derivation. For example, using the visual representation it is possible to automatically validate existing feature constraints or to derive potential new feature constraints. The effectiveness of our method is demonstrated by presenting two case studies of optimizing the variability of two large industrial software product lines.

Kurzfassung

Der umfassende Einsatz des Produktlinienansatzes in Unternehmen, die Software für eine Vielzahl von Kunden entwicklen, wird motiviert durch signifikante Verbesserungen der Produkteinführungszeiten, der Produktivität und der Qualität. Allerdings stehen diese Unternehmen sehr häufig vor der Herausforderung, die zunehmende Komplexität zu beherrschen, die durch die Variabilität in ihren Produktlinien verursacht wird. Bei Bosch ist diese Komplexität das Resultat einer großen Zahl von Features und Varianten. Beispielsweise bestehen Produktlinien für moderne elektronische Steuergeräte aus mehr als 1000 Features. Theoretisch lassen sich aus dieser Zahl von Features mehr als eine Milliarde Varianten ableiten. Dieser hohe Grad an Variabilität erschwert das Variabilitätsmanagement und die Produktableitung in zunehmendem Maße.

Eine der Ursachen hierfür ist, dass durch die kontinuierliche Evolution der Produktline eine große Anzahl neuer variabler Features und Konfigurationsparameter eingeführt werden, jedoch obsolete Variabilität nicht entfernt wird. Zum Beispiel ist es theoretisch möglich von einer Produktlinienkomponente, die nur 16 Features besitzt, $2^{16} = 65.536$ Varianten abzuleiten. Dieses Beispiel veranschaulicht, dass bereits eine kleine Anzahl an Features zu einer kombinatorischen Explosion der Varianten führt. Daher ist es dringend notwendig, Methoden zu entwickeln, welche die minimale Anzahl variabler Features garantieren, die zur Ableitung existierender und zukünftiger Produkte von der Produktlinie benötigt werden.

Um dieses Problem zu addressieren, wurde in dieser Arbeit eine semi-automatische Methode und ein Prozess zur Variabilitätsoptimierung entwickelt. Das Hauptziel der Methode ist, die vorhandene Variabilität zu vereinfachen ohne dabei die Konfigurierbarkeit der Produktlinie für bestehende und zukünftige Produkte einzuschränken. Die in dieser Arbeit vorgestellte Methode besteht hierbei aus vier Phasen: Dokumentation, Vorhersage, Analyse und Vereinfachung der Variabilität.

Hauptelemente der Methode sind die Verwendung des mathematischen Verfahrens Formale Begriffsanalyse (FCA) zur Herleitung einer Visualisierung der vorhandenen Variabilität in Form von Begriffsverbänden sowie eine Menge von Restrukturierungstransformationen zur Minimierung der Anzahl benötigter variabler Features für bestehende und zukünftige Produkte. Darüber hinaus kann diese Visualisierung für eine Vielzahl wichtiger Aufgaben des Variabilitätsmanagements und der Produktableitung eingesetzt werden. Beispielsweise lassen sich mit Hilfe der Visualisierung bereits bestehende Abhängigkeiten zwischen Features validieren sowie noch nicht bekannte potentielle Abhängigkeiten zwischen Features entdecken. Die Effektivität der in dieser Arbeit vorgestellten Methode zur Optimierung der Variabilität wurde in zwei Fallstudien nachgewiesen.

Contents

List of Tables

List of Figures

Chapter 1

Introduction

In this chapter, we describe the background promoting the application of software product lines and variability management. We begin with the presentation of the motivation and importance for variability evolution in general and variability optimization in particular. After that we elaborate on the research objectives and delimitations of this work. Finally, we give an overview of the outline of this work.

Overview. Section 1.1 explains the background of our work. The motivation and importance for variability maintenance and evolution in general and for variability optimization in particular are presented in Section 1.2. Section 1.3 describes the research objectives and delimitations of our work. This chapter is concluded by an outline of the following chapters of this work in Section 1.4.

1.1   Background

Several years ago embedded systems have been solely used for a small range of high-tech-products and production systems, but today these systems have become prevalent in almost every industry sector. Examples for embedded systems are electronic control units (ECUs) in cars, household appliances, cell phones, personal digital assistants, entertainment devices, as well as televisions and medical systems. Common for all of these systems is that their functionality, quality, and value is mainly driven by software. Therefore, these systems are often referred to as *software-intensive systems*.

Over the last decade, many organizations developing software-intensive systems have identified a conflict in their software development. On the one hand, the amount of software necessary for their products is constantly increasing. On the other hand, there is a constant pressure to increase the number of different products put out on the market in order to better serve various market segments. For many organizations, the only feasible way forward has been to adopt a *software product line approach*. This trend has been motivated by order-of-magnitude improvements in time to market, cost, productivity, and quality [CN01].

In a software product line, software products are developed in a two-stage process, i.e., a *domain engineering stage* and a concurrently running *application engineering stage*.

1

Domain engineering involves, amongst others, identifying commonalities and differences between a set of related products and implementing a set of shared software artifacts (e.g. components or classes) in such a way that the commonalities can be exploited economically, while at the same time the ability to vary the products is preserved. During application engineering individual products are derived from the product line, using a subset of the shared software artifacts.

Although the product line approach promises order-of-magnitude improvements in time to market, cost, productivity, quality, and other business drivers by effectively reusing common artifacts across a set of products, managing the variability required to facilitate differences of the product line artifacts (e.g. requirements, architectures, reusable components, and test-cases) has become the predominant challenge for many organizations developing software product lines.

Variability management encompasses the activities of introducing variability into software artifacts during domain engineering, explicitly representing variability in software artifacts throughout the lifecycle, and supporting the instantiations of variability [SJ04].

1.2 Motivation

Methods for managing variability during the initial development of software product lines and during the product derivation phase have been extensively discussed in the literature and are currently applied in industry [KCH$^+$90, SGB01, GB02, TH02a, TH02b, HK03, PS03, SDNB04a, SDNB04b, DGR07, SD07]. However, it is not sufficient to consider the development and product derivation phase of a product line alone. The evolution phase of a software product line, i.e., the time frame during which the product portfolio changes and during which the product line has to be adapted, is considerably longer than for a single product. Managing the provided variability of a software product line during this phase is vitally important for the future success of the software product line [DSNB04]. It needs to be addressed and treated in a systematic way. Otherwise the software product line will loose its ability to effectively exploit the similarity of its products [DSNB04]. However, the following observations from industry indicate that this is not yet the case:

- *Unsuitable methods used*: Managing variability during the evolution phase, i.e., variability maintenance and evolution, requires a different approach than variability management during the initial development of a software product line. The constant analysis and restructuring of the provided variability due to an evolving product portfolio rises to critical importance. Although there is a growing awareness of this issue in industrial organizations, methods to face this challenge have not yet been implemented [DSNB04].

- *Increasing amount of variability*: Despite the use of variability management methods during domain and application engineering, the amount of variability provided by the software product line in terms of variable features and variation points continues to rise unabated in most cases. This very often leads to high overhead costs for variability management and product derivation tasks. Currently no methods are applied to limit the increase and to minimize the amount of variability [STB+04, DSB04, TMKG07].

- *Insufficient decision basis*: Decisions in variability management in general and during variability maintenance and evolution in particular, have far-reaching effects on the current and the future scope of the product line and should therefore only be made after careful consideration of all available information. However, in most organizations the information needed to make these decisions is not available. As a consequence necessary maintenance on the provided variability of a software product line is not carried out [DSNB04, DSB04, RR03].

Due to these difficulties, organizations wish for a structured method for managing variability during the evolution phase of software product lines. This method should address the aforementioned challenges. In particular it should provide means to analyze the provided variability and its use in actual products in order to minimize the amount of variability that is required to derive the set of current and future products. We refer to these means as *variability optimization*.

1.3 Research Objectives and Delimitations

1.3.1 Research Objectives

The challenges of variability management in general and variability management during software product line evolution in particular have been described in the last section. The goal of this thesis is to provide an answer to these challenges. This goal can be formulated as an academic and as an industrial research objective:

- *Academic objective - Structure topic academically* The problem of variability management during software product line evolution, i.e., variability maintenance and optimization, has not been clearly defined yet. The objective is to define it, to position it in the context of variability management, to develop a structured method for solving it, and to evaluate the applicability, the appropriateness, and the utility of this method in several case studies.

- *Industrial objective - Provide decision support* Variability management during software product line evolution deals with analyzing the provided variability of a software product line and making changes if necessary to match variability required by the products to be derived from the product line. Currently this analysis is performed in an ad-hoc manner and necessary changes are typically only made if new variability is to be introduced [DSNB04]. Obsolete variability is not removed because of insufficient decision support. As a result the amount of variability provided by the product line is constantly increasing. Therefore, a method is to be provided that can be applied repeatedly to analyze the provided variability and to limit the amount of provided variability to the amount of variability which is actually required by the products. Using this method, the decision maker should be able to quantitatively analyze and visualize how the provided variability is used by current and future products in order to make informed decisions about the optimization of the provided variability. Such a method, which should also be automated to a large extent, is to be provided in this work.

These two general research objectives can be broken down into the following concrete research objectives:

1. To position variability management during software product line evolution in the context of software product line engineering in general and variability management in particular.

2. To describe a method for the analysis of the provided variability that provides the necessary support for making informed decisions about its optimization.

3. To present a process for variability optimization that shows how variability analysis can be used in practice to optimize the variability of the product line.

4. To specify and implement tools that support the variability optimization process.

5. To evaluate the applicability, the appropriateness, and the utility of variability optimization for the task of variability management during software product line evolution in several case studies.

1.3.2   Delimitations

The field of variability management in software product lines is a large field of research and affects all process phases of software product line engineering including the initial development of a software product line during domain engineering, the derivation of products during application engineering, and the maintenance and evolution of the software product line. In order to focus more closely on the research objectives stated above, we do not further develop the following aspects in this work:

- *Initial development of a software product line*: There is extensive coverage in the literature of methods how to deal with variability during the initial development of a software product line [KCH+90, SGB01, TH02a, TH02b]. It is therefore presumed in this thesis that some of these methods have been used to initially develop reusable generic assets providing variability that can be bound during the derivation of products from the product line.

- *Methods for product derivation*: Methods for deriving products from reusable variable assets during application engineering have also been described to a large extent in existing literature [GB02, HK03, PS03, SDNB04a, SDNB04b, SJ04, Dhu06, DGR07, SD07]. Since the focus of our work is on variability maintenance and optimization of an already existing software product line, we do not further develop these methods. However, we assume that one of these methods has been used to derive products from the product line.

1.4 Outline

The research objectives stated above are pursued in a structured way as shown in the outline in Figure 1.1.

In Chapter 1, the background promoting the application of a software product line approach is described. The motivation and importance for variability management in general and variability maintenance and evolution in particular are presented. The resulting research objectives and delimitations are stated.

Chapter 2 serves to present the fundamentals of software product line engineering that are the basis of this thesis. Challenges and problems of software product line engineering are discussed.

Chapter 3 describes the state of the art in variability management. Existing methods for variability management during domain engineering and during application engineering are presented.

In Chapter 4, we describe our method for variability analysis. This method includes the extraction and visualization of the variability currently provided by the product line and the actual use of variability in the products. This visualization serves as a basis for making informed decision about the maintenance and optimization of variability during software product line evolution.

Chapter 5 describes the preparation and implementation of variability restructuring for variability that has been realized using a SCM system.

In Chapter 6, we present our process for variability optimization, i.e., the systematic documentation, prediction, analysis, and restructuring of the provided variability of a software product line. Furthermore, we describe the tools supporting the process and the architecture of the tool chain.

In Chapter 7, we present two case studies that we conducted in order to evaluate and validate our method for variability analysis and optimization. The results of these case studies serve to assess the applicability, the appropriateness, and the utility of our method for the problem of variability maintenance and optimization.

In Chapter 8, we conclude by summarizing the main contributions of our work and give an outlook on future research avenues in the field of variability management during software product line evolution.

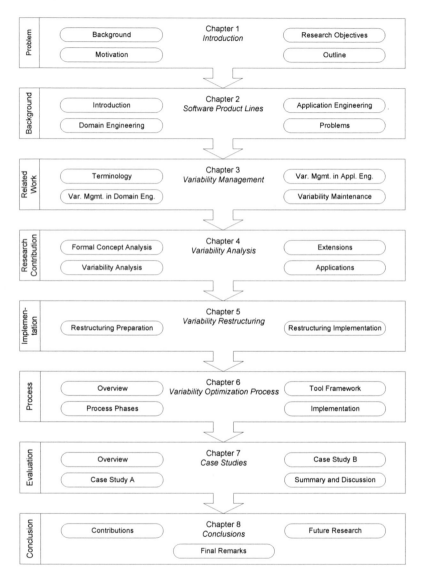

Figure 1.1: Outline.

In Appendix A, we describe general concepts of software configuration management (SCM) and the specific concepts of the SCM system ClearCase [Leb94]. We recommend readers who are not familiar with SCM concepts to read the Appendix before reading the Chapters 4 and 5.

Chapter 2

Software Product Lines

In this chapter, we describe the concept of software product lines, its terminology, as well as the software product line engineering process.

Overview. Section 2.1 gives a short introduction into software product lines, their history, and the two-stage process that is used for product line engineering. In Section 2.2, we describe the first phase of this process, i.e., domain engineering in detail. Section 2.3, presents the main steps of the second phase of the process, i.e., application engineering. In Section 2.4, we describe several problems and their causes in product line engineering. We conclude this chapter by a summary which is presented in Section 2.5.

2.1 Introduction

In the sixties of the last century a phenomena called "software crisis" appeared. Rapid increases in computer power made previously unthinkable applications theoretically possible. Software at this time could not follow the pace at which hardware evolved. This resulted in projects running over-budget and in low software quality. The causes of the software crisis were linked to the overall complexity of the software process and the relative immaturity of software engineering as a profession.

One of the reasons was that, compared to hardware, reuse of software artifacts in these days was limited. The emerging software engineering discipline started to think about how a system could be built from reusable parts [McI68]. The idea to develop so-called *program families* originated in 1976 when Parnas discovered that many problems of software reuse were related to the fact that traditional programming methods were intended for the development of single programs. He discovered that it might pay off to look not only at one problem at a time but to consider similar problems simultaneously. Parnas defines a *program family* as follows [Par76]:

> *We consider a set of programs to constitute a family, whenever it is worthwhile to study programs from the set by first studying the common properties and then determining the special properties of the individual family members.*

9

Since then the concept of program families evolved into practical approaches that promote reuse of core assets across related software products. Such approaches are often referred to as *software product family engineering* [Bos00, JRvdL00, vdL02] or *software product line engineering* [CN01, PBvdL05] and have received attention in both academia and industry since the early 1990s. The term *software product line*, as given in [CN01], is defined as:

> *A software product line is a set of software-intensive systems sharing a common, managed set of features that satisfy the specific needs of a particular market segment or mission and are developed from a common set of core assets in a prescribed way.*

The terms *product line* and *program family* are closely related, but have different meanings. The definition of a product line is based on a marketing strategy rather than technical similarities between its members as it is the case in Parnas' definition of program families. A *domain* encapsulates the knowledge needed to build the products of a program family or a product line. More precisely, program families and product lines constitute two different scoping strategies for domains.

The idea behind the software product line approach is that the initially high investments required to develop the reusable assets during domain engineering, are outweighed by the benefits in deriving individual products during application engineering [DSB05]. Although the initial investments for the development of a domain model, a product line architecture and reusable product line components are significantly higher than the investments required to develop a small number of individual products, there exists a point in time at which the cumulative costs for product line engineering are lower than for single systems engineering as shown in [WL99, KMB$^+$02, BCM$^+$04]. Figure 2.1 illustrates this fact. As one can see from this figure, initially the costs for single systems engineering (SSE) are lower than the costs for product line engineering (PLE). However, from a certain point on (in this example the break-even point is at three products), the costs for PLE will be much lower than for SSE due to savings in reusing already created artifacts.

In a software product line context, software products are developed in a two-stage process, i.e., a *domain engineering* stage ("engineering for reuse") and a concurrently running *application engineering* stage ("engineering with reuse"). This separation into two independent process stages is different from "traditional" process models like the waterfall model [Roy70], the spiral model [Boe88] or the Rational Unified Process [JBR99] in which there exists only one concurrently running process stage. The domain engineering stage comprises all activities to create reusable assets of the product line. During the application engineering stage individual products are derived from the product line using a subset of the previously created reusable assets.

In the following two sections, we will describe domain engineering and application engineering in more detail. This description includes the individual steps of each phase as well as the working products.

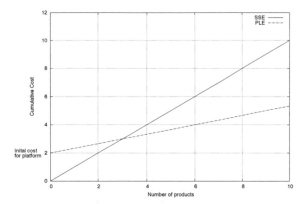

Figure 2.1: Single Systems Engineering (SSE) vs. Product Line Engineering (PLE)

2.2 Domain Engineering

According to Czarnecki and Eisenecker [CE00], domain engineering is

> ... *the activity of collecting, organizing, and storing past experience in build-ing systems or parts of systems in a particular domain in the form of reusable assets (i.e., reusable work products), as well as providing an adequate means for reusing these assets (i.e., retrieval, qualification, dissemination, adapta-tion, assembly, and so on) when building new systems.*

Domain engineering itself consists of the phases *domain analysis*, *domain design*, and *domain implementation*. Each of these phases has a strong relation to its corresponding phases in application engineering because the work products created during domain engineering phases are reused in corresponding application engineering phases. Figure 2.2 depicts this relation of domain and application engineering.

Compared to conventional software engineering that concentrates on satisfying requirements for a *single system*, domain engineering concentrates on providing *reusable* artifacts for a *family of systems* [CE00]. This involves, amongst others, identifying commonalities and differences between product line members and implementing a set of reusable software artifacts (e.g. components) in such a way that the commonalities can be exploited economically, while at the same time the ability to vary the products is preserved. Table 2.1 compares conventional software engineering and domain engineering based on their work products.

2.2.1 Domain Analysis

The term *domain analysis* was first defined by Neighbors in his Ph.D. work on Draco [Nei80] as *"the activity of identifying objects and operations of a class of similar systems*

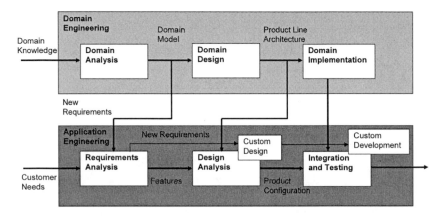

Figure 2.2: Relation of domain and application engineering (based on [CE00]).

Software Engineering	Domain Engineering
Requirements Analysis	*Domain Analysis*
Produces requirements for one system	Produces reusable, configurable requirements for a class of systems
System Design	*Domain Design*
Produces design of one system	Produces reusable design for a class of systems and a production plan
System Implementation	*Domain Implementation*
Produces system implementation	Produces reusable and configurable components, reuse infrastructure, and production process

Table 2.1: Comparison of conventional software engineering and domain engineering (taken from [CE00]).

in a particular problem domain". Thus, domain analysis is mainly concerned with defining the *problem domain*. The term *problem domain* describes similar but slightly different problems the products that are derived from the product line have to solve.

The goal of domain analysis is to select and define the domain of focus, i.e., the problem domain, and to collect the relevant information to integrate it into a coherent *domain model*. The sources of domain information include existing systems in the domain, domain experts, system handbooks, experiments, already known requirements on future systems, current or potential customers, market studies, technology forecasts, standards, and so on.

In order to be able to create a coherent model for a domain, the stakeholders have to agree on what the domain actually is. Therefore, the first activity of domain analysis is to define the *scope of the domain*, i.e., to define and characterize its contents by giving examples of existing systems in the domain, counterexamples (i.e., systems outside the domain), and generic rules of inclusion or exclusion (e.g. "Any system having the capability X belongs to the domain."). The scope of the domain is influenced by several factors, such as the stability and the maturity of the candidate areas to become parts of the domain, available resources for performing domain engineering, and the potential for reusing the domain engineering results within and outside an organization [CE00]. In order to meet the business objectives of the organization, *domain scoping* also involves a business and risk analysis, and the identification of stakeholders and their goals.

It is important to note, that the scope of a domain not only needs to be established, but also maintained afterwards. Typically, adaptation of the domain scope is necessary because of new business opportunities, market and technology trends, new insights during other activities of domain and application engineering, changing customer requirements, and several other factors. Interestingly enough, most of the existing approaches for domain engineering do not address the problem of adapting the scope during evolution of the product line.

The next activity in domain analysis is to create a *domain model*. A domain model is an explicit representation of the *commonalities*, i.e., the things that are common to all problems or subsets of them and the *variabilities*, i.e. the things that differentiate the problems in the domain. This information can be used to evaluate the scope definition with respect to the range of problems included. For example, if the number of commonalities is high and only a very small number of variabilities exists, the scope of the product line might be too small to justify the investments in domain engineering. If there are only a low number of commonalities the scope might be too wide, so that it will not be possible to effectively reuse large parts of the system.

In general, a domain model consists of a *domain definition* that defines the scope of the domain, a *domain dictionary* that defines the terms used in the domain, *concept models* that describe the common concepts in a domain in an appropriate modeling formalism, and the results of the commonality and variability analysis. The specific practices for eliciting and documenting relevant domain information very much depend on the chosen analysis processes and methods. Most methods use a graph-like notion to describe commonalities, variabilities, and their relation [KCH+90, KKL+98] but there also exist other possibilities to represent this kind of information such as lists [WL99] or tables [BFK+99].

2.2.2   Domain Design

The purpose of domain design is to develop a *product line architecture* for the set of products in the domain and to create a *production plan* using the domain model that has been created during domain analysis [CE00].

A *product line architecture* describes the structure of the product line using subsystems and components. Subsystems and components are typically specified in different views (e.g. logical, process, physical, and deployment view as described in [Kru95]) to show the relevant functional and non-functional properties of the product line. A strong product line architecture is considered as one of the key success factors of a product line [CN01]. Therefore, the goal of domain design is to come up with a flexible product line architecture that satisfies all important requirements and still leaves large degrees of freedom for the implementation. The product line architecture represents a reference architecture for the individual products that are derived from the product line. Therefore, a product line architecture not only has to include a description of the components but should also include an explicit representation of the variability, i.e., configurability it covers [CE00].

The second artifact to be developed during domain design is the *production plan*, which describes how concrete products will be derived from the product line [CE00]. The production plan describes the interface to the application engineers deriving concrete products, the process of assembling the components, the process of handling change requests and custom development, and the measuring, tracking, and optimizing of the production processes [CE00].

2.2.3   Domain Implementation

During domain implementation the product line architecture and the components are implemented using appropriate technologies [CE00]. Besides traditional technologies for the description of architectures, modularization techniques for source code (e.g. object-oriented programming), it is important to choose an appropriate *variability realization technique* to implement variable features in the source code. In Chapter 3, we provide a detailed description of these techniques.

Besides the implementation of the architecture and its components, the production plan needs to be implemented as well. This may require development of a reuse infrastructure, i.e., an infrastructure supporting component retrieval, qualification, dissemination, configuration and packaging of components for releases. Furthermore, if the production process should be automated, a mapping between features described in the domain model and the components of the product line architecture and their variation points has to be established.

2.3 Application Engineering

Application engineering is the process of building products using a subset of reusable assets (domain model, product line architecture, and product line components) created during domain engineering [CE00]. Thus, application engineering is a counterpart to domain engineering [Beu03].

The application engineering process usually consists of the phases *requirements analysis*, *product derivation*, and *integration and testing*. These phases are depicted in Figure 2.2. As the results of product derivation and integration and testing are very often not satisfactory after the first run, these phases can be iterated until the product is deemed to be ready.

2.3.1 Requirements Analysis

The first phase during application engineering is to identify and analyze the requirements for a new concrete product to be derived from the product line. During this analysis, we take advantage of the existing domain model and describe the product requirements directly in terms of features, i.e., reusable requirements from the domain model. Thus, the domain model helps the application engineer during requirements analysis as it already contains the relevant common and variable features for the given domain.

The analysis process can be supported by appropriate tools that allow to establish traceability links between requirements and features of the domain model. Usually there is a n-to-m relationship between features and requirements. This means that a particular requirement (e.g. a performance requirement) may apply to several features and that a particular feature may meet more than one requirement (e.g. a functional requirement and a number of quality requirements).

During requirements analysis new requirements may emerge which are not yet represented by features in the domain model. In that case, it is necessary to decide if these requirements should either be implemented by evolving the platform through additional features (*reactive evolution*) or by product specific features (*product-specific adaptation*) [DSB05]. This decision depends on the effort of implementing these features and the expected use of the features in other products. If the effort of implementing these features is low and these features are expected to be used in other products as well, it is advisable to extend the platform and make those features variable. However, if the effort is high and these features are expected to be only used in this specific product, the effort for implementing these features in the platform does not pay off and these features should rather be implemented separately for each product. The latter leads to *custom design* and *custom development* as shown in Figure 2.2.

2.3.2 Product Derivation

The second phase during application engineering is called *product derivation*. During this phase a concrete product is assembled out of the reusable assets created during domain implementation. These assets are selected based on the list of identified features during the first step of application engineering. We can distinguish between three automation levels of the product derivation process [Coh99]:

- *Manual product derivation*: The list of selected features is manually mapped to product line components implementing these features. Products are assembled from components manually.

- *Automated product derivation support*: The product derivation process is supported by various tools including configuration management, component browsing and search tools that help the application engineer to assemble the components. The mapping of features to components however is still performed manually.

- *Automatic product derivation*: This is the most mature level, where a set of tools supports the process of automatically deriving a product by a given list of features. Typically these tools provide an automated mapping of high-level features to product line assets or component implementing these features. Furthermore, these tools include product derivation knowledge such as constraints and dependencies that have to be met for a given selection of features.

Depending on the existing automation level of product derivation in a particular organization, the individual steps for product derivation are performed either manually, semi-automated or fully automated. Independent on the level of automation, at least the following steps are performed:

1. *Feature Selection*: Based on the customer requirements the features for a product to be derived from the product line are selected. This process involves making decisions about optional and alternative features that are provided by the product line and observing constraints that may exist between features. Output of this step is a list of features for the product to be derived with all existing constraints resolved, i.e., if the features in this list require other features, these features have been included as well.

2. *Asset Selection and Configuration*: Based on the list of features suitable software entities (e.g. product line components) implementing these features are selected from a central repository and configured according to these features.

Thus, three important prerequisites for efficient product configuration are:

- A *feature model* consisting of mandatory, optional, and alternative features and feature constraints that model the variability at the specification level.

- An *asset model* consisting of software entities and variation points that model the variability at the realization level.

- A mapping between these two models that allows for tracing features to assets and variation points implementing them.

If these prerequisites are fully met, the product configuration process can be automated to a large extent. However, in most cases in practice this level of automation is not fully achieved due to missing prerequisites such as a complete feature model with all feature constraints, missing asset models of the implemented variability including dependencies, and a mapping of features to variation points or software entities implementing them. In these cases, the product configuration process is mostly performed manually, or if it is automated to some extent, errors that occur due to incompleteness and imprecision of the models still require manual intervention.

The output of the product derivation phase is a suitable list of software entities implementing the required features for a product. Ideally, this list can be directly used in the subsequent phase to integrate and test the product from the list of software entities. Existing variability in software entities should have been resolved at the end of the product derivation phase, i.e., the software entities should be free of variation points.

2.3.3 Adaptation

In the case that customer requirements cannot be fulfilled by reusing existing features that are provided by the platform, there exist the following two possibilities for accommodation [DSB05]:

Product-specific adaptation: The customer requirements are implemented in product specific artifacts (e.g. product architecture and product specific component implementations). To this purpose product line engineers use the shared artifacts provided by the platform as basis for further development or develop new artifacts from scratch. The disadvantage of product specific adaptation is that the implemented functionality is not incorporated in the shared artifacts. The product specific adaptation scenario is depicted in Figure 2.2 by the steps *Custom Design* and *Custom Implementation*.

Reactive evolution: The customer requirements that cannot be fulfilled by reusing existing features of the platform are implemented by adapting shared artifacts of the platform. This has the advantage that these features can be reused in subsequent products. However, reactive evolution increases the variability and the size of the platform. Therefore, one should decide carefully if the benefits of implementing a functionality in the platform outweigh the negative effects on increasing complexity and size of the platform.

2.3.4 Integration and Testing

During the last phase of the application engineering process, the application engineer integrates the product based on the list of software entities that has been created for the product during the product derivation phase and the adapted or newly created software entities during adaptation. Integration typically involves checking out software entities from software configuration management, compiling and linking them.

If these steps have been fully completed, the integrated, compiled, and linked product is tested in order to check if the product fulfills the customer requirements.

In the case that an error occurs during the integration and testing phase, the application engineer needs to check the selection and configuration of assets based on the list of selected features. After the error is found, the integration and testing phase needs to be performed again.

2.4   Problems in Product Line Engineering

The fundamental reason for investing in software product lines is the expected savings in time, effort, and cost during application engineering. However, several organizations that employ software product lines are becoming increasingly aware of the fact that, despite their high investments and efforts in domain engineering, deriving individual products from their shared software assets is a time and effort consuming activity [DSB04, DSB05].

Figure 2.3 illustrates this problem by comparing the actual cumulative costs for product line engineering (APLE) to the expected costs for product line engineering (EPLE) and the costs for single systems engineering (SSE). Figure 2.3 can be obtained by predicting the cumulative product line costs (EPLE) and by measuring the actual cumulative costs (APLE) using one of the economic models for software product lines described in [Coh03, BCM+04, CMC05, LJG05]. As one can see from this Figure, the actual costs (APLE) are higher than the expected costs (EPLE), although the initial investments for domain engineering are the same. The reason for this is that the product derivation costs for APLE are higher than for EPLE. As a consequence the break-even point for product line engineering is achieved later. In the example shown in Figure 2.3 product line engineering (APLE) only pays off if at least 8 products are derived from the product line. This number is higher than the expected break-even point for product line engineering (EPLE) which is 3 products.

In order to identify the problems, core issues, and underlying causes that are responsible for a time and effort consuming product derivation process, Deelstra *et al.* analyzed the product derivation process in several organizations [DSB04, DSB05]. Their case study was part of the first phase of ConIPF (Configuration in Industrial Product Families), a research project sponsored by the IST-programme. In this case study, the product line derivation processes of two business units of Robert Bosch GmbH and of one business unit of Thales were analyzed in detail. The analysis process was mainly guided by interviewing experts that are involved in product derivation, amongst others, system architects, software engineers and requirement engineers. The interviews were complemented by documentation provided by the two organizations.

The authors categorized the problems they observed after analyzing the interviews into three problem areas. These three areas are *knowledge externalization*, *variability management*, and *scoping and evolution*. In the following subsections, we describe the problems observed by the authors and their underlying causes in more detail. This description is based on [DSB05].

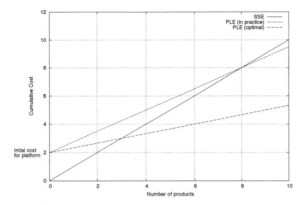

Figure 2.3: Comparison of actual costs for product line engineering (APLE) vs. expected costs for product line engineering (EPLE) and single systems engineering (SSE).

2.4.1 Knowledge Externalization

Organizations that employ software product line engineering use tacit, documented, and formalized knowledge to derive individual product line members from the shared software assets [DSB05]. The term *knowledge externalization* refers to the process of converting tacit knowledge into documented or formalized knowledge.

Observed Problems

Deelstra et al. [DSB05] identified the following problems in the context of knowledge externalization:

- *High workload of experts.* The experts involved during product derivation tend to experience a very high workload. On the one hand, the pressure on experts is sometimes experienced as negative by the experts themselves. On the other hand, other staff often mentioned the lack of accessibility of these experts.

- *Large number of human errors.* During product derivation a large number of human errors is made. This is not only caused by the large amount of variation points but mainly because of implicit dependencies between variation points.

- *Identical errors in successive projects.* Mistakes during product derivation that have been made in previous projects keep reoccurring in successive projects.

- *Missing traceability of relevant information.* Missing traceability of information that is of particular interest for deriving a specific product was identified as a problem.

Causes

Many of the observed problems are related to the lack of externalized, i.e., documented or formalized knowledge. Deelstra et al. [DSB05] identified the following causes for the observed problems:

- *Insufficient documentation.* Many of the errors during product derivation are caused by insufficient documentation. Implicit dependencies that are not documented and only exist in the heads of experts lead to errors during the derivation of a product and very often to identical errors in successive projects.

- *Irrelevant and voluminous documentation.* Although problems with documentation are usually associated with the lack of it, a large amount and irrelevance of documentation may cause problems such as traceability of relevant information.

- *Erosion of documentation.* Documentation has to be actively maintained in order to keep it useful. During the original development of software artifacts, the documentation can be correct, or at least intended to be correct. If in a later stage an artifact is changed, the documentation should also be changed accordingly. However, very often after artifacts are changed the documentation is not updated accordingly. As a consequence the documentation is becoming less and less useful because it does not correctly describe the implementation anymore.

2.4.2   Variability Management

The ability to derive various products from a software product line is referred to as variability. Variability in software product lines is realized through variation points that are introduced at various stages of the lifecycle of a software artifact, both during domain engineering and application engineering. During product derivation the variability that is present in the software artifacts is bound, i.e., for each variation point a suitable variant is selected. Managing the ability to handle the differences between products at the various phases of the lifecycle is referred to as variability management.

Observed Problems

Deelstra et al. [DSB05] identified the following problems in the context of variability management:

- *Unmanageable number of variation points.* Many organizations face the problem that their product line has a very high complexity in terms of the number of variation points. For example, a product line of industrial size can easily incorporate thousand variable features [STB+04]. This cognitive complexity causes the process of setting and selecting variants to become time consuming, error prone, and in some cases even unmanageable.

- *Consequences of variant selection unclear.* Software engineers often do not know all consequences of the choices they make in the derivation process. Sometimes, in later phases of product derivation, earlier selected variants complicate the product derivation process because these earlier choices have negative effects.

- *Variability negatively affects testability.* The large number of variation points and variants makes it virtually impossible to test all combinations during development. As a consequence, shared product line assets are only tested for a small number of configurations and not for all possible configurations.

- *Non-optimal realization of variability.* The number of different variability realization techniques used by organizations is often very limited and not always suited well for the problem at hand.

- *No uniform treatment of variation points over the lifecycle.* Variation points at different lifecycle phases (e.g. domain analysis, domain design, domain implementation) are dealt with by different experts. As a consequence, there is a limited interaction between these experts and traceability between variation points in different lifecycle phases is very low. Therefore, variation points are treated only in the context of the respective lifecycle phases.

Causes

Many of the problems associated with managing variability are related to the realization of variation points in shared software artifacts and their usage. Deelstra et al. [DSB05] identified the following causes for the observed problems in variability management.

- *Lack of first-class and formal representation of variation points and dependencies.* The lack of first-class and formal representation of variation points and dependencies makes it hard to assess the impact of selections during product derivation and of changes during evolution, as it is unclear how variability in requirements (e.g. features) are realized in the implementation. If formalized, first-class representations of variation points and dependencies enable tool support that may significantly reduce costs and increase efficiency of product derivation and evolution.

- *Variation points not organized hierarchically.* One of the reasons why the large number of variation points and variants is a problem, is the fact that very often variation points are not organized in a hierarchical fashion (as for example employed in feature diagrams [KCH+90]). As a consequence, during product derivation, application engineers are required to deal with many variation points that are either not at all relevant for the product that is currently being derived, or that refer to the selection of the same higher level variant.

- *Variability realization.* The realization of variability, i.e., the technique used to implement variation points and variants, typically has a large impact on the performance and flexibility of shared software assets. Therefore, a well considered choice should be made when a technique for variability realization is selected, based on a number of different aspects such as the size of involved software entities, when the variability should be introduced and when it needs to be bound to a particular variant. In practice, however the number of different variability realization techniques used is often very limited and not always best suited for the problem at hand. The reasons for this are:

– Software architects often do not know the advantages and disadvantages of certain variability realization techniques. Very often they only choose variability realization techniques they know [BFG+01].

– The available choices for variability realization techniques may be limited by the technology that is used. For example, the programming language C does not allow to implement variability using inheritance or polymorphism.

– Customer requirements may require a certain variability realization technique to be used, whereas this technique is not recommended from a technology point of view.

Although the selection of only a few techniques for realizing variability simplifies design and implementation, disregarding other choices may lead to problems regarding the understandability, complexity, maintainability, and evolution of variability in software product lines. This problem is increased by the fact that an optimal choice of the variability realization technique very often depends on the concrete properties of the variation point that should be implemented.

2.4.3 Scoping and Evolution

The last problem area that has been identified by Deelstra et. al [DSB05] is *scoping and evolution*. Managing the provided variability of a software product line during this phase is vitally important for the future success of the software product line [DSNB04]. It needs to be addressed and treated in a systematic way otherwise the software product line will loose its ability to effectively exploit the similarity of its products [DSNB04].

Observed Problems

Deelstra et al. [DSB05] observed the following problems:

• *Repetition of development.* The organizations identified that, despite their reuse efforts, development effort is spent on implementing functionality that highly resembles functionality already implemented in reusable assets or in previous projects.

• *Non-optimal scoping during product derivation.* During product derivation, it often turns out that new features are required for the product being derived. The interviews showed that it is difficult to decide whether a new feature should be implemented product specifically (no additional variation points and variants) or whether it should be part of the shared artifacts (possible reuse). Furthermore, it turned out that in most cases no explicit scoping activity existed that continuously interacted with product derivation. Due to this problem non-optimal scoping decisions are made for a considerable amount of functionality. This either results in more variation points and variants than actually needed or in repetition of development in different projects.

- *Obsolete variability not removed.* Changes in the domain during evolution may cause variability and variation points to become obsolete. An obsolete variation point is a variation point for which in each derived product the same variant is chosen, or in case of an optional variant, not used anymore. Often these obsolete variation points are not removed and keep being visible in the derivation process. These obsolete variation points contribute to the problem of cognitive complexity.

Causes

According to Deeelstra et al. [DSB05], the main causes for the observed problems are related to three types of evolution, namely *product specific adaptation*, *reactive evolution*, and *proactive evolution*.

- *Product specific adaptation versus reactive evolution.* During product derivation, changes can be handled by product specific adaptation or reactive evolution. Both types of evolution have their advantages and disadvantages, which are discussed below:

  - *Product specific adaptation.* The first approach, i.e., handling changes through product specific adaptation, has the advantage that the cognitive complexity of the product line is not increased because no additional variation points are introduced in the platform. Furthermore, product specific changes are generally cheaper and less time consuming than reactively evolving shared product line assets. However, product specific changes cannot be reused unless an old product configuration is copied and adapted. Furthermore, product specific changes may lead to repetition of development in subsequent projects because these projects are not aware of the functionality that is already implemented.

  - *Reactive evolution.* The second approach, i.e., handling changes through reactive evolution, has the advantage of making these changes available for all subsequent products, thus improving reuse and decreasing overall cost for implementing common functionality. However, a disadvantage of reactive evolution is that the changes are potentially more expensive than actually needed for the product under derivation. Furthermore, functionality that is implemented in shared assets but not reused in other products unnecessarily increases the cognitive complexity of the product line.

- *Proactive evolution* Another cause for the observed problems is proactive evolution, i.e., the evolution of the reusable assets without exact knowledge of the requirements of the products that are to be derived from the product line. In fear of missing important variability that is required to derive a set of specific future products, the platform engineers tend to implement more variability and more variation points than are actually required. Very often these variation points are not evaluated with respect to their actual use in products. This leads to the existence of obsolete variation points, i.e., variation points for which in each derived product the same variant is chosen, or in the case of optional variants, they are not used anymore. Often these obsolete variation points are left intact because it is not fully clear whether they are needed or not.

2.5   Summary

The initial contribution of the software product line approach is to promote the reuse of core assets across a set of related software products in order to save time and cost in building these products. The basic idea behind this approach is that the initially high investments required to develop reusable assets during domain engineering, are outweighed by the benefits in deriving individual products during application engineering.

However, as we have seen in this chapter, there exist several problems in product line engineering that make the derivation of products from reusable assets a time consuming and error prone task despite the high investments made in domain engineering. In our opinion, the high amount of variability and the changing scope of the software product line due to evolution are the main causes for this problem. As you will see in the next chapter, these issues are currently not addressed in the state of the art in variability management which mainly focuses on variability management during domain engineering and application engineering. Therefore, we address these issues in our thesis by presenting a method for variability analysis and optimization.

Chapter 3

Variability Management - State of the Art

Variability management *"encompasses the activities of introducing variability into software artifacts during domain engineering, explicitly representing variability in software artifacts throughout the lifecycle, managing dependencies among different variabilities, and supporting the instantiations of variability during application engineering"* [SJ04]. We argue that variability management also includes the maintenance and evolution of variability. This is shown in Figure 3.1.

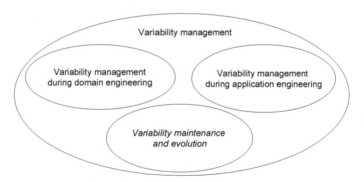

Figure 3.1: Relevant fields of variability management.

These three fields are required for effectively managing the variability during the lifecycle of the software product line. They have a great influence on its success. An understanding of these three fields is required for the following chapters of this thesis.

Overview. In Section 3.1, we present the terminology of variability that is used throughout this thesis. In Section 3.2, we describe methods for managing variability during domain engineering. This includes techniques for variability modeling and variability realization. Section 3.3 presents the most important techniques for managing variability during application engineering. In Section 3.4, we give an overview of existing literature on variability maintenance and evolution. We conclude this chapter by presenting a summary and discussion of the state of the art in variability management.

3.1 Terminology

When reading about variability in general and variability management in particular, there still seems to be some amount of confusion how different terms should be defined and interpreted. To avoid confusion, we present a list of terms and concepts in this section that we use throughout this thesis. This is provided to give the reader the necessary background information to understand the subsequent chapters of this thesis.

3.1.1 Variability

Variability is defined as *"the ability of a software system or artifact to be configured, customized, extended, or changed for use in a specific context"* [SDNB04a]. In a broader sense, the term *variability* refers to *"the whole area of how to manage the parts of a software development process and its resulting artifacts that are made to differ between products"* [SGB01].

Variability is concerned with many topics, ranging from the development process itself to the various artifacts created during development, such as requirements specifications, design documents, architecture descriptions, source code, test cases, calibration data, and executable binaries [SGB01]. Variability in software artifacts is typically associated with *features*, *variation points*, *variability mechanisms*, and *variability constraints*.

3.1.2 Feature

There exist many definitions for the term *feature*. The following definitions of the term *feature* can be found in literature:

- An end-user-visible characteristic of a system [KCH+90].

- A distinguishable characteristic of a concept that is relevant to some stakeholder of the concept [SCK+96].

- A logical unit of behavior that is specified by a set of functional and quality requirements [Bos00].

- A realized functional or non-functional requirement of a system [EKS03].

- An observable behavior of the system that can be triggered by the user [EKS03].

These definitions look at the term *feature* from different viewpoints. We argue that all of these definitions accurately describe the term feature. However, in this thesis, we look at the term *feature* from the following two viewpoints:

1. As a logical unit of behavior that is specified by a set of functional and quality requirements [Bos00], i.e., features in this sense are an abstraction from requirements. This is the viewpoint during domain analysis.

2. As a realized functional or non-functional requirement of a system [EKS03], i.e., features in this sense are represented by components, software modules, or source code lines in the implementation. This is the viewpoint during domain design and domain implementation.

To distinguish these two different viewpoints, people use the term *abstract feature* when they refer to a feature as an abstraction from requirements, and the term *implemented feature* when they refer to features as realized functional or non-functional requirements. However, very often this distinction is not made and the actual meaning of the term *feature* can only be inferred from the context in which it is used.

Another important aspect of features is that they are very often used to discuss the commonalities and variabilities between the products that should be derived from the product line. Consequently, a software product line must support *variability* for those features that differ from product to product. For example, a software product line for cell phones that should run on phones using different network frequencies should support variability for the features that implement the network communication in order to be configurable for the different network frequencies. This variability is expressed by *variable features*, i.e., *optional* or *alternative features* during domain analysis and by so called *variation points* during domain design and domain implementation. The mapping of variable features to variation points implementing them is typically performed during *variability design* and *variability implementation* (see Section 3.2.1 for details).

3.1.3 Variation Point

The term *variation point* was first introduced in [JGJ97] and identifies *"one or more locations at which variation will occur"*. In other words, a variation point is a location in a product line artifact (e.g. requirements specification, feature diagram, product line architecture, or source code) at which a choice is made as to which variant to use. If there is only one variant available the choice refers to whether this variant is included or not.

Variation points have been identified as the elements that facilitate systematic description of variability in variability models [KCH+90, Beu03, SDNB04a, SDNB04b], traceability throughout development [SDNB04a], assessment and evolution [DSNB04].

Although most literature about variation points has itself confined to code and design level, variation points occur in all phases of the development lifecycle. Variation points at lower abstraction levels, e.g., architecture and source code, are typically related to variation points at higher abstraction levels, e.g., an optional architectural component may realize an optional feature in the feature diagram. Usually, there is a $n-$to$-m$ relation between variation points at different abstraction levels. The concrete realization of high level variation points by lower level variation points depends on the chosen *variability realization technique* also referred to as *variability mechanism*, e.g., conditional compilation using preprocessor directives or permanent variants in software configuration management.

3.1.4 Variability Types

The term *variability types* [SGB01] refers to the different kinds of variabilities, as depicted in Figure 3.2.

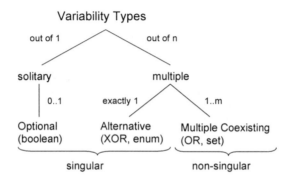

Figure 3.2: Variability Types.

In the simplest case, there is only one candidate (*out of 1*), which can be selected or not (*optional*). This kind of variability can be represented by a *boolean-type* of variation point. In the other cases more than one candidate exist (*out of n*):

1. Either, these candidates are mutually exclusive so that exactly one is selectable (*alternative*). This XOR-kind of variability can be represented by an *enumeration-type* of variation point, i.e., exactly 1 out of n candidates has to be selected.

2. Or, these candidates are not mutually exclusive so that one or more than one can be selected. This OR-kind of variability can be represented by a *set-type* of variation point, i.e., m out of n candidates can be selected. Thus, in the product multiple coexisting candidates of this set can be present.

Table 3.1 summarizes these variability types. In contrast to features that typically describe commonality by *mandatory* features and variability by *optional* and *alternative* features, the three types in Table 3.1 only refer to the variability of a software product line. Usually, they are used to describe the implemented variability of a software product line, i.e., variability that is expressed in terms of variable software entities or variation points.

Variability Type	Description	Selection
optional (boolean)	0..1 out of 1	singular
alternative (XOR)	1 out of n	singular
multiple coexisting (OR)	1..m out of n	multiple

Table 3.1: Variability types.

3.1.5 Variability Realization Technique

A *variability realization technique* also known as a *variability mechanism* is a means that can be used to implement variability. Typically, variability is first modeled using a *variability modeling technique* (see Section 3.2.2 for details) before it is implemented using a variability realization technique. There exist a large number of techniques that can be used for realizing variability in software product lines [SGB01, AG01]. In Section 3.2.3, we present a number of these techniques in more detail.

3.1.6 Variability Management

There exist multiple definitions for the term variability management. According to [SJ04], variability management *"encompasses the activities of introducing variability into software artifacts during domain engineering, explicitly representing variability in software artifacts throughout the lifecycle, managing dependencies among different variabilities, and supporting the instantiations of variability during application engineering"*.

Heina [Hei99] distinguishes between the following four different activities in variability management:

- *Variability generation*: If more utility can be created by providing more variety to the customers, additional variability may be introduced into the software product line. In doing so, one should strive to minimize the resulting complexity costs.

- *Variability prevention*: Potential new variability is analyzed in order to prevent unprofitable variability from entering the product line.

- *Variability handling*: This includes all measures that are taken to better handle the existing amount of variability, e.g., the introduction of a configurator to carry out product derivation more efficiently.

- *Variability reduction*: In variability reduction, existing variability is eliminated from the software product line with the intent of minimizing complexity costs.

Thus, variability management not only includes variability generation and prevention but also variability handling and reduction, i.e., variability maintenance and evolution. The focus of variability management on one or more of the different activities described above changes as a function of the lifecycle of the software product line. As one can see from Table 3.2, *variability generation* and *variability prevention* are in the focus of variability management during the development phase (domain engineering) and during the market phase (application engineering) whereas *variability handling* and *variability reduction* become the main focus of variability management during the market phase (application engineering) and during the evolution phase of the software product line.

Activity	Development Phase	Market Phase	Evolution Phase
Variability generation	X	X	
Variability prevention	X	X	
Variability handling		X	X
Variability reduction		X	X

Table 3.2: Focus of variability management on different activities during the software product line lifecycle [Hei99].

Interestingly, most literature focuses on variability generation during domain engineering [KCH+90, KKL+98, GFd98, CE00, CK05, AMS06, SGB01] and on variability handling during application engineering [Beu03, PS03, HK03, HKW+06, Kru02, AMS07, DGR07]. A small amount of research is devoted to variability prevention during initial development [CHW98, DS99]. Despite our observations in industry that clearly indicate a great demand for methods to reduce the amount of existing variability in a software product line, this problem has not yet been addressed in literature in a systematic and explicit way. Therefore, the focus of this thesis is to provide a method for variability optimization, i.e., the systematic analysis, visualization, and reduction of variability.

In the following Sections we describe the state of the art in variability management during domain and application engineering, before we discuss existing literature in variability maintenance and evolution in Section 3.4.

3.2   Variability Management in Domain Engineering

During the initial development of a software product line, variability needs to be managed in various phases during domain engineering to enable the product line assets to be configurable for a large number of products.

3.2.1   Process

In [SGB01], a generic process for variability management during domain engineering is presented. This process consists of the following phases:

1. Variability Identification

2. Variability Modeling

3. Variability Design

4. Variability Implementation

In the following, we describe each of these phases in more detail.

Variability Identification

Management of variability in software product lines usually starts with the *identification of the variability* required for the product line members. During this task, the requirements of all product line members are analyzed and classified into common and variable requirements. Typically, techniques for *domain analysis*, e.g., *scoping* and *commonality and variability analysis* [CHW98] are used for this task.

Variability Modeling

After the required variability has been identified it is modeled using a *variability modeling technique*. The goal of these techniques is to represent the variability in terms of choices that enable engineers to extend, change, customize, or configure product line artifacts for use in a specific context. Most of these techniques use the concept of *features* to model variability [KCH+90, KKL+98, KLD02, CK05], but there also exist other possibilities for representing variability such as *lists* [WL99] or *tables* [BFK+99, DS99]. We present some of these techniques in Section 3.2.2.

Variability Design

Once the variability of the software product line has been identified and modeled, it needs to be explicitly designed. According to Svahnberg et al. [SGB01] the first step of designing variability is to decide at which time in the development process the variability should be introduced. The next step is to decide when and how variants should be added to the product line. Finally, for each variation point a *binding time*, i.e., when a particular variant is selected for a variation point, should be chosen. Table 3.3 gives an overview of possible binding times for variation points.

After the variability has been identified, modeled, and the decisions for designing variability have been taken, the variability needs to be implemented. In general there is a $n-$to$-m$ relationship between features and software entities implementing them, i.e., a feature may be implemented by one or more software entities and one software entity may implement one or more features. In order to ensure traceability, the mapping of features to software entities implementing them should be documented.

Variability Implementation

Based on the variability design, a suitable realization technique can be selected for implementing the variability. However, the decisions taken for mapping features to software entities, for the introduction time, for the time of adding variants and for the binding time will influence the available choices for a suitable variability realization technique. In Section 3.2.3, we present a number of variability realization techniques.

Binding Time	Description
Configuration	The variation point is bound by generating or configuring an implementation where the variation is already removed. Typically, configuration management tools are involved in this process and most of the mechanisms are working with larger software entities introduced during architectural design.
Compilation	The compiler of an implementation language binds the variation point to a particular variant. This binding cannot be changed later. Examples are conditional compilation, parametric polymorphism, macros and aspects.
Linking	The time at which linking begins and ends depends on what programming and runtime environment is used. In some cases, linking means binding variation points directly after compilation, in other cases linking means binding variability at the start time. In other systems again, the running system can link and re-link at will.
Run time	The application can change the variation during run time. The collection of variants can be closed at runtime, i.e., it is not possible to add new variants, but it can also be open, in which it is possible to extend the system with new variants at runtime.

Table 3.3: Binding times for variability.

3.2.2 Variability Modeling Techniques

Over the past few years, a large number of methods and tools for variability modeling have been developed, e.g., FODA [KCH+90], FORM [KKL+98], FeatuRSEB [GFd98], Cardinality-Based Feature Modeling (CBFM) [CK05], Koalish/Forfamel [AMS06], van der Hoek et al. [vdH04], Gomaa and Webber [GS02, GW04], COVAMOF [SDNB04b], VSL [BGGB01], OVM [PBvdL05], DecisionKing [Dhu06], GEARS [Kru02], PureVariants [Beu03], ConIPF [HKW+06], Kumbang [AMS07], DOPLER [RDG06], Coplien et al. [CHW98], and Schmid et al. [SJ04].

These methods and tools aim at representing the variability in a software product line in an explicit way so that software engineers can handle variability during domain and application engineering more easily.

According to [Asi04], they can be classified into three different categories. The first category consists of methods based on *features*. As the SEI [CN01] defines a software product line as "a set of software-intensive systems sharing a common, managed set of features" features are a natural candidate for modeling variability in software product lines.

Furthermore, there exist a number of researchers that emphasize the role of a product line architecture for modeling variability. Therefore, *architecture-based methods* represent the second category.

Besides features and architecture, a number of researchers have developed *orthogonal approaches* to variability modeling which describe variability independently from features and architectural entities. This represents the third category.

Although our work mainly focuses on variability in terms of features at different abstraction levels, we will describe all three categories in the following to give the reader an overview of the different variability modeling approaches.

Feature-Based Methods

A number of feature-based variability modeling methods have been suggested [KCH+90, KKL+98, GFd98, CE00, CK05, AMS06]. All of these methods are based on the notion of a *feature model* which has been proposed by Kang et al. [KCH+90]. A feature model describes the common and variable features of a software product line. Individual products are distinguished from each other through the features they deliver. Feature models of industrial software product lines can be very large, consisting of hundreds or even thousands of features [FFB02, STB+04].

In the following we describe Feature-Oriented Domain Analysis (FODA) in detail. The other methods will only be presented briefly because most of these methods have been defined as an extension of FODA. Furthermore, FODA is the *de-facto* standard reference feature modeling method.

Feature-Oriented Domain Analysis (FODA)

Feature-Oriented Domain Analysis (FODA) is a domain analysis method based on identifying the prominent or distinctive features of a class of systems. FODA resulted from an in-depth study of other domain analysis approaches at the Software Engineering Institute (SEI) [KCH+90]. The method is known for the introduction of feature models and feature modeling. Later, FODA became a part of SEI Framework for Software Product Line Practice [SEI].

The FODA process consists of three phases. First, in *context analysis*, the goal is "to define the scope of a domain that is likely to yield useful domain products".

Feature modeling, or *analysis*, as it is called in the context of FODA, is part of the second phase, *domain modeling*, the other parts of domain modeling include *entity-relationship modeling*, and *functional analysis*. The purpose of entity-relationship modeling is to represent the domain knowledge in terms of domain entities and their relationships. The purpose of feature modeling is to capture the customer's or end user's understanding of the general capabilities or features of the class of systems in the domain.

The third phase of FODA is the *architecture modeling phase*. This phase provides a software "solution" to the problems defined in the domain modeling phase. The solution is an architectural model that is a high-level design of the applications in a domain. Additionally, this phase focuses on identifying concurrent processes and domain-oriented common modules. It defines the process for allocating the features, functions, and data objects defined in the domain models to the processes and modules. Although initially defined, this last phase of FODA is practically not used except in FORM [KKL+98] an extension of the FODA method.

The central element of the FODA method is the *feature model*. A *feature model* represents the common and the variable features of concept instances and the dependencies between the variable features [CE00]. A *feature* in FODA is defined as *an end-user-visible characteristic of a system*. A FODA feature model consists of *feature descriptions* and *feature diagrams*.

A *feature description* consists of a *feature definition* explaining the characteristics of the feature and a *rationale* that documents the reasons or trade-offs for choosing or not choosing a particular feature. Based on the purpose of a feature, FODA distinguishes between *context features* describing the usage patterns of an application, *representation features* describing how information is viewed by a user, and *operational features* describing the active functions carried out. Finally, FODA features are classified according to their binding time into *compile-time*, *activation-time*, and *runtime features* [KCH+90].

A *feature diagram* represents a hierarchical decomposition of features including the indication of whether or not a feature is *mandatory*, *alternative*, or *optional*. In general, a feature diagram is a tree in which the root represents the concept being described, the remaining nodes denote features and the edges between the features indicate whether they are optional, alternative or mandatory. FODA distinguishes between the following types of features:

1. *Mandatory features*: Mandatory features are features that must be included in every system.

2. *Optional features*: Optional features are features that may or may not be included in a system.

3. *Alternative features*: Alternative features describe a set of features from which one and only one alternative must be present in a system.

Table 3.4 explains the feature types and shows their representation in a feature diagram.

Type	Explanation	Representation
mandatory	Mandatory features f_2 and f_3 *must be included* in every product if the parent feature f_1 is included	
optional	Optional features f_2 and f_3 *may be included or not* in the product if the parent feature f_1 is included	
alternative	Alternative features are organized in alternative groups. If the parent feature f_1 is included in the product, then exactly one feature from the alternative group $\{f_2, f_3, f_4\}$ must be included	

Table 3.4: Types of FODA features and their representation in feature diagrams.

Figure 3.3 shows a simple feature diagram that will be used to illustrate the concepts of FODA. As you can see from Figure 3.3, our sample diagram contains *mandatory features*, e.g., all cars have a *brake*, *optional features*, e.g., a car may or may not have *air conditioning*, and *alternative features*, e.g., a car can only have an *automatic* or a *manual* transmission.

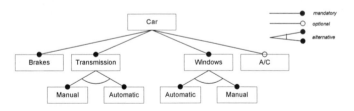

Figure 3.3: Example feature diagram showing features of a car (modified example from [KCH$^+$90]).

Feature dependencies or feature constraints are captured using *composition rules*. FODA describes two types of composition rules:

- *Requires rules*: Capture implications between features. For example, *"air conditioning* requires *automatic transmission"* [CE00].

- *Mutually-exclusive-with rules*: Capture constraints on feature combinations. An example of such a rule is *"manual transmission* is mutually-exclusive-with *automatic transmission"*. In our example, this rule is not needed because *manual* and *automatic* transmission are already marked as alternative features [CE00].

In FODA [KCH⁺90], feature models are mainly used for requirements engineering. The feature-oriented reuse method (FORM) [KKL⁺98] extends FODA to the software design phase and prescribes how the feature model is used to develop domain architectures and components for reuse. FORM distinguishes between a *feature space* containing the feature models and an *artifact space* containing descriptions of the product line architecture. During development a mapping between the feature space and the artifact space is established. Variability in FORM is expressed using features at the specification level and using architectural elements at the realization level. However, FORM is only semi-formal because it does neither include a formal description of variation points at the realization level nor a formal description of variability constraints.

Cardinality-based feature modeling (CBFM) [CK05] extends the original FODA notation [KCH⁺90] with a number of additional modeling concepts such as *feature cardinality*, *feature groups*, *feature attributes*, and *feature constraints*. In CBFM, features are hierarchically organized in a feature tree and each feature has a *feature cardinality* that specifies the number of times the feature may occur in one product, e.g., a cardinality of [0..1] specifies that a feature may be included not at all or once in a product. Features with the cardinality [1..1] are referred to as *mandatory*, whereas features with the cardinality [0..1] are called *optional*. Furthermore, features can be organized into *feature groups*, where each feature group has a *group cardinality*. The group cardinality denotes how many group members can be selected from the group, i.e., a group cardinality of [1..n] specifies that at least one and at most n features of the group can be selected. Another extension to the original FODA notation is that each feature can have a *feature attribute*, indicating that an attribute value can be specified during configuration. In addition to these extensions, CBFM also supports the formalization of feature constraints using the Object Constraint Language (OCL) [OMG03] or XPath [W3C05].

Architecture-Based Methods

Besides feature-based methods for modeling variability, a number of researchers have proposed approaches for modeling variability at the architectural level [DvdHT02, BGL⁺04, ASM04, vdH04, TH02a, TH02b]. These approaches have in common that they integrate variability into an existing architecture modeling language. In contrast to feature-based methods, the architecture-based methods describe variability in terms of components or interfaces between these components.

In [BGL⁺04] Bachmann and Bass describe a method for explicitly modeling and managing variability within software architectures. Their architectural description consists of *modules* that are connected by *depends-on* or *producer-consumer* relationships. They distinguish two main types of variability, namely *variability in architecture*, i.e., multiple alternative implementations of the same module, and *variability of relations*, i.e., different kinds of information exchanged between components. For the *variability in architecture*, they distinguish between four types of variability, namely *optional* (0..1 out of 1), *alternative* (1 out of n), *set of alternatives* (1..m out of n), *optional alternatives* (0..1 out of n), and *optional set of alternatives* (0..m out of n). For the description of variability in the architecture they use *variants*, i.e., placeholders for a set of different implementations of a software module. These different implementations are linked to their corresponding *variants* using *realization* relationships.

Koalish [ASM04] is a variability modeling method that enables variability modeling at the level of software product line architectures that are built using Koala [vOvdKM00]. Koala is a component model and architecture description language developed and used at Philips Consumer Electronics that uses *components* and *interfaces* to describe software product line architectures without variability. The component model describes what components exist and how these components are organized hierarchically. The interfaces specify how components interact with other components. For this purpose each component has a *required* and *provided* interface that specifies variables or methods that are imported from or exported to other components. Required and provided interfaces of different components are connected via *bindings*. Koalish extends Koala by providing so called *component types* that are instantiated as component instances. These component types can be used to model variability, i.e., optional and alternative Koala components. Similarly to Forfamel [AMS06], Koalish also allows to specify *constraints* concerning the combinations of architectural elements.

In [TH02a, TH02b] Thiel and Hein propose an extension to the IEEE P1471 recommended practice for architectural description. This extension includes *variation points* to model variability in the architectural description. Variation points in the architecture are characterized by specifying how and when a variation point applies. A variation point can be connected to the components that are affected by it using **arrows**. *Dependencies* between variation points can be modeled by connecting variation points with single lines in the architectural description. In order to map variation points in the architecture to features in the feature model, the variation points can be attached with *feature identifiers*.

Dashofy and van der Hoek [DvdHT02, vdH04] integrate concepts for variability modeling into the architecture description language xADL [DdHT01]. xADL is an extensible architecture description language that is built as a set of extensible XML schemas. In order to model product line architectures xADL has been extended by two new schemas, namely *options* and *variants* which provide facilities to model variability in xADL. The *options schema* allows elements in the architecture (e.g. components, connectors, and links) to be labeled as optional. Optional elements are accompanied by a *guard condition*. This condition is evaluated when the product line architecture is instantiated in a concrete product. If the condition is met, the optional element will be included in the product architecture, otherwise it is excluded. The *variants schema* allows the types of architectural elements to vary. In particular, it defines variant component and connector types. Variant types contain a set of possible alternatives. Like in the options schema, each variant type is accompanied by a guard condition. However, it is assumed that guard conditions for variant types are mutually exclusive.

Orthogonal Methods

A number of researchers have proposed orthogonal approaches to variability modeling which are independent from both feature and architectural descriptions. The main concept in these approaches is variability and thus *choices* or *decisions* and *constraints* are the first-class entities. Although these choices or decisions can refer to specific architectural entities or features, the choices and constraints in choice models are orthogonal to the structure of features and architectural entities. Choices are typically associated with a number of option entities of which zero or more can be selected for a product.

A prime example of such an approach is that proposed by Schmid and John [SJ04] which is independent from specific notations. In the approach, a *decision model* is used to represent the decisions needed to derive an individual member of the product line, and the dependencies between these decisions. In addition, the approach includes a mapping from the outcomes of the decisions into artifacts constituting the product line, i.e., the decisions are traced to variation points implementing these decision variables. The goal of modeling variability in a decision model is that the relevancies, selections, value ranges and constraints specified in a decision model must be obeyed by the set of value assignments during product derivation. This approach ensures that product configurations obeying the constraints are valid product configurations. Dhungana et al. [Dhu06, DRG+06, DRG07, DGR07] also use *decision models* for modeling variability independent of features and architectural elements.

Another example for orthogonal variability modeling is COVAMOF [SDNB04b] in which variation points and dependencies are used to model variability. Variation points in COVAMOF represent the locations at which a choice can be made and can appear at different abstraction levels, i.e., feature level, architecture level, or implementation level. This allows us to model variability uniformly across different abstraction levels. The mapping between different abstraction levels is achieved using *dependencies* that determine which variants or values at lower level variation points should be selected to realize the selection of variants or values at higher levels. A very similar approach is followed by Becker [Bec03, BGGB01] who explicitly interrelates variability at the specification and the realization level. In his approach, variabilities at the specification level are described using *variabilities*, *rationales* and *variants*. Variability at the realization level is described in terms of *variation points* and associated *variability mechanisms*. The relation between the two levels is explicitly modeled by linking variabilities to the variation points implementing them.

A major advantage of orthogonal methods for variability modeling is that they can be used to make variability explicit at all abstraction levels and development phases whereas feature-based methods and architecture-based methods are mainly focused to a single abstraction level or development phase.

3.2.3 Variability Realization Techniques

In this section, we present available techniques for variability realization in software product lines. In general, there exist a large number of techniques that can be used to realize variability in software product lines [SGB01, AG01]. Most likely, this section does not cover all available variability realization techniques, but we think that this section provides a good overview of the techniques that are most commonly used in industry. The techniques relevant for this thesis have been described in more detail than other techniques.

Preprocessor Directives

A *preprocessor* is a program that processes its input data to produce output that is used as input to another program. The output is said to be a *preprocessed* form of the input data, which is often used by subsequent programs like compilers. A common example is the preprocessing performed on source code before the next step of compilation.

Preprocessors can be classified into *lexical preprocessors, syntactic preprocessors*, and *general purpose preprocessors*.

Lexical preprocessors operate on the source code, prior to any parsing, by performing simple substitution of tokenized character sequences for other tokenized character sequences according to user-defined rules. The execution of the preprocessor is usually controlled by special commands called *preprocessor directives*. These preprocessor directives are not part of any programming language but have their own syntax.

The most widely used lexical preprocessor is CPP, the C preprocessor, used pervasively in C and its descendant, C++. This preprocessor performs the usual set of preprocessing services, namely *file inclusion* to insert the contents of a file into another file, *macro substitution* to replace instances of text with other defined pieces of text, and *conditional compilation* to evaluate conditions for deciding which sections of source code are included in the following compilation process. All these techniques can be used to realize variability in software product lines by separating the variant code from the common code. In the following we will describe each of these techniques in more detail.

File Inclusion. The most common use of CPP is the `#include` directive, which copies the full content of a file into the current file, at the point at which the directive occurs. These files usually contain interface definitions for various library functions and data types, which must be included before they can be used. Thus, the `#include` directive usually appears at the head of the file. The files so included are called *header files* for this reason. Variability can be achieved by providing different inclusion files, e.g., different headers which are generated for different execution platforms.

Macro Substitution. Macros are commonly used in C to define small snippets of code. During the preprocessing phase, each macro call is replaced, in-line, by the corresponding macro definition. If the macro has parameters, they are substituted into the macro body during expansion. Thus, a C macro can mimic a C function. The usual reason for doing this is to avoid the overhead of a function call in simple cases, where the code is lightweight enough that the function call overhead has a significant impact on performance. Similar to file inclusion, variability can be achieved by providing multiple implementations for a macro. Usually macros are defined in header files.

Conditional Compilation. The C preprocessor also offers conditional compilation. Conditional compilation enables control over the code segments to be included or excluded from program compilation. Directives mark the varying locations in the code [AG01]. Typically, conditional compilation is used to customize the program with respect to the compilation and execution platforms, the status (debugging code can be "defined out" in production code), as well as to ensure that header files are only included once.

Although conditional compilation is a very old variability realization technique, it is still widely used in industry especially for embedded systems. This has two reasons. First of all, embedded systems are often implemented in the C programming language. Thus, the CPP supporting conditional compilation is usually available. Second, other more advanced variability realization techniques such as inclusion polymorphism or parametric polymorphism are not supported by the C language and thus cannot be used.

Polymorphism

Another important variability realization technique is *polymorphism*. The word polymorphism is derived from the Greek language and means "the ability to have many forms". In computer science, it refers to the idea of allowing a single definition (variable, function) to be used with different types. As opposed to preprocessor-based techniques, polymorphism has direct programming language support, which simplifies the detection of programming errors.

Programming languages support polymorphism with many different mechanisms. The original definition of polymorphism by Strachey from 1967 distinguishes between *parametric* and *ad hoc polymorphism* [Str67]. *Parametric polymorphism* is obtained when a function works uniformly on a range of types; these types normally exhibit some common structure. *Ad-hoc polymorphism* is obtained when a function works, or appears to work, on several different types (which may not exhibit a common structure and may behave in unrelated ways for each type).

Cardelli and Wegner refined this definition in [CW85] as shown in Figure 3.4 by introducing a new form of polymorphism called *inclusion polymorphism* to model subtypes and inheritance in object-oriented languages. Parametric and inclusion polymorphism are classified as the two major subcategories of *universal polymorphism*, contrasted by *ad-hoc polymorphism* which contains *overloading* and *coercion*. The main differences between universal and ad-hoc polymorphism become clear if we look at universally polymorphic and ad-hoc polymorphic functions. Universally polymorphic functions will normally work on an *infinite number of types* (all the types having a given common structure) and will typically execute the *same code*, whereas ad-hoc polymorphic functions normally work on a *finite number of different and potentially unrelated types* and may execute *different code* for each type of argument.

Figure 3.4: Classification of polymorphism by Cardelli and Wegner [CW85].

All four types of polymorphism shown in Figure 3.4 can be used as a variability realization technique. In the following we will describe each of these types in more detail.

Parametric Polymorphism

In *parametric polymorphism*, a polymorphic function has an implicit or explicit type parameter which determines the type of the argument for each application of that function [CW85]. Suppose we want to write a function for squaring a number. The pseudo code for this function could look like this:

```
sqr(x)
return x * x
```

In a dynamically typed language, such as Smalltalk, this pseudo code can be typed in almost "as is":

```
sqr: x
  ^x * x
```

Thus, the type parameter that defines the type of variable x is *implicit*, i.e., it does not need to be statically defined.

However, if we want to implement this function in a statically typed language, we have to declare the type of variable x and the return type of the function, for example, in C++:

```
int sqr(int x)
{ return x * x; }
```

Thus, the type of variable x is *explicit*.

This latter implementation in C++, however, works only for x of type int, that is, it is more special than the pseudo code or the Smalltalk code, which work for any type of x including the operation "*". To overcome this limitation, many statically-typed programming languages such as Ada, C++, Eiffel, and Java provide mechanisms called *generics* or *templates*. Generics or templates refer to the ability to parameterize types (class templates) and functions (function templates) with types. Thus, these mechanisms implement the concept of parametric polymorphism.

In C++, we can implement the squaring function as a function template:

```
template <class T>
T sqr(T x)
{ return x * x; }
```

The idea is that the compiler will automatically generate an appropriate concrete function for each parameter type the function is called with, for example:

```
int a = 3;
double b = 5.0;
int aa = sqr(a); // sqr() for T = int
double bb = sqr(b); // sqr() for T = double
```

Using templates, the C++ implementation of the square function will work for any type of x that supports the operation "*", just as the Smalltalk implementation of the square function. However, there is a difference between these implementations. The C++ square template is statically type-checked and no runtime errors of the form "operation * not found" are possible, whereas the Smalltalk version is dynamically type-checked and a runtime error is possible if an object that does not provide "*" is passed to the function.

Parametric polymorphism in the form of generics or templates can be used to express variability. An example is a Stack class with a generically parameterized base type. This Stack class can be instantiated as a Stack of integer values, a Stack of any fundamental or used defined type, and even as a Stack of Stacks. In this example, the generic base type represents a variation point that can be bound to any fundamental or user-defined type. Thus, parametric polymorphism is a very flexible variability realization technique because it allows for the addition of an arbitrary number of new variants (types).

Inclusion Polymorphism

In *inclusion polymorphism*, an instance of a subtype can be manipulated by the same functions or methods that operate on the supertype [CW85]. Typically inclusion polymorphism corresponds to subtype polymorphism in object-oriented languages, that is, variables of a given type can also hold objects of its subtypes.

Subtype polymorphism is implemented in object-oriented languages by defining one abstract class or interface as a common point of access and several concrete subclasses for the implementation of the alternative behavior. Thus, subtype polymorphism is mainly used to implement XOR-kind of variability, i.e., having different implementations of the same method in multiple subclasses that can be accessed using the same interface provided by the abstract superclass. A typical example of subtype polymorphism is given by sets, bags, and tuples. A *set* has no repeated members and no order. A *bag* allows repetition but has no order. A *tuple* has repetition and order. Since *bag* and *tuple* are subtypes of *set*, they can all be referred to as type of set. For example, we can call the method *addElement* on an object that has the static type *set*. In a polymorphic language the call to this method will be dispatched to the correct method depending on the runtime type of the object, i.e., it will be dispatched to the addElement method of the set, bag, or tuple class.

Subtype polymorphism as a variability realization technique imposes two kinds of drawbacks concerning quality attributes. First, as subtype polymorphism is applied dynamically (its binding time is runtime), an extra level of indirection appears in the executable code, which has a negative performance impact. Second, and worse, subtype polymorphism restricts reusability [Bas96]. In contrast to generic implementations, it only allows to effectively add one kind of variability at the same time, for example by subclassing.

Overloading

Overloading is a feature found in various statically typed languages (e.g., C++ and Java; however, C and Pascal do not support user-defined overloading) that allows the creation of several functions with the same name which differ from each other in terms of the argument types and/or the return type [CE00]. Overloading on the return type is not supported in the C-family because a function can be called "just for its side effects" without actually using its return value.

Like parametric polymorphism, overloading is also a static variability realization technique, i.e., the variants will be bound at compile time.

Frame Technology

Paul Basset's Frame Technology [Bas96] provides the means to maximize code reusability through the definition and use of adaptable entities called *frames*. These frames can be assembled in a hierarchy to build a reuse library. Frames are source files equipped with preprocessor-like directives which allow parents (overlying frames) to copy and adapt children (underlying frames). A parent that wants to adapt a child must copy the complete code from the child. The adaptation is achieved in terms of (1) inserting or replacing code at predefined locations or (2) setting frame parameters.

Frame processing is performed at precompile-time, i.e., the frame processor translates the files with the frame-directives into ordinary source files that can be compiled.

Refinement Techniques

Recently emerging approaches combine several of the aforementioned polymorphism techniques with nesting techniques. In these post-object-oriented techniques, fragments of classes are encapsulated as components, instead of entire classes. Svahnberg et al. [SGB01] call these emerging techniques *refinements*. Refinements itself can be distinguished into *collaboration-based* and *aspect-oriented techniques*.

Collaboration-based techniques such as GenVoca [BST+94], Mixin Layers [SB98, SB02], and FOP [Bat03, ALRS05] have recently gained increased attention in the area of product lines and object-oriented frameworks. Whereas conventional object-oriented methods primarily view objects as instantiations of classes, in collaboration-based techniques collaborations of objects are emphasized in which the objects play certain roles. Classes are synthesized by composing the roles their instances play in different collaborations.

A second category of refinements comprises aspect-orientation, with several technologies like Aspect Oriented Programming (AOP) [KLM+97], Multi-Dimensional Separation of Concerns (MDSOC) [TOHS99], or Demeter/AP [LLM99]. Common to these techniques is the modularization of so called *crosscutting concerns* also called *aspects* which can be weaved into the normal code at multiple pre-defined locations called *joinpoints*. Examples of crosscutting functionality that can be handled with aspect-oriented methods are logging, synchronization and exception handling facilities. Aspect-oriented methods can be used for realizing variability in software product lines. For example it is possible to implement mandatory features as regular modules or classes in a system and optional features that crosscut the entire system as aspects. However, multiple options cannot easily be realized using aspects. For example, when logging is encapsulated as an aspect, some product line members may support logging. However, if the logging facility must be further enhanced in some products, the aspect code must be replicated and a new aspect version must be produced.

Software Configuration Management

A *software configuration management* (SCM) system is a repository that can be used to store multiple versions of software entities called *configuration items*. Depending on the intention of the creator, these versions of configuration items can be divided into *revisions* and *variants*. A *revision* typically represents a superseding version of the original version whereas a *variant* represents a coexisting *alternative* of the original version. A detailed description of software configuration management concepts is provided in Appendix A.

These variants are typically created to make the product configurable for different environments, i.e., they can be used to realize variability. This approach is widely used in industry to realize variability in software product lines. Its details will be explained in Chapter 5.

Static Libraries

A *static library* is a collection of object files containing functions, classes, or resources that an external program can use after being compiled to complement its functionality. The program and the library code will be linked together in a single executable and loaded at startup in the same memory space. The signatures of the functions are known to the compiled code and therefore must remain unchanged. However, the implementation of these functions can be changed by selecting different libraries during linking.

Thus, static libraries provide a technique for realizing variability. The latest binding time for static libraries is *link time* and the software entities involved are typically modules or set of modules.

Dynamic Libraries

A *dynamic library* is a collection of object files containing functions, classes, or resources that is loaded into an application program at runtime, rather than being linked in at link time, and remains as a separate file on disk. Only a minimal amount of work is done at link time. The linker records what library routines the program needs and the index names or numbers of the routines in the library. The majority of the work of linking is done at the time the application is loaded (load time) or during execution (runtime). The necessary linking code, called a *loader*, is actually part of the underlying operating system. At the appropriate time the loader finds the relevant libraries on disk and adds the relevant data from the libraries to the memory space of the program.

Like static libraries, dynamic libraries can be used for realizing variability by selecting different implementations for a library during load time or run time. The advantage over static libraries is that with dynamic libraries the behavior of the program can be changed during runtime. Thus, the latest binding time for dynamic libraries is *run time*.

Reflection

Reflection is the ability of a program to observe and manipulate its structure and behavior during its own execution. Generally, we can distinguish between ROM-reflection, i.e., the program only observes its structure and behavior, and RAM-reflection, i.e., the program not only observes but also modifies its structure and behavior.

In the case of RAM-reflection, this allows not only to bind new variants at runtime but also to create new variants at runtime. Contrary to the runtime type identification (RTTI) [Str86], the compiler of a reflective program does not need to know about the modules to be controlled at runtime.

Thus, reflection is the most flexible technique for realizing variability because base functionality can be "reflected" and manipulated according to a configuration which can also be generated at runtime (RAM-reflection). Nevertheless, reflective programs are from their nature difficult to understand, to debug and to maintain. Reflection as a variability realization technique is therefore only recommended for special systems and its use in other systems should be handled with care.

3.3 Variability Management in Application Engineering

Recently, a number of methods for variability management during application engineering have been proposed [Beu03, PS03, HK03, HKW+06, Kru02, AMS07, DGR07]. Compared to the techniques for variability management during domain engineering these methods not only support the creation and implementation of a variability model at the specification and realization level but also provide special support for the use of the variability model during the application engineering process, i.e., the task of making decisions for the choices and the effectuation of these decisions in the implemented product line artifacts. In the following we describe some of these methods in more detail.

Pure::Variants

PureVariants [PS03] is an integrated variability modeling and product derivation method which is based on the CONSUL approach [Beu03]. It provides four types of models, i.e., *feature models, family models, variant description models,* and *result models* which are depicted in Figure 3.5.

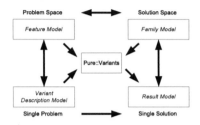

Figure 3.5: Variability models in Pure::Variants (based on [PS03])

All of these models have a similar structure. They are based on typed *elements* that may have *attributes*. Furthermore, elements can have directed *1:n relations* to other elements, such as, *requires, requiredFor, conflicts, recommends,* or *discourages.* In addition to relations, the availability of elements in configurations may be limited by so called *restrictions,* e.g., *hasFeature(x).* Restrictions are described using a logic expression syntax closely related to OCL notation [OMG03]. The evaluation of restrictions is done using Prolog.

Feature Models. Feature models in PureVariants describe the variability of the problem space in terms of FODA-like features with feature elements and attributes. PureVariants supports four types of features, i.e., *mandatory, optional* (0..1 out of 1), *alternative* (1 out of n), and *or* (i..j out of n) features. *Alternative* and *Or* features are grouped in feature groups such that one parent feature group can only have one *alternative* or one *or* feature group. Feature attributes can be used to describe features in terms of values which can be pre-defined, pre-calculated or set during configuration.

Family Models. Family models describe the structure and variability in the solution space, i.e., the reusable software (architectural) entities of the product line. The main elements in family models are *components* that contain *components* and/or *parts* which itself contain parts and/or *source elements* that map to actual software modules containing source code. Elements in the family model can be linked with *relations* and can be constrained by *restrictions.* These relations and restrictions are also used to link elements of the family models to the features of the feature models. For example, a component A in the family model might have a relation *requires(B)* which indicates that component A also requires component B. Furthermore, component A might have a restriction *hasFeature(X)* which indicates that component A is automatically included if feature X is selected in a configuration.

Variant Description Models. A variant description model describes a single configuration of a product that is derived from the feature model by selecting features and setting user specified attribute values. Thus, a variant description model contains all features that have been automatically selected by PureVariants due to its feature type (e.g. mandatory features) or because of relations and restrictions in the feature model as well as all optional or alternative features that have been selected by the user. PureVariants automatically checks the selection of features by the user and solves problems or reports them if they cannot be solved automatically.

Result Models. A result model describes all elements of the family model that are included in a product which is described by a variant description model. A result model is obtained from the family model and a variant description model by selecting all components whose *hasFeature()* restrictions are true under the given selection of features in the variant description model. In other words, a result model is a product dependent clipping of the family model which is determined by the selected features in the corresponding variant description model. For example, the family model contains component A which is restricted by *hasFeature(X)*, component B which is restricted by *hasFeature(Y)*, and component C which is restricted by *hasFeature(Z)* and the variant description model contains only features X and Y. Then, the result model will contain components A and B, but not C because the restrictions of component A and B evaluate to true under the given variant description model, but the restriction of component C evaluates to false.

ConIPF

The core idea of the ConIPF methodology [HK03, HKW$^+$06] is to provide automated support for product derivation using knowledge-based configuration technologies. For this purpose, ConIPF provides a so called *configuration model* that is a logical model describing the complete space of possible configurations. It contains a description of the variability that is provided by the product family assets in terms of *features* and *artifacts* (e.g. subsystems or hard- and software components) that are grouped into a *feature layer* respectively an *artifact layer*. Relations within these layers define the compositional and hierarchical structures of the features and the artifacts, whereas relations between these layers define how artifacts realize the features. The relations are specialized into several types, e.g., *has-context*, *has-features*, *has-hardware*, *has-subsystems*, and *has-software*.

GEARS

GEARS [Kru02] is a software product line development tool that covers variability modeling and product derivation. GEARS provides three types of models for variability modeling, i.e., *feature declarations*, *product definitions*, and *variation points*:

- *Feature models* model the variability of the software product line in terms of features. GEARS support four types of features, i.e., *optional features* (modeled by a boolean variable), *alternative features* (modeled by an enumeration), *or-features* (modeled by a set), and *value features* (modeled by integer or string variables). In addition to features GEARS also supports to model so called *assertions*, i.e., constraints on the values of features.

- *Product feature profiles* model the product instances that can be derived from the feature models. The product feature profile stores the selected features for a specific product. Assertions that have been modeled together with the feature declarations are automatically checked.

- *Variation points* encapsulate source code variants at the level of files that exist in the software product line and the logic for selecting among variants. The selection of these variants is controlled by simple if-then rules that map selections of features to the selection of particular variants, e.g. `if (featureX == true) then select variant Y`.

To support the product derivation process, GEARS provides a configurator that automatically assembles and configures the software assets for a specific product, guided by the product feature profiles.

Kumbang Configurator

Kumbang Configurator [AMS07] is a tool supporting the configuration task for configurable software product lines. Kumbang Configurator uses the Kumbang language that combines Forfamel [AMS06] and Koalish [AMS06] into a single integrated variability modeling language for software product lines. Hence, Kumbang enables variability modeling simultaneously from a feature and architectural point of view. In order to link Forfamel and Koalish, Kumbang allows the user to specify how features are *implemented* by architectural entities using *implementation constraints* that must hold for the architecture in order for the product individual to provide the specific feature.

   Kumbang Configurator takes a *configuration model* in the Kumbang language as input which is used as a basis for the configuration task. The configurator offers a graphical user interface through which the user can make *selections* that modify the configuration. Configurations are automatically checked for *consistency*, i.e., the configuration does not violate any rules and *completeness*, i.e., the configuration contains all necessary selections. Furthermore, Kumbang Configurator deduces the direct consequences of the configuration selections made so far.

ProjectKing

ProjectKing [RDG06, RGD07, RDG07] is a tool supporting the configuration and derivation of products from a product line whose variability has been modeled using decisions (see Section 3.2.2 for details). It uses a wizard-based approach in which the application engineer can make the decisions that are required to derive the product. These decisions are then effectuated in the generic product line artifacts.

3.4   Variability Maintenance and Evolution

During the market phase of the software product line, variability management rises to critical importance. However, the focus of variability management shifts from variability generation (domain engineering) and variability handling (application engineering) to variability maintenance and evolution. This involves *adaptive*, *corrective* and *perfective* maintenance tasks [Swa76] such as adding new variants to existing variation points, changing the realization of variation points, and pruning old variation points and unused variants. Furthermore, variable features may be removed altogether, as the requirements change, new products are added and old ones are removed from the product line [BFG+01].

Existing literature does recognize the importance of variability maintenance and evolution [KS94, Sne96, RU98, WL99, DS99, CN01, NI01, BFG+01, BM01, KMPY05]. However, when it comes to actually providing decision support in determining the necessary changes to the existing variability of a software product line the works cited above lack the necessary precision.

Krone and Snelting [KS94, Sne96] were the first to use Formal Concept Analysis [GW96] to analyze the relationship of preprocessor directives and code segments in order to better understand and decompose source code files that make heavy use of the C preprocessor. In [Sne96], they briefly mention the simplification of the configuration space by removing obsolete preprocessor symbols. However, they do not elaborate on how this knowledge can be obtained.

Baxter et al. [BM01] describe how obsolete conditional compilation directives can be removed by partial evaluation. Their work is related to our work of variability restructuring. However, they do not describe a method for analyzing the use of conditional compilation directives in product configurations in order to determine which of these directives can be removed.

In the SEI's Product Line Practices and Patterns book [CN01], Clements et al. quote evaluation of variation points with respect to appropriateness, flexibility, and performance as an example of an important evaluation. The book, however, does not present a detailed technique to perform these evaluations. It only suggests modifying existing architecture assessment methods to accomplish this goal.

Related work explicitly dealing with determining necessary changes to the existing variability is COSVAM [DSNB04], a technique developed by Deelstra et al. to identify mismatches between the provided and the required variability during software product line evolution. They argue that *"variability needs to undergo continual and timely change, or a product family will risk loosing the ability to effectively exploit the similarities of its members"*. This statement provides a general basis and motivation for research in variability maintenance and evolution in general and for our work in particular.

The paper of Eisenbarth et al. [EKS02] on the analysis of product maps is most similar in concepts and thus closely related to our work. They were the first authors who applied formal concept analysis [GW96] to analyze so called *product maps* which relate products and features in order to determine the scope of the product line during domain analysis and evolution.

Our work is based on and extends the work of Eisenbarth et al. [EKS02] by applying formal concept analysis on the problem of variability maintenance and optimization. This includes extraction of information about the provided variability of the software product line, visualization of this information in a human-understandable form, analysis of the usage of variability in product configurations, derivation and validation of feature constraints, as well as restructuring and simplification of the existing variability. Thus, our work provides a framework for variability optimization including the necessary support for making informed decisions regarding variability maintenance.

3.5   Related Work

There exist several publications which are related to this thesis in the broader sense. They deal with reengineering in the context of software product lines rather than explicitly with variability maintenance and optimization. The goal of these techniques is to consolidate several existing product variants which are closely related into a software product line [BGW+99, KMPY05, KMPY06, FKBA07] or to reactively introduce product specific adaptations into the product family [MBKM08]. Simon et al. [SE02, EKS03, Sim05] describe a process for the evolutionary introduction of software product lines by identifying feature-component relationships using formal concept analysis. The underlying scenario for these techniques is that product variants have been created using copy&paste to a large extent.

Bayer et al. [BGW+99] propose the RE-PLACE framework to leverage existing assets by integrating them in a product line architecture during the domain engineering phase. This includes an analysis of the commonalities and variabilities of existing assets. However, they do not describe of this analysis can be performed.

Kolb et al. [KMPY05, KMPY06] describe a case study in which an existing software component is systematically refactored for reuse in a software product line. Among several steps they identify obsolete preprocessor constants that are then to be removed from the component.

Frenzel et. al [FKBA07] describe an approach to consolidate existing product variants which are closely related into a software product line using clone detection to identify similar functions and an extension of hierarchical reflexion models [KS03] to reconstruct the variant product architectures and a common software product line architecture.

Mende et. al [MBKM08] use clone detection to support the grow- and-prune model [FV03], i.e., to reactively integrate product specific variants into the generic product line assets. They calculate the Levenshtein distance to measure the similarity of cloned function pairs in multiple software variants in order to identify candidates for reintegration into the common asset base of the software product line.

Simon et al. [SE02] describe a process for the evolutionary introduction of software product lines using existing features of products. In order to locate these features in existing assets, i.e., to identify the relationship of features and components implementing them, Eisenbarth and Simon apply dynamic analysis of execution traces, formal concept analysis, and static analysis [EKS01, ES01b, ES01a, EKS03, Sim05]. Feature location is related to our work. For example, it can be applied for the analysis of feature implementations during variability restructuring if the relationship between features and source code has been lost or is not clear.

3.6 Summary and Discussion

As we have seen in this Chapter, the state of art in variability management is mainly focused on domain engineering, i.e., the identification, modeling, and implementation of variability, as well as on application engineering, i.e., the handling of variability during product derivation. Although the importance of variability maintenance and evolution is recognized in existing literature, some works lack precision when it comes to actually providing decision support in determining the necessary changes to the existing variability of a software product line. None of the methods described in Section 3.4 has been conceived specifically for the task of variability optimization, i.e., minimizing the amount of existing variability.

However, as stated in Chapter 1, industrial organizations wish for a structured method for variability maintenance and evolution. In particular this method should provide means to analyze the provided variability and its use in actual products in order to take informed decisions about minimizing the amount of variability that is required to derive the set of current and future products.

The resulting research gap can be closed by answering the following research question:

> What is an operational and structured method to analyze the provided variability and its use in actual products that allows the decision maker to make informed decisions regarding its maintenance and optimization?

Different approaches can be taken to provide such a method. One approach is to adapt existing general purpose methods for the task of variability analysis and optimization. The second approach is to develop new methods. In our variability analysis and optimization framework which is described in the subsequent chapters we use both approaches, i.e., our framework is a combination of adapted general purpose methods and new methods.

Chapter 4

Variability Analysis

In the previous chapter, the research question has been laid down. Our variability analysis approach which provides the first part of the answer to this question is presented in this chapter. The basic idea of our approach is to analyze the relationship of product configurations and features to draw conclusions about the provided variability of the software product line. First, we analyze product configurations in order to construct a matrix that precisely documents the usage of realized variable features in these product configurations. Using a mathematical clustering method, called Formal Concept Analysis (FCA), a visual representation of this matrix in the form of a *concept lattice* is derived that factors out which features are commonly used and which features are only used in specific product configurations. This powerful visual representation allows us to analyze the actual degree of variability that the existing product configurations exhibit and to derive important knowledge about the configuration of products. This knowledge can be used for a number of different tasks that are related to variability management and product derivation. In particular, this knowledge can be used to optimize the existing variability in a software product line. Parts of this chapter have been published in [LP07b].

Overview. In Section 4.1, we present the general theory of Formal Concept Analysis (FCA) that is necessary to understand our approach for variability analysis. Section 4.2 gives an overview of our variability analysis approach and describes how formal concept analysis can be used to analyze variability that is represented in terms of features. In Section 4.3, we describe several extensions that make our approach for variability analysis more practicable. In Section 4.4, we give an overview of the most common applications for variability analysis. We conclude this chapter by a Summary which is presented in Section 4.5.

4.1 Formal Concept Analysis

4.1.1 Context and Concept

Formal Concept Analysis (FCA) [Bir79, GW96] is a mathematical method that provides a way to identify meaningful groupings of *objects* that have common *attributes*.

The starting point for concept analysis is a so called *formal context* $C = (\mathcal{O}, \mathcal{A}, \mathcal{I})$, consisting of a set of *objects* $\mathcal{O}$, a set of *attributes* $\mathcal{A}$, and a relation $\mathcal{I} \subseteq \mathcal{O} \times \mathcal{A}$, stating which attributes are possessed by each object.

For any set of objects $O \subseteq \mathcal{O}$, the set of *common attributes* is defined as

$$\sigma(O) = \{a \in \mathcal{A} \mid \forall o \in O \; : \; (o, a) \in \mathcal{I}\} \tag{4.1}$$

Similarly, for any set of attributes $A \subseteq \mathcal{A}$, the set of *common objects* is defined as

$$\tau(A) = \{o \in \mathcal{O} \mid \forall a \in A \; : \; (o, a) \in \mathcal{I}\} \tag{4.2}$$

A formal context can be easily represented by a rectangular *cross table* denoted by $\mathcal{T}$. In this table the row headings represent the objects and the column headings represent the attributes. An object o_i and an attribute a_j are in relation $\mathcal{I}$, if there is a cross ($\times$) in row i and column j. Table 4.1 shows an example of a formal context represented by a cross table. For example, in this context, the following equations hold: $\sigma(\{o_1\}) = \{a_1, a_4, a_5\}$ and $\tau(\{a_1, a_4, a_5\}) = \{o_1, o_2, o_4\}$.

	a_1	a_2	a_3	a_4	a_5
o_1	$\times$			$\times$	$\times$
o_2	$\times$		$\times$		
o_3		$\times$		$\times$	
o_4	$\times$			$\times$	$\times$
o_5		$\times$	$\times$		

Table 4.1: Example formal context represented by a cross table.

A pair of objects and attributes $c = (O, A)$ is called a *concept*, iff:

$$A = \sigma(O) \; and \; O = \tau(A) \tag{4.3}$$

Thus, a concept is a maximal collection of objects that share a common set of attributes. In other words, all $o \in O$ have all attributes in A, and all attributes $a \in A$ fit to all objects in O. A concept $c = (O, A)$ has *extent* $ext(c) = O$ and *intent* $int(c) = A$. Informally, a concept corresponds to a *maximal rectangle* of filled table cells in $\mathcal{T}$ modulo column and row permutations. Table 4.2 shows all concepts that can be derived from the context shown in Table 4.1.

4.1.2   Concept Lattices

The set of all concepts that can be derived from the formal context forms a *complete partial order* via the order relation $\leq$. The order relation $\leq$ between tow concepts $c_1 = (O_1, A_1)$ and $c_2 = (O_2, A_2)$ of the formal context is defined as follows:

$$c_1 \leq c_2 \Leftrightarrow O_1 \subseteq O_2 \tag{4.4}$$

c_0	$(\{o_1, o_2, o_3, o_4, o_5\}, \{\emptyset\})$
c_1	$(\{\emptyset\}, \{a_1, a_2, a_3, a_4, a_5\})$
c_2	$(\{o_1, o_3, o_4\}, \{a_4, a_5\})$
c_3	$(\{o_1, o_4\}, \{a_1, a_4, a_5\})$
c_4	$(\{o_3\}, \{a_2, a_4\})$
c_5	$(\{o_2, o_5\}, \{a_3\})$
c_6	$(\{o_5\}, \{a_2, a_3\})$
c_7	$(\{o_2\}, \{a_1, a_3\})$
c_8	$(\{o_3, o_5\}, \{a_2\})$
c_9	$(\{o_1, o_2, o_4\}, \{a_1\})$

Table 4.2: All concepts for formal context shown in Table 4.1.

or, equivalently,

$$c_1 \le c_2 \Leftrightarrow A_1 \supseteq A_2 \tag{4.5}$$

Note that (4.4) and (4.5) imply each other by definition. If, $c_1 \le c_2$, we call c_1 a *subconcept* of c_2 and c_2 a *superconcept* of c_1. In this case, c_2 has at least as many objects as c_1 in its extent, and inversely, c_1 has at least as many attributes as c_2 in its intent.

Given a formal context $C = (\mathcal{O}, \mathcal{A}, \mathcal{I})$, the set of all concepts $\mathcal{L}(C)$ that can be derived from the context and the partial order $\le$ form a complete lattice, called the *concept lattice*:

$$\mathcal{L}(C) = \{(O, A) \in 2^{\mathcal{O}} \times 2^{\mathcal{A}} \mid A = \sigma(O) \land O = \tau(A)\} \tag{4.6}$$

Concept lattices can be represented by *Hasse diagrams*, also called *line diagrams*. These diagrams visualize the $<$ relation between concepts that is defined as follows:

$$c_1 < c_2 \Leftrightarrow c_1 \le c_2 \text{ and there is no concept c } (\ne c_1, c_2) \text{ fulfilling } c_1 \le c \le c_2 \tag{4.7}$$

The concepts of $\mathcal{L}$ are depicted by nodes in the diagram with objects and attributes attached to it by labels. If $c_1, c_2 \in \mathcal{L}$ with $c_1 < c_2$ the node corresponding to c_2 is depicted above the node corresponding to c_1, and the two nodes are joined by a line segment. From such a diagram we can read off the order relation as follows: $c_1 < c_2$ if and only if the node representing c_2 can be reached by an ascending path from the node representing c_1.

The *infimum* ($\sqcap$) of two concepts in this lattice is computed by intersecting their extents as follows:

$$(X_1, Y_1) \sqcap (X_2, Y_2) = (X_1 \cap X_2, \sigma(X_1 \cap X_2)) \tag{4.8}$$

Similarly, the *supremum* ($\sqcup$) is determined by intersecting the intents:

$$(X_1, Y_1) \sqcup (X_2, Y_2) = (\tau(Y_1 \cap Y_2), Y_1 \cap Y_2) \tag{4.9}$$

In other words, the *infimum* describes the greatest common subconcept of two concepts and contains the set of common attributes for the set of objects of the both concepts. The *supremum* describes the smallest common superconcept of two concepts and contains the set of common objects for the set of attributes of the both concepts.

Obviously a labeling of nodes in the line diagram with full extents and intents will contain many redundant listings of objects and attributes and therefore becomes too complicated to be understandable at a glance for a large number of objects and attributes.

In order to avoid these redundant listings of objects and attributes, the concepts in a line diagram can be visualized in a more readable equivalent way as follows: a concept is labeled with object $o \in O$, if it represents the most special concept that has o in its extent. Analogously, a concept is labeled with $a \in A$, if it is the most general concept that has a in its intent. The unique element in the concept lattice labeled with a is therefore:

$$\mu(a) = \sqcup\{c \in \mathcal{L}(C) \mid a \in int(c)\} = (\tau(a), \sigma(\tau(a))) \qquad (4.10)$$

and is called *attribute concept* of a. The unique concept labeled with o is:

$$\gamma(o) = \sqcap\{c \in \mathcal{L}(C) \mid o \in ext(c)\} = (\tau(\sigma(o)), \sigma(o)) \qquad (4.11)$$

and is called *object concept* of o.

We call a line diagram representing a concept lattice using this labeling strategy a *sparse representation* of the lattice. Figure 4.1 shows the sparse representation of the concept lattice for the formal context shown in Table 4.1.

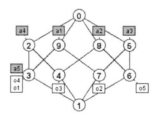

Figure 4.1: Sparse representation of concept lattice for context shown in Table 4.1.

In this sparse representation the attribute labels of a concept c are denoted by $\alpha(c)$, and the object labels of c are denoted by $\omega(c)$. Using this definition, the full extent of c can be obtained by collecting all objects which appear as labels at c and at all concepts *below c*. Thus:

$$ext(c) = \bigcup_{c' \leq c} \omega(c') \qquad (4.12)$$

The full intent of c is obtained by collecting all labels at c and at all concepts above c. Thus:

$$int(c) = \bigcup_{c' \geq c} \alpha(c') \qquad (4.13)$$

4.1.3 Subcontexts and Filtering

Sometimes concept lattices can get very large in terms of the number of concepts and edges that connect concepts. In this case, it seems reasonable to examine only a part of the overall context by excluding some objects or attributes from the examination. In this section we describe the effects of this procedure on the concept lattice [GW96].

If $C = (O, A, \mathcal{I})$ is a context and if $O' \subseteq O$ and $A' \subseteq A$, then $C' = (O', A', \mathcal{I} \cap O' \times A')$ is called a *subcontext* of C and C is called a *supercontext* of C'.

The question is how the concept lattice of the subcontext C' is related to the concept lattice of the supercontext C. If we only exclude attributes from the analysis, i.e., if for a set $A' \subseteq A$ we consider the subcontext $C' = (O, A', \mathcal{I} \cap O \times A')$, the modification remains transparent. Every attribute extent of C' is an attribute of C, and since the concept extent is the intersection of attribute extents, we obtain:

Proposition. Let $C = (O, A, \mathcal{I}$ and $C' = (O, A', \mathcal{I} \cap O \times A')$ with $A' \subseteq A$, then every extent of a concept of $\mathcal{L}(C')$ is an extent of a concept of $\mathcal{L}(C)$ [GW96].

According to this proposition, each extent within the subcontext will show up in the supercontext. This can be made plausible with the relation table: removed attributes (columns) will never change existing attributes (columns), so the maximal rectangles forming concepts will only shrink in horizontal direction (if columns represent attributes).

This proposition on the invariability of extents of subcontexts that only differ in the set of attributes results in a simple mapping of concepts from the subcontext to the super-context as follows: For $A' \subseteq A$, the map

$$\mathcal{L}(O, A', I \cup O \times A') \rightarrow \mathcal{L}(O, A, I) \tag{4.14}$$

$$(O, A) \rightarrow (O, \sigma(O)) \tag{4.15}$$

is a $\sqcap$-preserving order-embedding, i.e., the partial order relation of concepts is completely preserved. Dually, for $O' \subseteq O$, the map

$$\mathcal{L}(O', A, I \cup O' \times A) \rightarrow \mathcal{L}(O, A, I) \tag{4.16}$$

$$(O, A) \rightarrow (\tau(A), A) \tag{4.17}$$

is a $\sqcup$-preserving order-embedding, i.e., the partial order relation of concepts is completely preserved.

Example. Consider the context shown in Table 4.1 divided into two subcontexts (part 1 and 2) as shown in Table 4.3. If we analyze the first part using concept analysis, we obtain the concepts listed on the left side of Table 4.4. According to definition (2.15) all extents for concepts shown on the left side can be found as extents of concepts on the right side, e.g., $\text{ext}(c_2') = \text{ext}(c_9)$. The resulting concept lattices for the subcontext and the full context are shown in Figure 4.2. Although, the concept lattice for the full context (on the right side) contains three more concepts and the numbering of concepts is changed, the structure of both concept lattices remains stable. For example, if you compare concepts #3, #5, #6 on the left side with concepts #5, #6, #7 on the right side, you will see that the structure remains stable.

	Part 1			Part 2	
	a_1	a_2	a_3	a_4	a_5
o_1	×			×	×
o_2	×		×		
o_3		×		×	
o_4	×			×	×
o_5		×	×		

Table 4.3: Division of formal context shown in Table 4.1 into two subcontexts (part 1 and part 2).

c_0'	$(\{o_1, o_2, o_3, o_4, o_5\}, \{\emptyset\})$
c_1'	$(\{\emptyset\}, \{a_1, a_2, a_3\})$
c_2'	$(\{o_1, o_2, o_4\}, \{a_1\})$
c_3'	$(\{o_2\}, \{a_1, a_3\})$
c_4'	$(\{o_3, o_5\}, \{a_2\})$
c_5'	$(\{o_5\}, \{a_2, a_3\})$
c_6'	$(\{o_2, o_5\}, \{a_3\})$

c_0	$(\{o_1, o_2, o_3, o_4, o_5\}, \{\emptyset\})$
c_1	$(\{\emptyset\}, \{a_1, a_2, a_3, a_4, a_5\})$
c_2	$(\{o_1, o_3, o_4\}, \{a_4, a_5\})$
c_3	$(\{o_1, o_4\}, \{a_1, a_4, a_5\})$
c_4	$(\{o_3\}, \{a_2, a_4\})$
c_5	$(\{o_2, o_5\}, \{a_3\})$
c_6	$(\{o_5\}, \{a_2, a_3\})$
c_7	$(\{o_2\}, \{a_1, a_3\})$
c_8	$(\{o_3, o_5\}, \{a_2\})$
c_9	$(\{o_1, o_2, o_4\}, \{a_1\})$

Table 4.4: Concepts for first subcontext (left) of formal context shown in Table 4.3 and concepts for the full context (right).

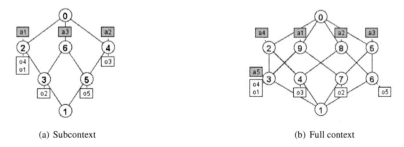

(a) Subcontext   (b) Full context

Figure 4.2: Concept lattices for subcontext 1 (a) and the full context (b).

4.1.4 Implications

A formal context and a concept lattice are alternate views on the same information but they provide different insights. In addition to these two views there is yet another view: a set of *implications between attributes*, i.e., statements of the following kind: "Every object with attributes $a, b, c, \ldots$ also has the attributes $x, y, z, \ldots$". Formally, for any two attribute sets $A, B \subseteq \mathcal{A}$ and a formal context $C = (\mathcal{O}, \mathcal{A}, \mathcal{I})$, we say A *implies* B (written $A \rightarrow B$), iff any object o having all attributes in A also has all attributes in B:

$$A \rightarrow B \Leftrightarrow \forall o \in \mathcal{O} : (\forall a \in A : (o, a) \in \mathcal{I}) \Rightarrow (\forall b \in B : (o, b) \in \mathcal{I}) \qquad (4.18)$$

For $B = \{b_1, \ldots, b_k\}$, $A \rightarrow B$ holds iff $A \rightarrow \{b_i\}$ for all $b_i \in B$. Implications show up in the lattice as follows: $A \rightarrow b$ holds, iff $\mu(b) \geq \sqcap \{\mu(a) \mid a \in A\}$. This means that we have to check in the concept lattice whether the concept denoted by b is located above the infimum of all concepts denoted by an a of A. Informally, implications between attributes can be found along upward paths in the lattice.

4.2 Variability Analysis

4.2.1 Overview

In the most general form, variability in software product lines is represented by *choices* that provide one or several *options* that can be chosen. The choices and options are typically represented in a *variability model* using one of the variability modeling techniques described in Chapter 3. For our variability analysis approach, we assume that the variability has been modeled in terms of features that can either be included or excluded in a product configuration.

During product derivation, a subset of features described in the feature model are selected for a product. The decision which features to include is either based on implicit knowledge of the product developers or on documented knowledge about correct configurations. The list of selected features for a product is typically stored in a *product configuration* in order to reproduce the product.

The general idea of our variability analysis approach is similar to the analysis of product maps using formal concept analysis which has been first presented by Eisenbarth et al. [EKS02]. Similarly to their approach we interpret the information that a product configuration uses a specific feature as a relation in order to derive a concept lattice which can be interpreted to identify shared and distinct features. However, we extend the interpretation by providing a classification of the features which allows the analyst to make informed decisions about the maintenance and optimization of the provided variability.

In Subsection 4.2.2, we discuss several assumptions for the application of our approach. In Subsection 4.2.3, we introduce an example which is used throughout the following subsections to illustrate our approach. In Subsection 4.2.4-4.3.2, we describe the application of concept analysis and the interpretation of the resulting concept lattice. In Subsection 4.2.6, we describe how the concept lattice can be used to classify the features into four different classes that allow the analyst to make informed decisions regarding the maintenance and optimization of variability.

4.2.2   Assumptions

For the application of our variability analysis approach, we make the following assumptions:

1. All features are known before the analysis. We only require that this information is available, i.e., we do not prescribe how this information is obtained. For example, the list of features can be obtained from different information sources such as existing feature models, expert knowledge, or a set of product configurations.

2. All existing product configurations are known before the analysis.

3. The relation between features and product configurations is available and precise, i.e., for each product configuration it is known which features it contains.

4.2.3   Running Example

In order to illustrate our variability analysis approach, we present a running example in this subsection. We use the ICC feature group which has been inspired by our case study of the engine control software product line (see Section 7.2). The engine control software is embedded in so called electronic control units (ECUs), i.e., boxes that contain the hardware and interfaces to sensors and actuators that are needed to control the engine of a diesel passenger car. The engine control software product line is divided in subsystems. One of these subsystems controls the injection of fuel into the engine.

The *ICC* feature group offers a high degree of variability which is required to configure the subsystem IS for different customer requirements. In total, ICC offers 21 features that can be used for configuring the subsystem IS for different customer requirements. The list of features that are offered by the ICC feature group was obtained by consulting existing documentation and asking experts. In order to analyze the usage of these features in different products, we obtained a set of 11 product configurations, i.e., configurations of products that use the ICC feature group.

4.2.4   Setup of Formal Context

In order to analyze the usage of features in product configurations using Formal Concept Analysis (FCA), we first need to define the formal context (objects, attributes, relation table) and then interpret the resulting concept lattice accordingly.

As described in [EKS02], we interpret the product configurations p as objects o of the formal context. Features f are interpreted as attributes a. The relation $\mathcal{R}$ of the formal context is defined by the product-feature matrix $\mathcal{M}$. The product-feature matrix $\mathcal{M}$ is a simple table relating product configurations and features, i.e., $\mathcal{M} \subseteq \mathcal{P} \times \mathcal{F}$. If a feature f is used in a product configuration p the corresponding cell in the product-feature matrix is marked with a cross. The mapping of terms for variability analysis to the general terms of formal concept analysis is shown in Table 4.5.

Variability Analysis $[\mathcal{P} \times \mathcal{F}]$	Formal Concept Analysis $[\mathcal{O} \times \mathcal{A}]$
Product configuration p	Object o
Set of product configurations P	Set of objects O
All product configurations $\mathcal{P}$	All objects $\mathcal{O}$
Feature f	Attribute a
Set of features F	Set of attributes A
All features $\mathcal{F}$	All attributes $\mathcal{A}$
Product-feature matrix $\mathcal{M}$	Relation $\mathcal{R}$
Product configuration concept $\gamma(p)$	Object concept $\gamma(o)$
Feature concept $\mu(f)$	Attribute concept $\mu(a)$

Table 4.5: Mapping of terms for variability analysis to general identifiers of formal concept analysis.

If $\mathcal{P}$ represents the set of all product configurations, $\mathcal{F}$ represents the set of all features, and $\mathcal{M}$ represents the product-feature matrix, i.e., the uses-relation of features in product configurations, then we can define the formal context $C_{PF} = (\mathcal{P}, \mathcal{F}, \mathcal{M})$.

Using the definitions of Section 4.1.1, the *common features* of a set of products $P \subseteq \mathcal{P}$ can be identified as $\sigma(P)$:

$$\sigma(P) = \{f \in \mathcal{F} \mid (p, f) \in \mathcal{M} \text{ for all } p \in P\} \tag{4.19}$$

Similarly, the set of *common product configurations* $\tau(F)$ that possess a given set of features $F \subseteq \mathcal{F}$ can be identified as:

$$\tau(F) = \{p \in \mathcal{P} \mid (p, f) \in \mathcal{M} \text{ for all } f \in F\} \tag{4.20}$$

A concept $c = (P, F)$ with $F = \sigma(P)$ and $P = \tau(F)$ thus represents a set of product configurations $P \subseteq \mathcal{P}$ using all features $f \in F$ or equivalently a set of features $F \subseteq \mathcal{F}$ that is used in all product configurations $p \in P$.

The set $\mathcal{L}$ of all concepts and the partial order $\leq$ as defined in Section 4.1.2 form the concept lattice:

$$\mathcal{L}(C) = \{(P, F) \in 2^{\mathcal{P}} \times 2^{\mathcal{F}} \mid F = \sigma(P) \text{ and } P = \tau(F)\} \tag{4.21}$$

Example. The product-feature matrix for ICC is shown in Table 4.6. The features that are offered by the feature group ICC are shown in the rows. The product configurations are shown in columns. A cross at row r_i and column c_i in the product-feature matrix indicates that the feature at row r_i is used in the product configuration at column c_i. In order to quickly find a feature in the product-feature matrix, the features are sorted alphabetically by their name. Note, that the product-feature matrix can contain empty rows, i.e., features that are not used in any of the product configurations and full rows, i.e., features that are used in all of the product configurations. Although these rows do not have an influence on the structure of the concept lattice, they are important for variability analysis because these rows indicate features that are always used or never used as we shall see in subsection 4.2.6.

	P1	P2	P3	P4	P5	P6	P7	P8	P9	P10	P11
A1	x	x	x	x	x	x	x	x	x	x	x
A1_A				x				x			
A1_T	x	x	x		x	x	x		x	x	x
A1_R	x	x	x	x	x	x	x	x	x	x	x
A2	x	x	x	x	x	x	x	x	x	x	x
A2_A				x				x			
A2_T	x	x	x		x	x	x		x	x	x
A2_R	x	x	x		x	x	x		x	x	x
A2_SC	x	x	x	x	x	x	x	x	x	x	x
A2_CC											
A3	x	x	x	x	x			x	x	x	x
A3_R	x		x	x	x			x			
B1	x	x	x	x	x	x	x	x	x	x	x
B1_R	x	x	x	x	x	x	x	x	x	x	x
B2	x	x	x	x	x	x	x	x	x	x	x
B2_A	x		x	x				x	x		
B2_T		x			x	x	x			x	x
B2_R	x	x	x	x	x	x	x	x	x	x	x
Q	x	x	x	x	x	x	x	x	x	x	x
Z	x	x	x	x	x	x	x	x	x	x	x

Table 4.6: Product-feature matrix $\mathcal{M}$ for the feature group ICC. Product configurations are shown in columns and features are shown in rows.

The resulting concept lattice for the product-feature matrix in Table 4.6 is shown in Figure 4.3. To improve the legibility, we use the *sparse representation* of the concept lattice. Each product configuration p is attached to the smallest concept c that has p in its extent, i.e., $p \in ext(c)$. Although all concepts above this concept also contain the product configuration p, p is not shown at these concepts anymore. Similarly, each feature f is attached to the largest concept c that has f in its intent, i.e., $f \in int(c)$. Although all concepts below this concept also contain the feature f, f is not shown at these concepts anymore.

4.2.5   Interpretation of the Concept Lattice

Concept analysis applied to the formal context defined in the last subsection yields a concept lattice from which the following interesting facts about the relationships of fea-

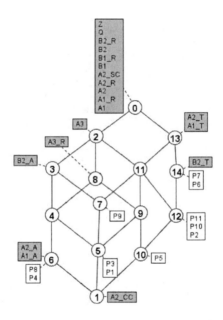

Figure 4.3: Sparse representation of concept lattice $\mathcal{L}$ for ICC.

tures and product configurations can be derived. Some of these facts have been already described in [EKS02]:

1. **Feature concept.** The feature concept $\mu(f)$ is the largest concept with feature f in its intent. A feature f is contained in all concepts that appear at or below the feature concept $\mu(f)$, i.e., all concepts c with $c \leq \mu(f)$. As a result of the product-feature matrix $\mathcal{M}$, it follows that the feature f is used in all product configurations p that appear at or below the feature concept $\mu(f)$ in the sparse representation of the concept lattice. If a full representation is used, the set of features can be directly obtained by reading of the extent of the feature concept $\mu(f)$.

   In the concept lattice shown in Figure 4.3 the feature B2_A can be found at the feature concept $\mu(B2\_A)$ = concept 3. This feature is used in product configurations P9 (at concept 7), P4 and P8 (at concept 6), and P1 and P3 (at concept 5).

2. **Product concept.** The product concept $\gamma(p)$ is the smallest concept with product configuration p in its extent. A product configuration p is contained in all concepts that appear at or above the product concept $\gamma(p)$, i.e., in all concepts c with $c \geq \gamma(p)$. As a result of the product-feature matrix $\mathcal{M}$, it follows that the product configuration p uses all features f that appear at or above the product configuration concept $\gamma(p)$ in the sparse representation of the concept lattice. If a full representation is used, the set of features can be directly obtained by reading of the intent of the product concept $\gamma(p)$.

   In the example shown in Figure 4.3 the product configuration P6 can be found at the product concept $\gamma(P6)$ = concept 14. Product configuration P6 uses the features B2_T (at concept 14), A1_T and A2_T (at concept 13), and all features that appear at concept 0.

3. **Shared features.** Features shared by a set of product configurations $\{p_1, \ldots, p_n\}$ can be identified at the supremum of the product concepts $\gamma(p_i)$, i.e.,

$$c_{sup} = \sqcup\{\gamma(p_i) \mid i \in \{1..n\}\}$$

   This concept is the smallest concept that has all product configurations $\{p_1, \ldots, p_n\}$ in its extent. The intent of this concept contains exactly those features that are shared by these product configurations. In the concept lattice the supremum c_{sup} is the first common superconcept of all product concepts $\gamma(p_i)$ towards the top concept. If a sparse representation is used for the concept lattice, the shared features are those features which appear at the concept c_{sup} and at all concepts above c_{sup}.

   In the example shown in Figure 4.3 the shared features for product configurations P2 and P5 are the features A3 (at concept 2), A1_T and A2_T (at concept 13), and all features at concept 0 because these features appear at or above the supremum $c_{sup} = \gamma(P2) \sqcup \gamma(P5)$ = concept 11.

4. **Distinct features.** Features that are different between a set of product configurations $\{p_1, \ldots, p_n\}$ are those features for which the following conditions hold:

   (a) They appear at superconcepts of $\gamma(p_i)$

   (b) They have not been identified as shared features for $\{p_1, \ldots, p_n\}$

   In the example shown in Figure 4.3 the distinct features of P2 and P5 are the features A3_R (at concept 8) and B2_T (at concept 14) because these features appear at superconcepts of $\gamma(P5) = $ concept 10 and $\gamma(P2) = $ concept 2 and do not belong to the set of shared features of P2 and P5.

5. **Specific feature.** A feature f is specific to exactly one product configuration p if the following conditions hold:

   (a) Product configuration p uses feature f, i.e., $(p, f) \in \mathcal{M}$.

   (b) Product configuration p is the only product configuration on all paths from $\mu(f)$ to the bottom concept.

   In the example shown in Figure 4.3 there does not exist a feature that is specific to exactly one product configuration. However, the features A1_A and A2_A are specific features of product configurations P4 and P8 because these product configurations are the only product configurations on all paths from $\mu(A1\_A) = \mu(A2\_A)$ down to the bottom concept.

6. **Feature-offering product configurations.** Similarly to shared features, feature-offering product configurations for a set of features $\{f_1, \ldots, f_n\}$ can be found at the infimum of the feature concepts $\mu(f_i)$, i.e.,

$$c_{inf} = \sqcap\{\mu(f_i) \mid i \in \{1..n\}\}$$

This concept is the largest concept that has all features $f_1, \ldots, f_n$ in its intent. The extent of this concept contains exactly those product configurations that offer the features $\{f_1, \ldots, f_n\}$. In the concept lattice the infimum c_{inf} is the first common subconcept of all feature concepts $\mu(f_i)$ towards the bottom concept. If a sparse representation is used for the concept lattice, the feature-offering product configurations are those product configurations which appear at the concept c_{inf} and at all concepts below c_{inf}.

In the example shown in Figure 4.3 the feature-offering product configurations for the features B2_A and A1_T are the product configurations P9 (at concept 7), and P1 and P3 (at concept 5) because these product configurations appear at or below the infimum $c_{inf} = \mu(B2_A) \sqcap \mu(A1_T) = $ concept 7.

7. **More specific and more general features.** If the feature concept of feature f_1 appears below the feature concept of feature f_2, i.e., $\mu(f_1) < \mu(f_2)$, then f_1 is more specific than f_2 with regard to the product configurations of $\mu(f_1)$ because f_2 is also used in other product configurations than those of $\mu(f_1)$. Thus, the more general features in the sparse representation of a concept lattice can be found at higher concepts, while more specific features can be found at lower concepts in the lattice.

8. **Extended product configurations.** If the product concept of product configuration p_1 appears below the product concept of product configuration p_2, i.e., $\gamma(p_1) < \gamma(p_2)$, then product configuration p_1 extends product configuration p_2 because p_1 contains all features in the intent of $\gamma(p_2)$ plus additional features. Thus, the lower a product configuration appears in the sparse representation of a concept lattice, the more capable it is because it provides more features.

9. **Minimal number of required features.** A very interesting fact we discovered and which has not been mentioned in [EKS02] is that the concept lattice also reveals the minimal number of distinguishing features that is required to derive the set of analyzed products. This number can be easily derived from the concept lattice by counting the number of concepts that have at least one feature attached except top and bottom concept. Intuitively, this is the minimal number of features needed to facilitate the differences of the set of analyzed product configurations because the additional features that appear at these concepts are not required to facilitate the differences. By comparing this number to the total number of features, i.e., $|\mathcal{F}|$, we can calculate the optimization potential, i.e., the number of features that can be removed or combined with other features.

Summary. Primarily, the third, fourth, and fifth fact allow us to analyze how the features are used in product configurations. By using the third and fourth fact, the commonalities and differences for any set of product configurations can be determined. Furthermore, the concept lattice reflects the specificity of features, i.e., features that are used in a lot of product configurations appear towards the top element and features that are used only in a few, in one or in none of the product configurations appear towards the bottom concept (seventh fact). The ninth fact allows us to determine the degree of variability that is actually required for the derivation of the products whose product configurations have been analyzed. By comparing this number to the total number of features, we can exactly determine the optimization potential.

4.2.6   Feature Usage Classification

The interpretation of the concept lattice as described in the last subsection gives insights into the relationships between features and product configurations, i.e., it allows us to analyze how features are actually used in product configurations.

In this subsection, we show how the usage of the features in product configurations can be automatically classified into four different classes that allow the analyst to make informed decision about the maintenance and optimization of the existing variability. These four classes are:

I **Always used.** Features that are used in every product configuration $p \in \mathcal{P}$ can be found in the intent of the top concept because all product configurations are contained in the extent of this concept. Formally, a feature f belongs to class I, iff $\mu(f) = \top$.

In our example shown in Figure 4.3 these are the features A1, A1_R, A2, A2_R, A2_SC, B1, B1_R, B2, B2_R, Q, and Z at concept 0.

II **Not used.** Features that appear at the bottom concept in the sparse representation of the lattice are not used in any of the product configurations $p \in \mathcal{P}$ if the extent of the bottom concept does not contain product configurations. Formally, a feature f belongs to class II, iff $\mu(f) = \bot$ and ext($\bot$) = $\emptyset$.

In our example shown in Figure 4.3 the feature A2_CC is not used in any of the product configurations because it appears at the bottom concept and the bottom concept does not contain any product configurations.

III **Used together.** Features $\{f_1, \ldots, f_n\}$ that appear at the same concept, i.e., $\mu(f_i) = \mu(f_j)$ for $i, j \in 1..n$ are features that are used together in a set $P \subset \mathcal{P}$ of product configurations. The set P can be directly read off the extent of $\mu(f_i)$. The features $\{f_1, \ldots, f_n\}$ together form a group. In a concept lattice there exist $0..m$ of those groups. The class III (Used together) contains all features that belong to one of these groups except those features that belong to class I or class II.

In our example shown in Figure 4.3 the features A1_A and A2_A are used together in P4 and P8 as these features appear at the same concept (concept 6), i.e., they form the first group. The same applies to features A1_T and A2_T as they appear together at the same concept (concept 13), i.e., they form the second group. Thus, A1_A, A2_A, A1_T, and A2_T belong to class **used together**.

IV **Only used separately.** A feature f that does not belong to any of the classes I, II, or III is a feature that is used separately. This is the case if the following conditions hold:

(a) $\mu(f) \neq \top$ (f does not belong to class I)

(b) $\mu(f) \neq \bot$ (f does not belong to class II)

(c) $\forall g \in \{\mathcal{F} \setminus f\} : \mu(f) \neq \mu(g)$ (f does not belong to class III)

In our example shown in Figure 4.3 the features B2_A, B2_T, A3, and A3_R are used separately as all of the conditions above hold, i.e., they do not belong to any of the usage classes I, II, or III.

The feature usage classification as described above allows us to uniquely classify each feature $f \in \mathcal{F}$ into one of the classes I-IV as the classes I-IV are not overlapping, i.e., a feature f always belongs only to one of the classes I-IV. The process of feature usage classification can be fully automated because the information used for the classification is completely available in the concept lattice. The feature usage classification provides the basis for making informed decisions about the maintenance and optimization of variability. In Chapter 5, we describe how the feature usage classification is used for deriving restructuring strategies for the optimization of variability.

4.2.7   Derivation of Feature Constraints

Beyond the classification of features into feature usage classes, our approach also allows us to automatically derive *potential feature constraints* from the concept lattice.

A *feature constraint* is a restriction on the use of features in product configurations. Typically, we can distinguish between *requires constraints*, i.e., constraints describing which features require the presence of which other features, and *mutual-exclusion constraints*, i.e., constraints describing illegal combinations of features. A *requires constraint* on two features f_1 and f_2, written f_1 *requires* f_2, states that feature f_2 has to be always included in a product configuration if feature f_1 is included. On the other hand a *mutual-exclusion constraint* on two features f_1 and f_2, written f_1 *excludes* f_2, states that whenever feature f_1 is included in a product configuration p, feature f_2 is not allowed to be included in p.

Thus, feature constraints restrict the number of variants that can be theoretically configured out of a set of features $\mathcal{F}$. For example, for the set of features $\mathcal{F} = f_1, \ldots, f_5$ it is theoretically possible to configure $2^5 = 32$ different variants by including or excluding the features if there exist no feature constraints. If there exist feature constraints between these features, the number of variants that can be configured without violating any of the constraints is reduced. For example, let us assume that the following constraints exist:

1. $f_1 \rightarrow \{f_2, f_3\}$

2. f_4 *excludes* f_5

3. $f_3 \rightarrow f_4$

Then, the number of different variants that can be configured is reduced from 32 down to 8 because the other 24 variants violate one or more of the constraints above.

In order to derive potential *requires* and *mutual-exclusion constraints*, we can use the information about the relationships between features that is contained in the concept lattice.

Potential Requires Constraints

A *potential requires constraint* between two features f_1 and f_2 exists if there is an implication between f_1 and f_2, i.e., if every product configuration using feature f_1 also uses f_2: $f_1 \rightarrow f_2$. According to the definition of implications described in Section 4.1.4 this is the case if the following condition holds in the concept lattice:

$$\mu(f_1) \leq \mu(f_2) \tag{4.22}$$

The definition of implications can also be applied to sets of features, i.e., $A, B \subseteq \mathcal{F}$. An implication between two sets of features, i.e., $A \rightarrow B$ holds if and only if $A \rightarrow b_i$ for all $b_i \in B$. $A \rightarrow b$ holds, if and only if $\sqcap\{\mu(a) \mid a \in A\} \leq \mu(b)$. This is the case, if the infimum of the feature concepts $\mu(a_i)$ for all $a_i \in A$ appears below the feature concept of b in the concept lattice.

Note that this is a necessary but not a sufficient condition, i.e., a valid requires constraint always implies an existing implication:

$$f_1 \text{ requires } f_2 \Rightarrow \mu(f_1) \leq \mu(f_2) \tag{4.23}$$

but the existence of an implication does not necessarily imply a valid requires constraint:

$$\mu(f_1) \leq \mu(f_2) \not\Rightarrow f_1 \text{ requires } f_2 \tag{4.24}$$

Thus, the analyst needs to check implications for their validity. Some of them may be spurious. In order to help the analyst to validate the implications, we can calculate the *global support* and the *local support* for each implication. Given an implication of the form $A \rightarrow B$, the global support and local support are determined by:

$$global\ support = \frac{N_{A,B}}{N} = P(A\&B) \tag{4.25}$$

$$local\ support = \frac{N_{A,B}}{(N_A + N_B) - N_{A,B}} \tag{4.26}$$

Thus, the *global support value* indicates the relation of product configurations including all features from A and B ($N_{A,B}$) to the total number of product configurations (N) in the concept lattice. In other words, the global support value can be interpreted as the likelihood of an implication to be valid ($P(A\&B)$), i.e., to represent a *valid feature constraint*. In order to help the analyst to decide which implications to accept or reject, we can sort the list of found implications by their global support value. However, this has the disadvantage that implications between features that are rarely used likely appear at the bottom of the list and implications between features that are used in a majority of all products likely appear at the top of the list. In order to solve this problem, we can use the *local support value*. Instead of relating the number of product configurations that include all features from A and B represented by $N_{A,B}$ to the total number of product configurations represented by N, $N_{A,B}$ is related to the $(N_A + N_B) - N_{A,B}$, i.e., to the number of product configurations actually using A or B. If we sort the list of implications by their *local support value* we avoid the problem of missing potential requires constraints between features that are only used in a small number of product configurations. This effect becomes obvious if one looks at Table 4.7.

Furthermore, we can compute another value, the so called *confidence value* which is defined as:

$$\text{confidence} = \frac{N_{A,B}}{N_A} = P(B|A) \tag{4.27}$$

The *confidence value* indicates the conditional probability that a product configuration including the features of set A also includes the features of set B.

In our case, the confidence value is always 1 because of the partial order of concepts in the lattice, i.e., all features of set B appear above all features of set A in the concept lattice. Therefore, the confidence value cannot be used as criteria for determining whether an implication is likely to be a valid feature constraint or not.

Of course it is also possible to derive implications with a confidence value of less than 1 from the concept lattice. These kind of implications are also referred to as *association rules* [AS94]. However, we do not look at these kinds of implications during variability analysis.

Example. From the concept lattice shown in Figure 4.3, we can for example derive the following potential require constraints between features:

- $B2\_T \rightarrow \{A1\_T, A2\_T\}$ because $\mu(B2\_T) \leq (\mu(A1\_T) = \mu(A2\_T))$. This can be interpreted as $B2\_T$ *potentially requires* $A1\_T$ and $A2\_T$.

- $\{A1\_A, A2\_A\} \rightarrow B2\_A$ because $\mu(A1\_A) = \mu(A2\_A) \leq \mu(B2\_A)$. This can be interpreted as $A1\_A$ and $A2\_A$ *potentially require* $B2\_A$.

Table 4.7 shows all potential require constraints between features that can be derived from the concept lattice for the feature group ICC shown in Figure 4.3. The implications in the Table are sorted by descending global support value. As one can see from this Table, the global support value for some implications, e.g., $A2\_A \rightarrow A1_A$ is very low and the local support value is high whereas for other implications the global and the local support value are high, e.g., for the implication $A2\_T \rightarrow A1\_T$. An expert that validated the feature constraints confirmed that $A2\_A \rightarrow A1\_A$ and $A2\_T \rightarrow A1\_T$ are both valid feature constraints. This supports our argument that for the identification of likely feature constraints the local support value provides a good indicator while the global support value might be misleading.

Potential Exclusion Constraints

Similarly to potential require constraints between features, we can also use the concept lattice to derive *potential mutual-exclusive constraints* between features. A potential mutual-exclusive constraint between two features f_1 and f_2, written f_1 *excludes* f_2, exists if f_1

Premise		Conclusion	$N_{A,B}$	Global Support	Local Support
A2_T	$\rightarrow$	A1_T	9	81%	100%
A1_T	$\rightarrow$	A2_T	9	81%	100%
B2_T	$\rightarrow$	A1_T	6	55%	67%
B2_T	$\rightarrow$	A2_T	6	55%	67%
B2_A	$\rightarrow$	A3	5	45%	67%
A3_R	$\rightarrow$	A3	5	45%	55%
A2_A	$\rightarrow$	A1_A	2	18%	100%
A2_A	$\rightarrow$	A3	2	18%	40%
A2_A	$\rightarrow$	A3_R	2	18%	22%
A2_A	$\rightarrow$	B2_A	2	18%	40%
A1_A	$\rightarrow$	A2_A	2	18%	100%
A1_A	$\rightarrow$	A3	2	18%	40%
A1_A	$\rightarrow$	A3_R	2	18%	22%
A1_A	$\rightarrow$	B2_A	2	18%	40%

Table 4.7: Potential require constraints between ICC features.

and f_2 are used only mutually-exclusively, written $f_1 \oplus f_2$, in the analyzed set of product configurations $\mathcal{P}$.

The features f_1 and f_2 are used mutually exclusively, written $f_1 \oplus f_2$, if the following conditions hold:

1. $\mu(f_1) \sqcap \mu(f_2) = \bot$

2. $ext(\bot) = \emptyset$

The first condition states that the *infimum* of the feature concepts $\mu(f_1)$ and $\mu(f_2)$ is the bottom concept. The second condition states that the bottom concept ($\bot$) does not contain a product configuration.

Note that this is also only a necessary but not a sufficient condition, i.e., a valid exclusion constraint always implies that f_1 and f_2 are used mutually-exclusively:

$$f_1 \text{ excludes } f_2 \Rightarrow \mu(f_1) \oplus \mu(f_2) \Rightarrow (\mu(f_1) \sqcap \mu(f_2) = \bot \wedge \text{ext}(\bot) = \emptyset) \qquad (4.28)$$

but the fulfillment of the conditions for mutual-exclusive usage does not necessarily imply a valid exclusion constraint:

$$(\mu(f_1) \sqcap \mu(f_2) = \bot \wedge \text{ext}(\bot) = \emptyset) \Rightarrow (\mu(f_1) \oplus \mu(f_2)) \not\Rightarrow f_1 \text{ excludes } f_2 \qquad (4.29)$$

Therefore, the validity of potential mutual-exclusive constraints should be checked by an analyst.

Example. From the concept lattice shown in Figure 4.3, we can for example derive the following potential mutual-exclusive constraints between features:

- $B2\_A \oplus B2\_T$ because $\mu(B2\_A) \sqcap \mu(B2\_T) = \bot$. This can be interpreted as B2_A is *potentially mutually-exclusive with* B2_T.

- $\{A1\_A, A2\_A\} \oplus \{A1\_T, A2\_T\}$ because $(\mu(A1\_A) = \mu(A2\_A)) \sqcap (\mu(B2\_A) = \mu(B2\_T)) = \bot$. This means that A1_A is *potentially mutually-exclusive with* A1_T, A1_A is *potentially mutually-exclusive with* A2_T, A2_A is *potentially mutually-exclusive with* A1_T, and A2_A is *potentially mutually-exclusive with* A2_T.

Potential mutual-exclusion constraints between features that can be derived from the lattice are shown in Table 4.8.

A1_A	$\oplus$	A1_T
A1_A	$\oplus$	A2_T
A1_A	$\oplus$	B2_T
A1_T	$\oplus$	A2_A
A2_A	$\oplus$	A2_T
A2_A	$\oplus$	B2_T
B2_A	$\oplus$	B2_T

Table 4.8: Potential mutual-exclusion constraints between ICC features.

Summary

Note, that these potential require constraints and potential mutual-exclusive constraints are valid only for the analyzed product configurations. Although each potential constraint has a confidence level of 100% stating that if the premise is true, the conclusion will be true, the potential constraint is only valid for all $p \in \mathcal{P}$ but not necessarily for some other $p \notin \mathcal{P}$. As we have seen, the conditions for implications and mutual-exclusive usage are necessary but not sufficient for the existence of a requires or exclusion constraint. Therefore, the potential constraints need to be verified by an expert before they can be considered as universally valid constraints.

Interesting conclusions can be drawn if existing domain knowledge about feature constraints is compared with potential feature constraints identified by variability analysis. For example, if we know from existing domain knowledge that a feature constraint is valid and it is not identified as a potential feature constraint during variability analysis we know that some of the analyzed product configurations must exhibit a configuration error. In the case of mutual-exclusion constraints, we can even identify the product configurations that exhibit the configuration error. Those erroneous product configurations appear in the extent of the infimum of the two features that are supposed to be mutually exclusive.

4.3 Extensions

We extended the basic approach for variability analysis as described in Section 4.2 by several concepts that make the approach more practicable. These concepts include means that allow the user to manipulate the concept lattice and product-feature matrix during analysis, means that allow the user to reduce the size of the product-feature matrix in order to make the resulting concept lattices smaller and easier to interpret, and visual aids that help the user during manual inspection of the concept lattice.

4.3.1 User Manipulations

During the manual inspection of the concept lattice situations may arise in which the concept lattice does not fully represent the knowledge about features, product configurations, and their relationships. For example, it might be the case that there exist constraints between features which are not reflected in the concept lattice because none of the product configurations happens to exhibit the constraints. Such facts which can be derived from external information sources such as expert knowledge or existing documentation can be used for further iterations of variability analysis in order to improve the analysis results. In order to incorporate this knowledge, we allow the user to extend the product-feature matrix by additional rows (product configurations) or columns (features). The concept lattice, feature constraints, and the feature usage classification are automatically recalculated after the product-feature matrix has been extended by row or column.

4.3.2 Filters

Concept lattices grow with an increasing number of objects and attributes, i.e., in our case with an increasing number of product configurations and features. In practice, the number of features is often much larger than the number of product configurations. Therefore, it is helpful to exclude some of the features from the analysis in order to reduce the size of the resulting concept lattice. The software architects or other experts having specific domain knowledge usually define the set of features to be excluded from the analysis. For example, the software architect might decide to exclude all features from the analysis that do not belong to a specific architectural component or feature group.

These features can either be excluded before or after the construction of the product-feature matrix or even after formal concept analysis has been applied on the product-feature matrix. Excluding features before the construction of the product-feature matrix has the advantage that the construction and handling of the product-feature matrix will be easier because it is smaller. Filtering features after the construction of the product-feature matrix has the advantage that the product-feature matrix does not need to be reconstructed if the rules of the filtering change during subsequent analyses of the data. The last option, excluding features after formal concept analysis, has the advantage that the analyst can first get an overview of the size of the concept lattice before deciding which features should be excluded. However, it has the disadvantage that the product-feature matrix and the concept lattice need to be constructed with all features and all product configurations which may take considerably longer than excluding features before the analysis. It is important to note that filtering of features is an order-preserving transformation of the concept lattice as shown in Section 4.1.3.

The usage of filters is especially helpful if a large system with several hundred features has to be analyzed. In this case, the filters allow the analyst to analyze the system step by step, e.g., by focusing on specific subsystems in each step of the analysis. In addition, our approach provides the analyst with a great flexibility in the time when he wants to apply the filter. This allows him to analyze the system in a number of different ways. For example, he might decide to get an overview of the whole system first by analyzing the whole product-feature matrix before focusing his analysis on individual subsystems. Or he might decide to filter all features that do not belong to a specific subsystem before applying concept analysis on the product feature matrix to focus on the variability of this subsystem right from the beginning.

4.3.3   Visual Aids

The understanding of large concept lattices can be considerably eased by providing visual aids for the analyst to draw his attention to specific areas of the concept lattice. A relatively easy way to do so is to color the relevant concepts. Another way of drawing the attention to specific areas is to draw the nodes representing the concepts in the concept lattice in different sizes. In the following, we describe these two ways in more detail.

Coloring

During the manual inspection of concept lattices we found out that the coloring of concepts according to their type, according to specific features or product configurations and according to the feature usage classes helped considerably to enhance the understanding of the provided variability and its use in product configurations. We used the following coloring strategies to make the inspection of the concept lattice as easy as possible:

- **Coloring according to concept type.** In the sparse representation of a concept lattice there exist four different types of concepts, namely, *feature concepts* that contain one or more features, *product concepts* that contain one or more product configurations, *mixed concepts* that contain both features and product configurations, and *empty concepts* that neither contain features nor product configurations. In order to visually distinguish these different types of concepts in a large concept lattice, the following coloring scheme can be applied:

  - Feature concepts are half-filled with a specific feature color
  - Product concepts are half-filled with a specific product color
  - Mixed concepts are half-filled with the feature color and half-filled with the product color
  - Empty concepts are not filled at all

Using this coloring scheme, the concepts conveying information, i.e., feature concepts, product concepts, and mixed concepts, can be easily distinguished from empty concepts conveying no information.

Example. Figure 4.4 shows the concept lattice of the ICC feature group with concepts colored according to its type. Feature concepts are half-filled with gray, product concepts are half-filled with black, mixed concepts are half-filled with gray and half-filled with black, and empty concepts are not filled.

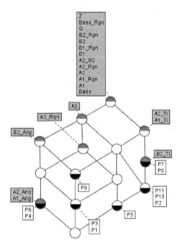

Figure 4.4: Coloring of concept types for ICC features.

- **Coloring according to features or product configurations.** Another strategy of coloring concepts is to color all concepts containing a specific feature or a specific product configuration with a certain color. This coloring of concepts can be used to quickly identify all features that are used in a specific product configuration or all product configurations that use a specific feature. Before the concepts are colored, a specific color for each feature or product configuration to be colored is chosen. In the next step, all concepts containing a specific feature f, i.e., all concepts c with $f \in int(c)$, or all concepts containing a specific product configuration p, i.e., all concepts c with $p \in ext(c)$ are colored with the chosen color for feature f or product configuration p.

Interesting insights in the usage of features in product configurations can be obtained if two product configurations p_1 and p_2 or two features f_1 and f_2 are colored at the same time. In this case, the concepts containing one of the product configurations p_1 or p_2 or one of the features f_1 or f_2 are respectively colored with their corresponding colors. If a concept contains both p_1 and p_2 or f_1 and f_2 it is colored with both colors of p_1 and p_2 or f_1 and f_2, respectively. This coloring scheme allows us to identify features that are shared between two product configurations p_1 and p_2 or product configurations that use two features f_1 and f_2 together. Furthermore, distinct features of two product configurations p_1 and p_2 or distinct product configurations for two features f_1 and f_2 can be identified as well.

Examples. Figure 4.5 shows the concept lattice of the ICC features in four different colorings. In subfigure (a), all concepts containing the feature B2_Ang are colored in black. In subfigure (b), the concepts containing feature B2_Ang and not A3_Rgn are colored in black, the concepts containing feature A3_Rgn and not B2_Ang are colored in gray, and the concepts containing both features are colored in both black and gray. In subfigure (c), all concepts containing product configuration P9 are colored in black. In subfigure (d), the concepts containing product configuration P9 and not P5 are colored in black, the concepts containing product configuration P5 and not P9 are colored in gray, and the concepts containing both product configurations P5 and P9 are colored in both black and gray.

- **Coloring according to feature usage classes.** The third strategy is to color the features according to the feature usage classes I-IV. For this, we need 4 different colors. Each feature is colored according to the usage class it belongs to. This coloring helps to get an quick visual overview of the distribution of features to feature usage classes.

  Example. Figure 4.6 shows the concept lattice for the ICC features with concepts colored according to the feature usage classes I-IV. As it is impossible to distinguish these colors in black and white rendition, we marked the concepts with the class numbers I-IV instead.

Node Size

Another way of drawing the attention of the analyst to specific areas of the concept lattice is to draw the nodes representing the concepts in different sizes. This is especially useful for large concept lattices in which the display of label boxes that show features and product configurations is turned off to increase the readability of the concept lattice. During the manual inspection of concept lattices, we found out that the following strategies of drawing the node size are especially helpful for an easier understanding of the concept lattice:

- **Fixed radius.** This is the standard way of drawing nodes that represent concepts. All nodes representing concepts are drawn with a fixed radius. Thus, none of the concepts receives special attention by the analyst.

  Example. Figure 4.7, Subfigure (a) shows the concept lattice for the ICC features in which each node has the same fixed radius.

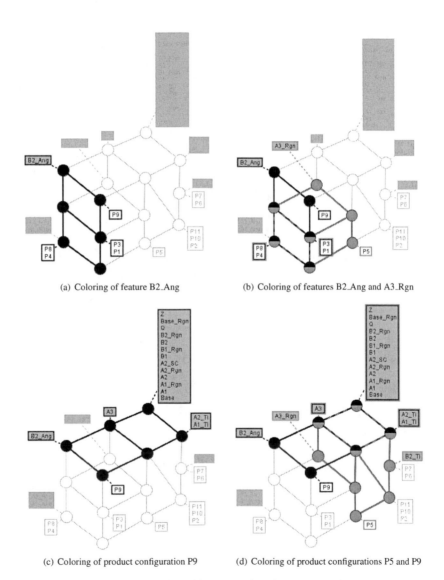

(a) Coloring of feature B2_Ang

(b) Coloring of features B2_Ang and A3_Rgn

(c) Coloring of product configuration P9

(d) Coloring of product configurations P5 and P9

Figure 4.5: Coloring of features and product configurations.

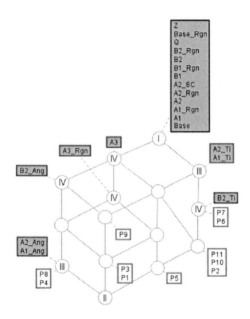

Figure 4.6: Coloring of concepts according to feature usage classes I-IV.

- **Proportional to number of attached features.** Another way of drawing the nodes is to adjust the radius of the nodes proportional to the number of features that are attached to the node. In other words, concepts that have a large number of features attached will be drawn bigger than concepts which have a smaller number of features or no features attached. Consequently, the attention of the analyst is drawn towards the bigger nodes, i.e., those nodes having a large number of features attached.

  Example. Figure 4.7, Subfigure (b) shows the concept lattice for the ICC features in which the radius of the concepts is drawn proportional to the number of attached features.

- **Proportional to number of attached product configurations.** Opposite to the last strategy, in this strategy the radius of the nodes is proportional to the number of attached product configurations. In other words, concepts that have a large number of product configurations attached will be drawn bigger in size than concepts which have a small number of product configurations or no product configurations attached. Consequently, the attention of the analyst is drawn towards the bigger nodes, i.e., those nodes having a large number of product configurations attached.

  Example. Figure 4.7, Subfigure (c) shows the concept lattice for the ICC features in which the radius of the concepts is drawn proportional to the number of attached product configurations.

4.4   Applications of Variability Analysis

The information contained in the concept lattice can be used for a number of important variability management and product derivation tasks. In particular, variability analysis can be applied to derive important knowledge about the correct configuration of products, to provide decision support for the optimization of variability, and to determine the future scope of the software product line.

4.4.1   Derivation of Configuration Knowledge

In industrial organizations it is very often the case that the necessary knowledge for product derivation is not fully documented. Some of this knowledge, especially the dependencies between variable features, is often only present in the head of software architects. Variability analysis allows the derivation of important configuration knowledge for the derivation of products. The concept lattice can be used to identify likely constraints between variable features that can then be documented to make this knowledge available for the derivation of future products. In addition this knowledge can be used to automatically check future product configurations for the inclusion of required features and the exclusion of mutually-exclusive features.

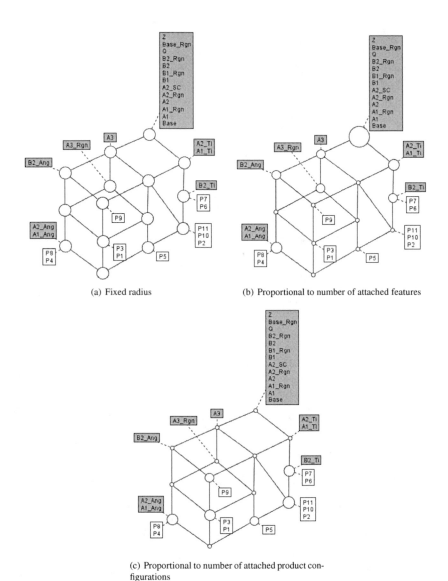

(a) Fixed radius

(b) Proportional to number of attached features

(c) Proportional to number of attached product configurations

Figure 4.7: Different strategies for drawing the radius of the nodes.

4.4.2 Decision Support for Variability Optimization

The variability provided by the software product line and the variability currently required by the set of analyzed products do not necessarily need to match. Due to changes in the product portfolio that should be supported by the product line or planning for the future, it often occurs that the provided variability in a product line is higher than the amount of variability actually required to derive the products from the product line.

In this case, variability analysis allows us to identify the minimal number of variable features needed to derive the existing set of products from the product line. Furthermore, using the feature usage classification a set of strategies for restructuring the existing variability, i.e., minimizing the number of features required to derive the set of products, can be derived. The restructuring of variability using the information that can be obtained by variability analysis is described in more detail in Chapter 5.

4.4.3 Determination of the Future Scope

The concept lattice also allows us to measure the usage of features in product configurations, i.e., for each feature the percentage of product configurations using it can be determined. This allows us to group the features by their usage, e.g., into the following three groups:

1. High Usage: used in 50-100% of all product configurations

2. Medium Usage: used in 10-50% of all product configurations

3. Low Usage: used in 0-10% of all product configurations

The distribution of features into these groups can be used as a basis for making informed decisions about the future scope of the software product line. For example, if there is a large number of features in the *low usage* group, we may come to the conclusion that these features should be implemented product-specifically in the future.

4.5 Summary

In this chapter, we presented our approach for variability analysis that provides the necessary decision support for the analyst in order to make informed decisions about the maintenance and evolution of the provided variability in the software product line. The approach applies formal concept analysis to derive a concept lattice from a table relating product configurations and features. Given an adequate interpretation, this concept lattice provides the analyst with a lot of information regarding the actual use of variability in the set of analyzed product configurations.

We showed that the concept lattice provides means to derive important configuration knowledge about the correct configuration of products, to determine the future scope of the product line, and to provide decision support for variability maintenance and evolution.

Furthermore, we presented several extensions to our approach that make variability analysis more practicable and enable its application to very large software product lines. These extensions include means that allow the user to manipulate the concept lattice and product-feature matrix during analysis, filters that allow the user to reduce the size of the product-feature matrix in order to make the resulting concept lattices smaller and easier to interpret, and visual aids that help the user during manual inspection of large concept lattices.

Chapter 5

Variability Restructuring

In this chapter, we describe how the provided variability of a software product line can be restructured. The goal of variability restructuring is to minimize the amount of variability provided by the features by restructuring their implementation without affecting the configurability of the software product line for current and future products. The variability restructuring process is divided into two parts, namely, *restructuring preparation* and *implementation of restructuring decisions*, and uses the main results of variability analysis, i.e., the feature usage classification and the concept lattice.

Overview. In Section 5.1, we describe how the feature usage classification is used to derive and validate so called restructuring decisions, i.e., decisions about the restructuring of the implementation of features. Section 5.2 explains the implementation of these restructuring decisions for features that have been implemented and whose variability has been realized by a software configuration management (SCM) system. In Section 5.3, we conclude this chapter by a summary of the main ideas.

5.1 Restructuring Preparation

Before the provided variability of the software product line can be restructured we need to make decisions about which features should be restructured and validate these decisions. In Section 5.1.1, we describe how the feature usage classification is used to derive hypotheses about the necessity of the variability provided by these features. Based on these hypotheses decisions are made whether to restructure the implementation of the features or not. The implementation of these restructuring decisions will result in the minimal number of features required to derive the analyzed product configurations. However, as the hypotheses and the resulting restructuring decisions are based solely on the analyzed product configurations, they need to be validated prior to their implementation. Therefore, we describe in Section 5.1.2 how the hypotheses and the restructuring decisions are validated by comparing them with additional explicit and implicit domain knowledge.

5.1.1 Derivation of Restructuring Decisions

As a starting point for variability restructuring we use the classification of feature usage as described in Section 4.2.6. The feature usage classes I-IV provide valuable hints for the restructuring of variability as they allow us to derive hypotheses about the intended use of the features by product line engineers. These hypotheses can then be used to decide whether the provided variability of the features is required or not. If the variability is not required the implementation of the features should be restructured to remove the variability. The following hypotheses and restructuring decisions can be derived for the feature usage classes I-IV:

I **Always used.** This class contains features that are used in every product configuration that has been analyzed. Therefore, it is very likely that the features of this class are *mandatory features*, i.e., features that have to be used in every product that is derived from the product line. As the variability provided by the implementation of these features apparently is not needed for the analyzed product configurations, it should be restructured. This will reduce the complexity of variability as the number of variation points that need to be managed and handled during product derivation is reduced.

II **Never used.** Features in this class are not used in any of the analyzed product configurations. Therefore, it is likely that these features are (a) new features that have not yet been used in any of the product configurations or (b) obsolete features that are not needed anymore. In case (a), the variability provided by these features is probably required for future product configurations and therefore the implementation of these features should not be restructured. In case (b), the provided variability by these features is not required anymore because the features have become obsolete. Therefore, the implementation of these features should be restructured.

III **Only used together.** This class contains clusters of features that are used together in a subset of all analyzed product configurations. The hypothesis is that features that are together in a cluster are likely features that cannot be used separately. If this hypothesis is accepted by the domain expert, the implementation of these features should be restructured to reduce the number of variation points.

IV **Only used separately.** This class contains features that do not belong to any of the classes I-III. Therefore, it is very likely that these features are needed for the differentiation of products, i.e., these features provide variability that is actually required by the analyzed product configurations. Therefore, the implementation of these features should not be restructured.

Table 5.1 shows a summary of the hypotheses and restructuring decisions that can be derived from the feature usage classes I-IV. The column "Variability"' in Table 5.1 shows whether the variability provided by the features in each class is actually required for the product family or not.

	Feature Usage Class	Hypothesis	Variability	Decision
I	Always used	Mandatory features	not required	restructure
II	Never used	(a) New features	(a) required	leave as is
II	Never used	(b) Obsolete features	(b) not required	restructure
III	Only used together	Cannot be used separately	combinable	restructure
IV	Only used separately	Variable features	required	leave as is

Table 5.1: Hypotheses for feature usage classes I-IV, necessity of variability provided by features in each class, and resulting restructuring decisions.

It is important to note that the hypotheses and the restructuring decisions are based only on the analyzed product configurations and strongly depend on the usage of features in these product configurations. The accuracy of the hypotheses can be improved by analyzing preliminary or planned product configurations in addition to existing product configurations (see Section 6.2 for details). Although this will reduce the likelihood of a wrong classification of features and wrong decisions about the necessity of the provided variability, the hypotheses and the restructuring decisions should always be checked by an analyst before the actual restructuring is performed (see Section 5.1.2 for details).

Example. In order to illustrate the derivation of restructuring decisions we use the ICC feature group which we already analyzed in Chapter 4. In Section 4.2.6, we derived the feature usage classification from the concept lattice. Table 5.2 shows a summary of this classification.

Class	Features	#
I	A1, A1_R, A2, A2_R, A2_SC, B1, B1_R, B2, B2_R, Q, Z	11
II	A2_CC	1
III	{A1_A, A2_A}, {A1_T, A2_T}	4
IV	A3, A3_R, B2_A, B2_T	4

Table 5.2: Usage classification of ICC features.

The last column of Table 5.2 shows the number of features in each class. Using the hypotheses of the intended usage, the necessity of the variability, and the restructuring decisions shown in Table 5.1, the classification of ICC features can be interpreted as follows:

- Class I: A1, A1_R, A2, A2_R, A2_SC, B1, B1_R, B2, B2_R, Q, and Z are very likely mandatory features. The variability of these features is not required for the analyzed product configurations. Therefore, the implementation of these features should be restructured to remove unnecessary variation points.

- Class II: A2_CC is either a new feature or an obsolete feature. In the latter case, the variability provided by this feature is not required and should be removed.

- Class III: The pairs {A1_A, A2_A} and {A1_T, A2_T} are very likely features that have to be used together. The variability of these single features is not required for the analyzed product configurations. However, the variability of subsets of these features is required, e.g., A1_A and A2_A or A1_T and A2_T are used in the product configurations. Therefore, the implementation of the features in class III should be restructured according to the distribution of features on the clusters, i.e., the implementation of A1_A and A2_A should be combined and the implementation of A1_T and A2_T should also be combined.

- Class IV: A3, A3_R, B2_A, and B2_T are features whose variability is required for the analyzed product configurations. Therefore, the implementation of these features should not be restructured.

The number of features whose variability is not required for the analyzed product configurations in total is 14 features (classes I, II, and III). This number is very high compared to the total number of 21 features that are provided by the ICC feature group. In other words, this means that the variability provided by the ICC feature group is much higher than the variability actually required to derive the product configurations {P1,...,P11}. Consequently, there is a great potential for restructuring the provided variability of the ICC feature group.

5.1.2   Validation of Restructuring Decisions

As the hypotheses and the restructuring decisions are based only on the analyzed product configurations and strongly depend on the usage of features in these product configurations, they should be validated by an analyst and corrected if necessary before the restructuring is performed. This validation can be done by comparing the classification of features, the derived hypotheses, and the necessity of the variability provided by features with domain knowledge that has not been inferred by variability analysis. For example, explicit domain knowledge in the form of variability models, architecture descriptions, prescriptions for the configuration of products or implicit domain knowledge in the form of expert knowledge can be used for this comparison. Furthermore, additional knowledge about the future of the product portfolio that should be supported by the product line is very helpful in this comparison.

The goal of comparing the classification of features, the hypotheses, and the derived restructuring decisions with explicit and implicit domain knowledge that has not been inferred by variability analysis is to accept or reject the hypotheses about the necessity of the variability provided by the features and the resulting restructuring decisions. In other words, we want to select those features for restructuring whose variability is truly not required for the intended product portfolio, i.e., the future scope of the product line. Furthermore, we want to avoid the application of restructuring transformations on the implementation of features whose variability is required from a domain perspective but is not required by looking at the feature usage classification and hypotheses alone.

The comparison of the feature usage classification with domain knowledge that has not been inferred by variability analysis can be automated to some extent if the domain knowledge is available explicitly and in a computer understandable form. However, in most cases the domain knowledge is only available implicitly or if it is available explicitly it is not in a form that can be easy processed by a computer. In these cases, the comparison has to be performed manually. However, the concept lattice and the feature usage classification simplify this manual comparison to a great extent because the hypotheses and possible restructuring decisions can be automatically derived from the feature usage classification and presented to the analyst.

In order to validate the restructuring decisions we proceed as depicted in Figure 5.1:

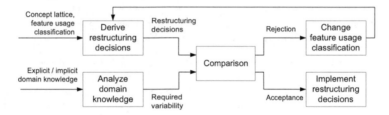

Figure 5.1: Validation process for restructuring decisions.

1. As a starting point for the validation of the restructuring decisions we use the feature usage classification, the hypotheses and the restructuring decisions that have been derived from the concept lattice. The concept lattice and the feature usage classes serve as a basis for selecting the features whose variability is not required from the viewpoint of a domain expert.

2. Explicit domain knowledge in the form of variability models, architecture descriptions, rules for the configuration of products and product roadmaps are analyzed and product developers are interviewed to obtain a detailed description of the variability that is required from the product line from a domain perspective. This description may include variability that is required for products which have not yet been derived from the product line but might be derived from it in the future.

3. In the following, the feature usage classification, the hypotheses, and the restructuring decisions that have been obtained in the first step are compared with the required variability obtained from domain knowledge. For each feature, the analyst either accepts the hypothesis, i.e., the feature usage class confirms with the additional domain knowledge about the features, or he rejects the hypothesis, i.e., the feature usage class does not confirm with the additional domain knowledge. In the first case, the restructuring decision is not changed and the implementation of the

features will be restructured as planned. In the latter case, the analyst is allowed to change the feature usage classification. Depending on the new class of the feature this change in classification will have an effect on the restructuring decision or not (see Table 5.4 for details).

For the adaptation of the feature usage classification, we allow the following changes:

I **Initially always used.** Features in this class are used in all analyzed product configurations. The hypothesis is that these features are *mandatory* features, i.e., they have to be used in every product configuration that is derived from the product line. Therefore, the resulting restructuring decision is to restructure the implementation of these features. However, the hypothesis and the resulting restructuring decision might not be valid from a domain perspective for specific features in this class. Therefore, we allow the analyst to change the class of features to class III (used together) or class IV (used separately). We do not allow the class to be changed to class II (never used) as this is in conflict with the analyzed product configurations.

II **Initially never used.** Features in this class are not used in any of the analyzed product configurations. The hypothesis is that these features are *obsolete* features, i.e., that they should be removed. However, this hypothesis might not be valid from a domain perspective. Therefore, we allow the analyst to change the classification of features from this class to class III (used together) or class IV (used separately). We do not allow the class to be changed to class I (always used) as this is in conflict with the analyzed product configurations.

III **Initially only used together.** Features in this class are used together with other features in a subset of all analyzed product configurations. The hypothesis is that these features cannot be used separately. However, this hypothesis might not be valid from a domain perspective for specific features in this class. Therefore, we allow the analyst to change the classification of features in this class to class IV (used separately). We do not allow other class changes because these changes would conflict with the set of analyzed product configurations.

IV **Initially only used separately.** Features in this class are used separately. Apparently, the variability provided by these features is needed to differentiate the products. Any change in the classification of these features conflicts with the set of analyzed product configurations. Therefore, we do not allow the analyst to change the classification of features belonging to this class.

For features that belong to class III (initially only used together) the features that are used together with them can be directly read off the concept lattice, i.e., these are the features that appear at the same concept. Therefore, the class III (initially only used together) is divided into groups, i.e., subsets of features of class III which are used together. Thus, whenever the classification of features that initially belong to classes I or II is changed to class III, the analyst needs to decide to which group the feature should be added. In the concept lattice this corresponds to moving attributes from the top concept downwards in the lattice or from the bottom concept upwards.

A summary of the allowed changes for each feature usage class is shown in Table 5.3. The initial classes are shown in the rows of the table and the new classes are shown in the columns. A *yes* in a table cell indicates that this change is allowed, a *no* in a table cell indicates that this change is not allowed because it is in conflict with the analyzed product configurations.

Initial Class	New Class			
	I	II	III	IV
I: Always used	-	no	yes	yes
II: Never used	no	-	yes	yes
III: Used together	no	no	-	yes
IV: Used separately	no	no	no	-

Table 5.3: Allowed changes of feature usage classification.

It is important to note that the changes that we allow affect the previously made restructuring decisions. Table 5.4 shows the effects that a change of the classification of a feature has on the previously made restructuring decision (n.a. indicates that this change is not allowed as specified in Table 5.3).

Initial Class	New Class			
	I	II	III	IV
I: Always used	-	n.a.	no effect	restructure $\rightarrow$ leave as is
II: Never used	n.a.	-	no effect	restructure $\rightarrow$ leave as is
III: Used together	n.a.	n.a.	-	restructure $\rightarrow$ leave as is
IV: Used separately	n.a.	n.a.	n.a.	-

Table 5.4: Effects of the change of classification on restructuring decisions.

From Table 5.4 one can see that whenever the feature usage class is changed to class IV (used separately) the previously made decision to restructure the implementation is revoked, i.e., the implementation will be left as is. All other changes do not affect the restructuring decision itself. However, these changes affect the implementation of the restructuring decision, i.e., the selection of an appropriate restructuring transformation. The derivation of restructuring transformations based on the changed feature usage classification will be described in Section 5.2.2.

In order to keep the validated hypotheses and restructuring decisions for repeated analyses, our variability analysis and restructuring tool VariAnT [Per07] allows the changed feature usage classification to be saved and reloaded.

In case of an incremental analysis of product configurations, i.e., product configurations are added or removed from the formal context, it may happen that the new feature usage classification which is based on the extended formal context (NEW INITIAL) contradicts with the feature usage classification changed by the analyst (ANALYST). In those situations, the ANALYST classification needs to be updated, i.e., the class of some features needs to be recalculated to match the NEW INITIAL classification. Of course this recalculation should keep as much information about the ANALYST classification as possible. Table 5.5 shows the recalculated classes of features for each possible combination of mismatches in the classification of features that may occur between the ANALYST classification and the NEW INITIAL classification. As one can see from Table 5.5, in

	ANALYST Class			
NEW INITIAL Class	I	II	III	IV
I: Always used	keep	I	keep/IV	keep
II: Never used	II	keep	keep/IV	keep
III: Used together	III/IV	III/IV	keep	keep
IV: Used separately	IV	IV	IV	keep

Table 5.5: Recalculation policy for each possible combination of conflicting feature usage classes after addition or removal of product configurations.

most cases the features can keep the classification that was chosen by the analyst. However, in some cases it needs to be updated to be in congruence with the new initial classification. For example, when a feature has been classified as being always used (class I) by the analyst and the new initial classification classifies this feature as being used separately (class IV), the classification of this feature needs to be changed from class I to class IV in the ANALYST classification.

Example. In order to illustrate the procedure for comparing the feature usage classification, the derived hypotheses, and restructuring decisions with additional domain knowledge we use the ICC feature group as an example again. In Section 5.1.1 we already derived several hypotheses and restructuring decisions for the features of the ICC feature group. The initial feature usage classification is shown in Table 5.2 and serves as a basis for the comparison with additional domain knowledge. Table 5.6 shows a summary of the restructuring decisions we made for the features of the ICC feature group based on the initial feature usage classification.

Decision	Features / Groups
Restructure	{A1, A1_R, A2, A2_R, A2_SC, B1, B1_R, B2, B2_R, Q, Z}, {A1_A, A2_A}, {A1_T, A2_T}, A2_CC
Leave	A3, A3_R, B2_A, B2_T

Table 5.6: Derived restructuring decisions for features of the ICC feature group based on the initial feature usage classification.

We analyzed explicit domain knowledge in the form of a feature model and interviewed the platform developers of the ICC feature group to obtain a description of the variability that is required for the ICC feature group from a domain perspective. The feature model for the ICC feature group is shown in Figure 5.2.

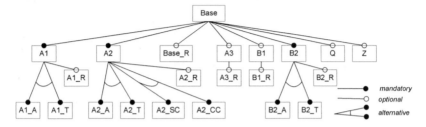

Figure 5.2: Feature diagram for ICC feature group.

From this feature model one can infer the following classification of features:

- **Mandatory features:** Base, A1, A2, B2

- **Optional features:** Base_R, A1_R, A2_R, A3, A3_R, B1, B1_R, B2_R, Q, Z

- **Alternative features:** {A1_A, A1_T}, {A2_A, A2_T}, {A2_SC, A2_CC}, and {B2_A, B2_T}

By interviewing the platform developers we obtained the following additional implicit domain knowledge which is not contained in the feature model:

- If regeneration mode shall be enabled, the features ending with _R have to be included. As A1, A2, and B2 are mandatory this means that if A1_R is included A2_R, and B2_R must be included as well. It is not possible to include one of these features alone as they work together to build the regeneration mode.

- If alternative A1_T is selected, the alternative A2_T must be selected as well.

- If alternative A1_A is selected, the alternative A2_A must be selected as well.

- Features Q and Z have been initially designed as optional features but are used in every product configuration.

- A2_SC and A2_CC are alternative features although almost all product configurations use feature A2_SC.

By comparing the initial feature usage classification shown in Table 5.2, the restructuring decisions shown in Table 5.6, the feature model shown in Figure 5.2, and the additional implicit domain knowledge that we obtained by interviewing the platform developers, we identified the following mismatches:

- The features Q and Z are shown as optional in the feature diagram but according
  to the feature usage classification they belong to class I (always used), i.e., the
  hypothesis is that these features are mandatory. The platform developer confirms
  this hypothesis by explaining to us that these features have become commodity
  features that are used in every product configuration. Therefore, we accept the
  hypothesis and do not change the classification of these features.

- The features A1_R, A2_R and B2_R belong to class I (always used) according to the
  feature usage classification, i.e., the hypothesis is that these features are mandatory
  features. In the feature model they are listed as optional features that may be selected independently. The platform developer tells us that if they are used they must
  be used together. Therefore, we reject the hypothesis and come to the conclusion
  that the class of these features should be changed from class I to class III and that
  they should form a new group.

- A2_CC and A2_SC are shown as alternative features in the feature diagram. According to the feature usage classification A2_SC belongs to class I (always used)
  and A2_CC belongs class II (never used). Thus the hypothesis for A2_SC is that it
  is mandatory and the hypothesis for A_CC is that it is obsolete. However, the platform developer states that A2_CC is still needed, i.e., he rejects the hypothesis that
  A2_CC is obsolete. Therefore, we change the classification of A2_CC from class II
  (never used) to class IV (used separately). Consequently, we also need to change
  the class of A2_SC from class I (always used) to class IV (used separately).

The changes in the feature usage classification affect the restructuring decisions as
already described above. Table 5.7 shows the new restructuring decisions that take the
changes in the feature usage classification into account. As one can see from Table 5.7
the validation of restructuring decisions and the resulting changes in the classification of
some features have increased the number of features whose implementation will be left
as is, i.e., whose implementation will not be restructured.

Decision	Features / Groups
Restructure	{Base, A1, A2, B2, Q, Z}, {A1_A, A2_A}, {A1_T, A2_T}, {Base_R, A1_R, A2_R, B2_R}
Leave	A2_SC, A2_CC, A3, A3_R, B1, B1_R, B2_A, B2_T

Table 5.7: Restructuring decisions for features of the ICC feature group based on the new
feature usage classification.

5.2   Implementation of Restructuring Decisions

In the last section we described the derivation and validation of restructuring decision.
This section deals with the implementation of these restructuring decisions. As the im-

plementation of the restructuring decisions depends on the implementation of features and the chosen variability realization techniques, we first need to analyze the implementation of features in order to derive suitable restructuring transformations for the implemented variability. The final step of restructuring is to apply the derived restructuring transformations on the implemented features.

In the following subsections, we will describe the implementation of restructuring decisions for variability that has been realized using the software configuration management (SCM) system ClearCase [Leb94].

In cases when the mapping of features to source code entities implementing them is not clear feature location as described in [EKS03, Sim05] may be used to identify the source code entities implementing specific features. In cases when preprocessor directives are used as a variability realization a technique called preprocessor conditional removal by simple partial evaluation may be used to implement the restructuring decisions [BM01].

5.2.1 Analysis of Feature Implementation

The first step of implementing the restructuring decisions for specific features is to analyze the implementation of these features and the chosen variability realization technique. In our case, the software configuration management (SCM) system ClearCase [Leb94] is used for the implementation of the features and for variability realization. Readers who are not familiar with SCM systems should read Appendix A that describes the basic concepts of SCM systems and the specific concepts of ClearCase before reading the following Section.

Feature Implementation and Variability Realization with ClearCase

In this Section, we describe how features are implemented and how their associated variability is realized using the SCM system ClearCase [Leb94]. We will illustrate this description using an example of variable features of a car. Figure 5.3 shows an example feature diagram for a car with mandatory, optional, and alternative features that is used for illustration purposes throughout this section. In Figure 5.3 one can see one mandatory feature, namely *Brakes*, one optional feature, namely *A/C*, and four alternative features, namely *manual transmission* or *automatic transmission*, and *manual windows* or *automatic windows*.

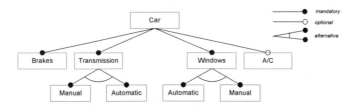

Figure 5.3: Example feature diagram of a car.

The abstract features described in the feature diagram are implemented by software entities which are *configuration items* in our case, i.e., files that are versioned by the SCM system. Table 5.8 shows the mapping of features to configuration items implementing them for the car example.

Features	Configuration Items
Car [C]	`car.c`
	`car.h`
	`ac.c`
	`ac.h`
Brakes [B]	`brakes.c`
	`brakes.h`
Air Conditioning [AC]	`ac.c`
	`ac.h`
Manual Transmission [MT]	`transmission.c`
	`transmission.h`
	`trans_man.c`
Automatic Transmission [AT]	`transmission.c`
	`transmission.h`
	`trans_aut.c`
Manual Windows [MW]	`windows.c`
	`windows.h`
	`windows_man.c`
Automatic Windows [AW]	`windows.c`
	`windows.h`
	`windows_aut.c`

Table 5.8: Mapping of features to configuration items.

Each feature is mapped to one or more configuration items that implement the feature as one can see in Table 5.8. As one can see from the table some configuration items are mapped to multiple features. For example, `ac.c` is mapped to *Car [C]* and *Air Conditioning [AC]*. However, the contents of the configuration item `ac.c` for feature *Car [C]* and for feature *Air Conditioning [AC]* are different, i.e., the configuration item `ac.c` exists in two different *permanent variants*, namely the variants *Car [C]* and *Air Conditioning [AC]*. In our case, the *Car [C]* variant of the file `ac.c` only contains empty functions whereas the *Air Conditioning [AC]* variant contains the full implementation for these functions.

To implement these different variants of configuration items, *named branches* in the SCM system are used. For each feature that appears in the feature diagram a corresponding branch is created. For example, the branch \b is created for the feature *Brakes [B]* at the configuration items `brakes.c` and `brakes.h`. If a configuration item appears more than once in the table above, as many branches as needed are created, e.g., for the configuration item `transmission.c` the branch \mt is created for the feature *Manual*

Transmission [MT] and the branch \at is created for the feature *Automatic Transmission [AT]*.

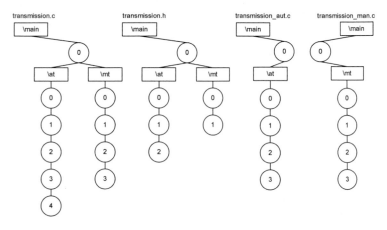

Figure 5.4: Version graphs of configuration items that implement the features *Automatic Transmission [AT]* and *Manual Transmission [MT]* in ClearCase [Leb94].

Figure 5.4 shows the version graphs of the configuration items that implement *Manual Transmission [MT]* and *Automatic Transmission [AT]*. The branches \mt and \at represent the features *Manual Transmission [MT]* and *Automatic Transmission [AT]* respectively. From Figure 5.4 one can see that transmission.c has the branches \at and \mt which indicates that this configuration item exists in two different variants, namely *Automatic Transmission [AT]* and *Manual Transmission [MT]*. Furthermore, one can see from Figure 5.4 that the configuration items specific to one of the alternative features, i.e., transmission_aut.c, and transmission_man.c only have one branch, namely either \at or \mt. This indicates that these configuration items only exist in one variant. By using branches and revisions each *permanent variant* of a configuration item can be evolved independently from other permanent variants at the same configuration item or other configuration items. In other words, the number of revisions of permanent variants of the same configuration item or other configuration items does not need to be the same, e.g., as shown in Figure 5.4 for configuration item transmission.c. This flexibility allows us to evolve each permanent variant separately and independently from other permanent variants.

Although having differing number of revisions for permanent variants allows a great flexibility for the evolution of these variants, it complicates selecting matching revisions of permanent variants across configuration items. In order to simplify this selection, *intensional versioning* with *labels* as described in Section A.1.3 is used.

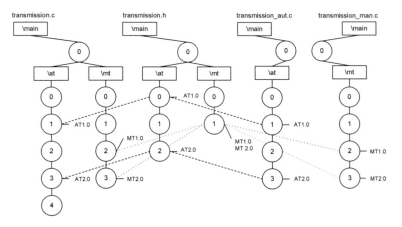

Figure 5.5: Selection of revisions of configuration items that implement the features *Automatic Transmission [AT]* and *Manual Transmission [MT]* using labels in ClearCase [Leb94].

Figure 5.5 shows the version graphs of the configuration items that implement the features *Automatic Transmission [AT]* and *Manual Transmission [MT]* including *labels* that are used to identify consistent sets of matching revisions of these configuration items.

As one can see in Figure 5.5 there are four *labels*, namely *AT1.0, AT2.0, MT1.0,* and *MT2.0*, which are attached to different revisions of multiple configuration items. The syntax of the labels is as follows:

- The first part describes the name of the feature which is represented by its corresponding branch, e.g., the label *AT* stands for the feature *Automatic Transmission [AT]* which is represented by branch \at.

- The second part describes the version number of the feature, e.g., *AT1.0* stands for version *1.0* of the automatic transmission feature.

For the attachment of labels to revisions of configuration items the following rules apply:

- As each label represents a version of a feature that is realized by a branch, labels should only be attached to revisions of configuration items in branches whose branch name corresponds to the first part of the label name, e.g., label *AT1.0* should only be attached to revisions in branch \at, but it is not allowed to be attached to revisions in branch \mt.

- It is allowed to attach multiple versions of labels to the same revision as long as the branch name matches the first part of the label, e.g., it is allowed to attach the labels *MT1.0* and *MT2.0* to revision *1* in branch *mt* of configuration item `transmission.h`.

- The version number of labels should increase with increasing revision numbers, e.g., label *AT1.0* is attached to revision 1 and label *AT2.0* is attached to revision 2, but it is not allowed to attach label *AT2.0* to revision 1 and label *AT1.0* to revision 2.

- A label for a feature should be attached to at least one revision of each configuration item that has been identified during the mapping of features to software entities. For example, the label *AT1.0* should be attached to at least one revision of the files `transmission.c`, `transmission.h`, `transmission_aut.c` as these configuration items *implement* the feature *Automatic Transmission [AT]* as shown in Table 5.8.

Using this syntax of labels and rules for their attachment, it is possible to implement and identify multiple versions of features in a consistent and easy way. This scheme is especially helpful in a situation when different versions of multiple features need to be supported for products, e.g., in one product the automatic transmission feature in version 1.0 is used and in another product the automatic transmission in version 2.0 is used. The knowledge about which feature versions are combinable, e.g., automatic transmission 1.0 can be combined with manual windows 5.0, is stored externally of the SCM system in a separate list.

Analysis of Feature Implementation

In the last section we described how features are implemented and how their associated variability is realized using the SCM system ClearCase [Leb94]. In this section, we will describe how this form of feature implementation and variability realization can be analyzed. This analysis is necessary for the correct application of restructuring transformations as we shall see in Section 5.2.3.

Usually, SCM systems provide commands to retrieve a list of all revisions and branches of configuration items that have a given configuration label attached. In most cases, the SCM system also provides a command to retrieve all configuration labels that are attached to all revisions inside the branches of a given configuration item. For example, ClearCase [Leb94] provides the command *lsvtree* to obtain the version graph, i.e., the branches, the revisions, and the configuration labels of a configuration item i. When this command is executed, ClearCase outputs a list of all branches, all revisions, and all configuration labels that are attached to specific revisions, e.g.:

```
foo.c@@\main\a\3 (A1.0)
foo.c@@\main\b\3 (B1.0)
```

The first part before the @@ shows the name of the configuration item, e.g., `foo.c`, the part after the @@-sign shows the *branch name*, e.g., \main\a, the *revision number* of the configuration item, e.g. 3. The information in brackets shows the *configuration labels* that are attached to this revision, e.g., A1.0.

Using these commands, we can obtain a matrix relating configuration items and configuration labels for a given set of configuration labels called *item-label matrix*. Similarly to the product-feature matrix we used in Chapter 4 for variability analysis, we can use the item-label matrix as a basis for the analysis of the implementation of features and apply Formal Concept Analysis on the matrix by interpreting the configuration items i as objects o of the formal context and the configuration labels l representing feature versions as attributes a. The relation $\mathcal{R}$ of the formal context is defined by the item-label matrix $\mathcal{M}$. The item-label matrix $\mathcal{M}$ is a simple table relating configuration items and configuration labels that represent feature versions, i.e., $\mathcal{M} \subseteq \mathcal{I} \times \mathcal{L}$. If a configuration item i has a revision with a configuration label $l \in \mathcal{L}$ attached, the corresponding cell in the item-label matrix is marked with a cross. It is important to note that a single feature has an associated set of feature versions which are represented by a corresponding set of configuration labels, e.g., if we have feature Q which exists in versions $1.0, 2.0$ and 3.0, the corresponding set of configuration labels is $\{$Q_1.0, Q_2.0, Q_3.0$\}$. In order to get meaningful analysis results, the matrix $\mathcal{M}$ shall only contain one version of each feature which is being analyzed. The mapping of terms for the analysis of feature implementation to the general terms of formal concept analysis is shown in Table 5.9.

Feature Implementation Analysis $[\mathcal{I} \times \mathcal{L}]$	Formal Concept Analysis $[\mathcal{O} \times \mathcal{A}]$
Configuration item i	Object o
Set of configuration items I	Set of objects O
All configuration items $\mathcal{I}$	All objects $\mathcal{O}$
Configuration label l	Attribute a
Set of configuration labels L	Set of attributes A
All configuration labels $\mathcal{L}$	All attributes $\mathcal{A}$
Item-label matrix $\mathcal{M}$	Relation $\mathcal{R}$
Configuration item concept $\gamma(i)$	Object concept $\gamma(o)$
Configuration label concept $\mu(l)$	Attribute concept $\mu(a)$

Table 5.9: Mapping of terms for feature implementation analysis to general terms of formal concept analysis.

If $\mathcal{I}$ represents the set of all configuration items, $\mathcal{L}$ represents the set of all configuration labels, and $\mathcal{M}$ represents the item-label matrix, i.e., mapping of configuration items to configuration labels representing feature versions, then we can define the formal context $C_{IL} = (\mathcal{I}, \mathcal{L}, \mathcal{M})$.

Using the definitions of Section 4.1.1, the *configuration labels* that are attached to revisions of a set of configuration items $I \subseteq \mathcal{I}$ can be identified as $\sigma(I)$:

$$\sigma(I) = \{l \in \mathcal{L} \mid (i, l) \in \mathcal{M} \text{ for all } i \in I\} \qquad (5.1)$$

Similarly, the set of *configuration items* $\tau(L)$ that have multiple branches with revisions with a given set of configuration labels $l \subseteq \mathcal{L}$ can be identified as:

$$\tau(L) = \{i \in \mathcal{I} | (i, l) \in \mathcal{M} \text{ for all } l \in L\} \tag{5.2}$$

A concept $c = (I, L)$ with $L = \sigma(I)$ and $I = \tau(L)$ thus represents a set of configuration items $I \subseteq \mathcal{I}$ that have revisions with labels $l \in L$ attached or equivalently a set of configuration labels $L \subseteq \mathcal{L}$ that are attached to revisions of configuration items $i \in I$.

The set $\mathcal{L}$ of all concepts and the partial order $\leq$ as defined in Section 4.1.2 form the concept lattice:

$$\mathcal{L}(C) = \{(I, L) \in 2^{\mathcal{I}} \times 2^{\mathcal{L}} \mid L = \sigma(I) \text{ and } I = \tau(L)\} \tag{5.3}$$

Example. As an example for the analysis of the implementation of features, we use the ICC feature group again. In Table 5.7, the final list of features and restructuring decisions is shown. In the following, we illustrate how the implementation of these ICC features is analyzed using formal concept analysis on the item-label matrix. Each feature of the ICC feature group is represented by a set of configuration labels that represent the different versions of the feature, e.g., feature Q in its different versions is represented by the set $\{Q\_1.0, Q\_2.0, Q\_3.0\}$ of configuration labels. These configuration labels are attached to revisions of the configuration items. We extracted the indirect relationships of configuration labels, revisions, branches, and configuration items and constructed an item-label matrix relating configuration items and configuration labels. A cross in the cell (i, l) of this matrix indicates that configuration item i has a revision r with configuration label l attached. Figure 5.6 shows the calculated concept lattice for a subset of feature versions of the ICC feature group, namely for the configuration labels {Base_2.0, A1_2.0, A2_2.0, B2_2.0 Q_2.0}.

Interpretation of the Concept Lattice

Concept analysis applied to the item-label matrix yields a concept lattice from which the following facts can be automatically derived:

1. **Mapping of configuration labels.** Each concept provides the mapping of configuration labels that represent realized features to configuration items which contain the actual implementation of the features.

2. **Configuration label concept.** The configuration label concept $\mu(l)$ is the largest concept with configuration label l in its intent. The configuration label l is in all concepts that appear at or below the configuration label concept $\mu(l)$, i.e., all concepts c with $c \leq \mu(l)$. As a result of the item-label matrix $\mathcal{M}$, it follows that the configuration label l is attached to at least one revision of all configuration items i that appear at or below the configuration label concept $\mu(l)$ in the sparse representation of the concept lattice. If a full representation is used, the set of configuration

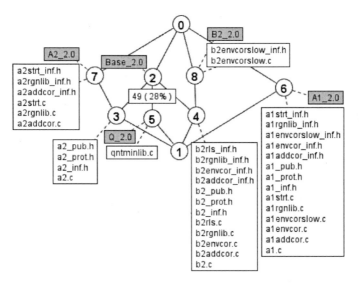

Figure 5.6: Partial concept lattice for configuration labels and configuration items of the ICC feature group. The configuration items at concept #2 are not shown due to space reasons. Instead the number of configuration items (49) and the percentage of the total number of configuration items (28%) is shown.

items can be directly obtained by reading of the extent of the configuration label concept $\mu(l)$.

In the example shown in Figure 5.6, the configuration label concept for the configuration label B2_2.0 is $\mu(B2\_2.0)$ = concept 2. This configuration label is attached to revisions of the configuration items at concept 8, and to revisions of the configuration items at concept 4.

3. **Configuration item concept.** The configuration item concept $\gamma(o)$ is the smallest concept with the configuration item i in its extent. A configuration item i is contained in all concepts that appear at or above the configuration item concept $\gamma(i)$, i.e., in all concepts c with $c \geq \gamma(i)$. As a result of the item-label matrix $\mathcal{M}$, it follows that the configuration item i has multiple branches that contain revisions that have the configuration labels l attached that appear at or above the configuration item concept $\gamma(i)$ in the sparse representation of the concept lattice. If a full representation is used, the set of configuration labels can be directly obtained by reading of the intent of the product concept $\gamma(i)$.

   In the example shown in Figure 5.6, the configuration item concept for configuration item qntminlib.c is $\gamma(\texttt{qntminlib.c})$ = concept 5. This configuration item has revisions with the configuration labels *Q_2.0* (at concept 5) and *Base_2.0* (at concept 2) attached.

4. **Shared configuration labels.** Configuration labels that are attached to revisions of a set of configuration items $\{i_1, \ldots, i_n\}$ can be identified at the supremum of the configuration item concepts $\gamma(i_k)$, i.e., $c_{sup} = \sqcup\{\gamma(i_k) \mid k \in \{1..n\}\}$. This concept is the smallest concept that has all configuration items $\{i_1, \ldots, i_n\}$ in its extent. The intent of this concept contains exactly those configuration labels that are attached to revisions of these configuration items. In the concept lattice the supremum c_{sup} is the first common superconcept of all configuration item concepts $\gamma(i_k)$ towards the top concept. If a sparse representation is used for the concept lattice, the shared configuration labels are those configuration labels which appear at the concept c_{sup} and at all concepts above c_{sup}.

   In the example shown in Figure 5.6, the shared configuration label for configuration item a2_pub.h (at concept 3) and b2rls.c (at concept 4) is the configuration label *Base_2.0* because it is the only configuration label that appears at or above the supremum $c_{sup} = \gamma(\texttt{a2\_pub.h}) \sqcup \gamma(\texttt{b2rls.c})$ = concept 2.

5. **Shared configuration items.** Configuration items that have multiple branches containing revisions which have a set of configuration labels $\{l_1, \ldots, l_n\}$ attached can be identified at the infimum of the configuration label concepts $\mu(l_i)$, i.e., $c_{inf} = \sqcap\{\mu(l_i) \mid i \in \{1..n\}\}$. This concept is the largest concept that has all configuration labels $\{l_1, \ldots, l_n\}$ in its intent. The extent of this concept contains exactly those configuration items that have a branch for each configuration label

$\{l_1, \ldots, l_n\}$ that contains a revision to which the configuration label is attached. In the concept lattice, the infimum c_{inf} is the first common subconcept of all configuration label concepts $\mu(l_i)$ towards the bottom concept. If a sparse representation is used for the concept lattice, the shared configuration items are those configuration items which appear at the concept c_{inf} and at all concepts below c_{inf}.

In the example shown in Figure 5.6, the shared configuration items for configuration labels *Base_2.0* (at concept 2) and *A2_2.0* (at concept 7) are all configuration items at concept 3 because they appear at or below the infimum $c_{inf} = \mu(Base_2.0) \sqcap \mu(A2_2.0) = $ concept 3.

Summary. The primary purpose of the concept lattice on the item-label matrix is to analyze the mapping of configuration labels that represent implemented feature versions to the actual configuration items containing the implementation of these feature versions (fact 1). Furthermore, the concept lattice allows the analyst to check whether two configuration labels are overlapping, i.e., whether they have shared configuration items (fact 5). This check is required to apply the restructuring transformations correctly because the configuration items that have multiple configuration labels to their revisions attached need special treatment during the application of restructuring transformations as we shall see in Section 5.2.3.

5.2.2   Derivation of Restructuring Transformations

Based on the analysis of the feature implementation and the variability realization technique, concrete restructuring transformations can be derived. In our case, the following restructuring transformations are used for simplifying the provided variability:

- **Combination of configuration labels** In this restructuring transformation, two or more configuration labels representing feature versions are combined. After the application of this restructuring transformation the individual configuration labels are not distinguishable anymore for the purpose of configuration, i.e., either the whole set of configuration labels is included for a product or not.

- **Marking configuration labels as obsolete** Another restructuring transformation is to mark a configuration label representing a feature version as obsolete and thus implicitly remove it from the list of provided configuration labels. After the application of this restructuring transformation the configuration label should not be included in future product configurations.

The next step is to map the features and groups of features that should be restructured according to the restructuring decisions to the appropriate restructuring transformations for their implementation. In our case, the allocation of features and groups of features to the appropriate restructuring transformations of their implementation is as follows:

- Class I: Combination of configuration labels.

- Class II: Marking configuration labels as obsolete.

- Class III: Combination of configuration labels.

- Class IV: No restructuring transformation is applied.

In order to keep already configured products and their associated product configurations intact, we need to identify the latest existing version sets of the features that shall be restructured. Typically this information can be obtained from the release documentation of feature sets.

5.2.3 Application of Restructuring Transformations

In the following, we describe the procedure for the application of the restructuring transformations. The concept lattice on the item-label matrix which has been described in Section 5.2.1 is used as a basis for guiding the application of restructuring transformations. The application of each restructuring transformation is hereby divided into smaller restructuring steps which are implemented by executing *basic commands* on the version repository of the SCM system, e.g., addition or removal of configuration labels, creation of new revisions, merging of revisions. These basic commands are provided by each SCM system that has a two-dimensional organization of the version space, i.e., a SCM system that provides the general concepts of configuration items, revisions, branches, and tags. As an example we describe the application of restructuring strategies and the basic commands for the SCM system ClearCase [Leb94]. Each restructuring step is illustrated by depicting the results of the basic commands on the version graphs of the configuration items.

Table 5.10 shows a list of basic commands that are provided by the SCM system ClearCase [Leb94]. The basic commands are sorted by the SCM elements on which they operate.

Combination of Configuration Labels

Combining configuration labels means to unify the set of revisions of configuration items these configuration labels point to. For example, if we want to combine the configuration labels $L\_1.0$ and $K\_1.0$ and $L\_1.0$ and $K\_1.0$ are attached to revisions of configuration items $\{a,b,c\}$ and to revisions of configuration items $\{d,e,f\}$ respectively then after the combination strategy has been applied the new combined label $L\_2.0$ will be attached to revisions of configuration items $\{a,b,c,d,e,f\}$. The original configuration labels $L\_1.0$ and $K\_1.0$ should be made obsolete after the combination of $L\_1.0$ and $K\_1.0$.

Example. In the following, we describe the restructuring steps for the combination of the configuration labels $A2\_2.0$ and $Base\_2.0$ of the ICC feature group. By analyzing Figure 5.6, we see that the configuration items at concept #2, at concept #3, and at concept #7 are affected by this restructuring transformation. In total, 59 configuration items are

Concept	Command	Description
Configuration Item	`mkelem`	Creates a new configuration item
	`rmelem`	Removes a configuration item and all its versions
Branch	`mkbranch`	Creates a branch on a given configuration item
	`lock -obsolete`	Locks the branch and marks it as obsolete
Revision	`checkout`	Creates a temporary modifiable copy of a revision.
	`checkin`	Creates a permanent new revision of a configuration item. The `checkin` command can only be issued on a previously checked out revision.
	`merge`	Merges two or more revisions. The target revision needs to be checked out before the merge can be applied.
Configuration Label	`mklabel`	Attaches a predefined configuration label to the specified revision of a given configuration item
	`lock -obsolete`	Locks the configuration label and marks it as obsolete

Table 5.10: Basic commands provided by the SCM system ClearCase [Rat03].

affected. Furthermore, we can infer that *Base_2.0* and *A2_2.0* have shared configuration items because they have a common infimum (concept 3). Each configuration item attached to concept #3 has a revision with configuration label *Base_2.0* and a revision with configuration label *A2_2.0*. Furthermore, these revisions are not in the same branch as this would violate the third rule that has been described in Section 5.2.1.

As it is impossible to show the application of the restructuring transformation for all 59 configuration items, we will choose one configuration item from each concept to illustrate how the application of the restructuring transformations affects the configuration item. Figure 5.7 depicts a layout of the version graphs for the configuration items a2strt.c (at concept 7), a2.c (at concept 3), and mi.c (at concept 2) before the first restructuring step.

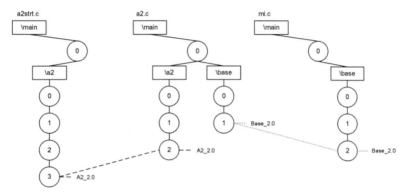

Figure 5.7: Original version graphs for configuration items a2strt.c, a2.c and mi.c before restructuring.

As one can see from Figure 5.7, the configuration item a2strt.c has a single branch, namely \a2 with 4 revisions. The label *A2_2.0* is attached to revision 3. The configuration item a2.c has two branches, namely \a2 and \base with 3 and 2 revisions respectively. The configuration label *A2_2.0* is attached to revision 2 in branch \a2 and the configuration label *Base_2.0* is attached to revision 1 in branch \base. The configuration item mi.c has a single branch, namely \base with 3 revisions. The configuration label *Base_2.0* is attached to revision 2 in the \base branch. The dotted and dashed lines indicate which revisions will be selected when the corresponding configuration label is used in a product configuration. If both configuration labels are used in a product configuration, the order of configuration labels in the product configuration determines which revision of configuration item a2.c will be selected. Thus, if the configuration label *A2_2.0* appears above the configuration label *Base_2.0* then revision 2 in branch \a2 will be selected. If the configuration label *Base_2.0* appears above the configuration label *A2_2.0* then revision 1 in branch \base will be selected. In our case, if both configuration labels are used, the configuration label *A2_2.0* needs to appear above the configuration label *Base_2.0* otherwise the product will not work correctly.

Before the configuration labels can be combined a new name and version number for the combined configuration label has to be chosen. This label will become the new configuration label for all configuration items after the application of the restructuring transformation. In our case, we selected the label *BaseA2_3.0*. In the following, we describe the individual steps for combining configuration labels:

- **Step 1: Creating branches.** During the first step we create the branch *base* on all configuration items that are shown at concept 7 in Figure 5.6 using the ClearCase command `mkbranch`. Figure 5.8 depicts the layout of the version graphs after the first restructuring step. Changes are shown in bold.

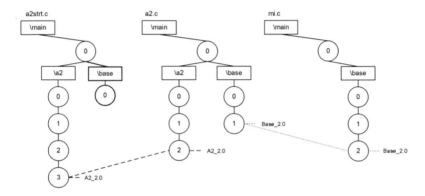

Figure 5.8: After Step 1: Version graphs for configuration items `a2strt.c`, `a2.c` and `mi.c`.

- **Step 2: Merging revisions.** During the second step the revisions in the branches *a2* and *base* of all configuration items that are attached to concept 3 and concept 7 are merged using the ClearCase command `merge`. The revisions in branch *a2* of the configuration items that are attached to concept 7 can be merged automatically because the revisions in branch *base* are empty. Thus, the contents of the revisions in branch *a2* simply need to be copied to the revisions in the newly created branch *base*. This is also called a *trivial merge*. On the other hand the merging of revisions for the configuration items that are attached to concept 3 can only be automated to some extent because the revisions that need to be merged might have overlapping code lines which cause merge conflicts. Section 5.2.4 describes some techniques for the resolution of merge conflicts.

Figure 5.9 shows the layout of the version graphs after the second restructuring step. Changes are shown in bold again. As you can see from Figure 5.9, revision 2 in branch *a2* of configuration item `a2strt.c` has been merged with revision 0 of branch \base and the result of this merge operation has been stored in revision 1. Furthermore, revision 2 in branch \a2 and revision 1 in branch \base of configuration item have been merged and the result has been stored in revision 2. The merge of these two revisions could be automated as there were no overlapping code lines.

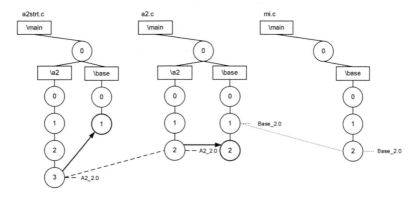

Figure 5.9: After Step 2: Version graphs for configuration items a2strt.c, a2.c and mi.c.

- **Step 3: Addition of new configuration labels.** During the third step, the new configuration label needs to be attached to all revisions which have been newly created by the merge operations during restructuring step 2 and to all old revisions that had the label *Base_2.0* attached but have not been merged with other revisions. Figure 5.10 shows the layout of the version graphs after the third step. The new configuration label *BaseA2_3.0* has been attached to revision 1 in branch \base of configuration item a2strt.c which has been created by the merge during the last restructuring step and to revision 2 in branch \base of configuration item mi.c which has not been merged and already has the label *Base_2.0* attached.

- **Step 4: Marking branches and configuration labels as obsolete.** During the fourth and last step, the branches and configuration labels which are not needed anymore after the restructuring are marked as being obsolete. In our case, the configuration label *A2_2.0*, the corresponding revisions and the branch \a2 as well as the configuration label *Base_2.0* are not needed anymore and therefore can be marked as obsolete. This can be done by issuing the lock -obsolete command on the branch \a2 and on the configuration labels *A2_2.0* and *B2_2.0*. Instead of marking these items as obsolete, we could also remove them. However, removing items would contradict the general idea of configuration management of keeping the history in order to be able roll back at any time if necessary.

Figure 5.11 shows the version graphs of the three configuration items after marking the configuration label *A2_2.0*, its associated revisions and the branch \a2 as well

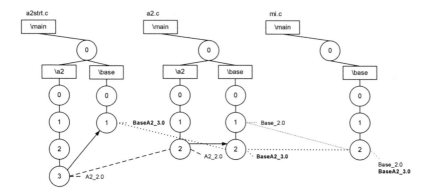

Figure 5.10: After Step 3: Version graphs for configuration items a2strt.c, a2.c and mi.c.

as the configuration label *Base_2.0* as obsolete. Obsolete items are shown in light gray in Figure 5.11.

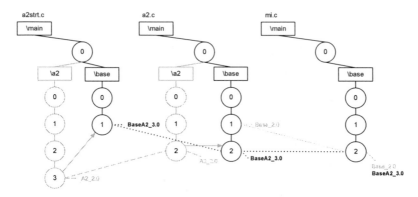

Figure 5.11: After Step 4: Version graphs for configuration items a2strt.c, a2.c and mi.c.

- **Step 5: Update of component description.** After the application of restructuring steps 1-4 the component description should be updated to reflect the changes. As we marked the configuration label *A2_2.0* and *B2_2.0* as obsolete, this should be reflected in the documentation. The functionality of the feature *A2* is from now on always activated when the configuration label *BaseA2_3.0* is used in a product configuration. Furthermore, the feature A2 should be marked as *mandatory* in the feature diagram.

Mark Configuration Labels as Obsolete

Another restructuring transformation that can be applied is to mark configuration labels and the revisions these configuration labels are pointing to as obsolete.

Example. In the following, we describe the restructuring steps for marking the configuration label *Q_2.0* of the ICC feature group as obsolete. By analyzing Figure 5.6, we can infer that *Q_2.0* has shared configuration items with the configuration label *Base_2.0* because they have a common infimum (concept 5). The configuration item attached to this concept has a revision with configuration label *Q_2.0* and a revision with configuration label *Base_2.0*. Furthermore, these revisions are not in the same branch as this would violate the third rule that has been described in Section 5.2.1. Figure 5.12 depicts the layout of the version graph for the configuration item qntminlib.c (at concept 5) before marking the configuration label *Q_2.0* as obsolete.

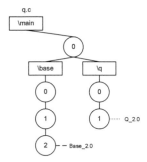

Figure 5.12: Version graph for configuration item qntminlib.c before restructuring.

- **Step 1: Mark configuration label as obsolete.** During the first restructuring step, the configuration label representing the obsolete feature version is marked as obsolete. In our case, we need to mark the configuration label *Q_2.0* as obsolete using the ClearCase command lock -obsolete. Figure 5.13 shows the version graph for configuration item qntminlib.c after the first restructuring step. As you can see in Figure 5.13 the configuration label *Q_2.0* is marked as obsolete (shown in light gray in the Figure).

- **Step 2: Mark branches and revisions as obsolete.** During the second step, the branches and revisions which are not needed anymore are also marked as obsolete. In our case, the revisions 0 and 1 in branch \q of configuration item qntminlib.c and the branch \q are not needed anymore and thus can be marked as obsolete. Figure 5.11 shows the version graph of configuration item qntminlib.c after the revisions 0 and 1 and the branch \q has been marked as obsolete (shown in light gray).

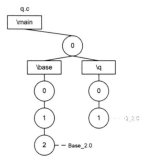

Figure 5.13: After Step 1: Version graph for configuration item `qntminlib.c`.

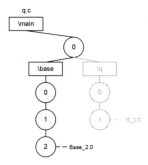

Figure 5.14: After Step 2: Version graph for configuration item `qntminlib.c` after restructuring.

- **Step 3: Update of component description.** After the application of restructuring steps 1 and 2 the component description should be updated to reflect the changes. As we marked the configuration label $Q\_2.0$ and the revisions it has been pointing to as being obsolete, the configuration label should be removed from the component description in future releases of the component to avoid that it is included in future products. Furthermore, the feature diagram should be updated and the feature Q should be marked as obsolete as well.

5.2.4 Resolution of Merge Conflicts

During the combination of configuration labels revisions need to be merged. Some of these merges are simple copies of revisions others are real merges in which merge conflicts may arise due to overlapping code lines between the revisions. ClearCase [Leb94] provides a textual three-way merge function which is very flexible because it can be applied to arbitrary text documents and source code files irrespective of the programming language in which they were written. However, an inherent limitation of this merge function is that only basic conflicts can be detected and the conflicts need to be manually resolved. Furthermore, the merge function gives often rise to unimportant conflicts such as changed code comments. This makes the resolution of merge conflicts a time-consuming and error-prone task in ClearCase [Leb94]. Fortunately, we encountered only a few merge conflicts when we applied the restructuring transformations on the ICC feature group. In cases when overlapping code lines were encountered, it was often possible for the platform developer to simply choose the appropriate revision due to the domain knowledge he had about the functionality.

In order to solve this problem, a number of automated techniques for conflict resolution have been proposed. Horwitz et al. [HPR89] propose a technique to automatically merge two noninterfering versions of a program using program dependence graphs. Munson and Dewan [MD94] propose a number of different merge strategies which can be applied for three-way merging and allow revisions to be merged automatically, semiautomatically, and interactively. The resolution strategies are implemented in a uniform way using so called merge matrices that can be fine-tuned by the user. For example, the *consolidation* strategy can be used if it is expected or known that most of the parallel changes are complementary, e.g., when the changes are made to different program modules or to different functions inside the source code. In case of deletions or additions, the merge proceeds automatically. In case of overlapping changes, one of both changes is chosen interactively.

Another strategy is to reduce the number of merge conflicts. Asklund et al. [MA96] propose to minimize the number of merge conflicts by using *fine-grained revision control* in which the software changes should be as small as possible. This idea is supported by Perry et al. [PSV98] who noticed in a large-scale industrial study that making large changes tends to lead to revisions whose merges are very time-consuming. Unfortunately, the granularity of versioning in ClearCase [Leb94] is on the file level. Thus, the above strategies cannot be applied unless the configuration management system is changed. Bruegge and Dutoit [BD99] give two simple heuristics for avoiding merge conflicts. First, changes to the main development line should be restricted to bug fixes, and important new changes should be carried out in development branches. Second, the number of coexisting branches that represent variants should be as small as possible.

A further discussion of available techniques for the detection, resolution, and reduction of merge conflicts can be found in the state-of-the-art survey on software merging [Men02].

5.3   Summary

In this chapter, we presented our approach for restructuring variability that has been realized using a SCM system. The description of the approach is divided into two parts, namely *restructuring preparation*, i.e., the necessary steps that need to be taken before the restructuring can actually be implemented and *implementation of restructuring decisions*, i.e., the necessary steps that are required for implementing the restructuring decisions. An advantage of separating the restructuring into preparation and implementation is that the preparation is independent of the concrete implementation of features and the used variability realization technique.

The preparation of the restructuring has been described in Section 5.1. We showed how the results of variability analysis were used to derive hypotheses about the intended use of features and decisions about which features should be restructured. The implementation of these restructuring decisions will result in the minimal number of features required to derive the analyzed product configurations. However, we found out that this kind of restructuring is too restrictive with regard to the future scope of the software product line. Therefore, we described in Section 5.1.2 how additional domain knowledge can be used to select only those features for restructuring whose variability is truly not required from a domain perspective.

In Section 5.2, we described the implementation of the restructuring decisions. As the implementation of these decisions is dependent on the implementation of the features and the chosen variability realization we first analyzed the feature implementation. We assumed that the features and the associated variability has been implemented using the SCM system ClearCase [Leb94]. In a next step, we derived concrete restructuring transformations for the feature implementation and showed the individual steps that need to be performed in order to apply these restructuring transformations on features that have been implemented using ClearCase [Leb94]. In Section 5.2.4, we described techniques to resolve merge conflicts which may arise during the combination of configuration labels.

Chapter 6

Variability Optimization Process

In the previous chapters, we described our approach to variability analysis and variability restructuring. In this chapter, we present a process for variability optimization that combines both variability analysis and variability restructuring into a general framework. The goal of the process is to describe the steps that are required to document the variability currently provided by the product line, to analyze the variability required by current and future products, and to derive necessary actions for restructuring the variability in case the provided variability is higher than the variability actually required by current and future products. Parts of this chapter have been published in [LP07a].

Overview. In Section 6.1, we give an overview of the process including the description of the prerequisites, the roles, the process phases, and the iterations of the process. Section 6.2 describes each process phase in more detail. In Section 6.3, we present the general architecture of the tool chain and the tools that are necessary to support the participants in performing different process activities. The chapter is concluded by a summary in Section 6.4.

6.1 Overview of the Process

An overview of the process that controls variability optimization is shown in Figure 6.1 in IDEF0 notation [IDE93]. The input to the process is the *provided variability*, i.e., the variability currently offered by the software product line in terms of variable features. The output of the process is an optimized version of the product line variability in which the number of variable features has been reduced and the set of products that can be reasonably derived from the product line has not been affected, i.e., the process does not affect the configurability of the product line assets for current and planned future products. The process is controlled by the analysis of the actual usage of variable features in current products and the prediction of the usage of variable features in future products.

The process is supported by several experts that fulfill different *roles* in the process. These roles are described in Section 6.1.2. Furthermore, the process is supported by several *tools* that are presented in Section 6.3.

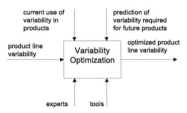

Figure 6.1: High-level overview of the variability optimization process in IDEF0 notation [IDE93].

6.1.1   Prerequisites

The prerequisites for the application of the variability optimization process are rather modest. We require an evolving software product line, i.e., a product line with an existing platform providing reusable software components that can be configured for a variety of products using variable features. Furthermore, we assume that a considerable number of products has already been derived from the product line and their product configurations are available. The variability provided by the platform is sufficient for the existing set of products, but not necessarily optimal with respect to the number of variable features required to derive the products. The specific variable features that could be combined or removed without affecting the configurability of the product line are not yet known.

6.1.2   Roles

The variability analysis and optimization process comprises the participation of several persons that fulfill the following roles:

1. The *product line manager* is the person who is responsible for the evolution and maintenance of the software product line. He is interested in finding out whether the variability currently provided by the product line matches the variability required by current and future products. He performs the variability analysis and derives possible restructuring strategies together with the platform developer in case the variability currently provided by the product line is higher than the variability required by current and future products.

2. The *platform developer* is the person who knows the variable features currently provided by a specific platform component or subsystem and the variability that is required for future releases of the platform component or subsystem. He assembles a list of variable features currently provided by a platform component or subsystem. He receives a list of required features for future releases of the platform component by product developers.

3. The *product developer* is the person who assembles a product out of reusable platform components and configures these platform components according to the customer requirements. He is familiar with existing product configurations and with the required features of future product releases. Together with the platform developers he decides about the required variability of the software product line for future product releases.

4. The *marketing expert* is the person who analyzes the market to provide predictions with regard to the variability required for future products.

The process only prescribes several roles but the mapping of these roles to concrete persons fulfilling them is not prescribed in the process. In other words, each of the roles described above can be fulfilled by a single person or multiple persons. On the other hand, it is also possible that a person fulfills different roles during the process.

6.1.3   Process Phases

The variability optimization process consists of the following four main phases that are illustrated in Figure 6.2:

1. Phase: **Variability Documentation.** Based on existing documentation of variable features and product configurations, the product-feature matrix relating product configurations and variable features is constructed which precisely documents the provided variability of the software product line.

   Participants: Product line manager, platform developer, and product developer

2. Phase: **Variability Prediction.** Using requirements of future products, the variability required by the product line in the future is predicted.

   Participants: Product line manager, marketing expert and product developer

3. Phase: **Variability Analysis.** The product-feature matrix is analyzed using Formal Concept Analysis (FCA) to determine the usage of features in current and in future product configurations. Features are classified according to their usage, feature constraints are identified, and the optimization potential is determined in the case that the provided variability of the software product line is higher than the variability required for current and future products. This phase conforms to the procedure described in Chapter 4 and can be performed repeatedly if necessary.

   Participants: Product line manager

4. Phase: **Variability Restructuring.** The data yielded by variability analysis is used to derive restructuring strategies to simplify the provided variability without affecting the configurability of the software product line for the products that have been analyzed. After consulting the market manager and platform developer, the product

line manager selects a set of the features for restructuring with the help of the feature usage classification. The restructuring strategies that have been derived during variability analysis are then applied by the platform developer to the selected features. Product configurations that are affected by the restructuring are updated by the product developer to reflect the performed changes in the platform components.

Participants: Product line manager, platform developer, and product developer

The phases 1, 3, and 4 are dependent on each other and need to be performed in this sequence during the first iteration of the process. Phase 2, namely variability prediction, may be performed or not depending on the availability of future product configurations. If phase 2 is performed it can either be performed before phase 3 or after phase 3 if phase 3 is repeated again. However, phase 2 should always be performed before phase 4 as the restructuring may be influenced by the variability prediction phase (phase 2).

6.2   Description of Process Phases

In this section, we describe the four process phases in detail. Each process phase consists of a set of single steps that are normally performed sequentially. In some cases it might be necessary to iterate a whole phase or specific steps of a single phase. These iterations are described in Section 6.2.5.

6.2.1   Variability Documentation

During the first phase of the variability optimization process the provided variability of the software product line is identified and documented. A complete and up-to-date documentation is the key to successful maintenance, evolution and optimization of variability. The input to this process phase are various information sources such as existing component documentations, product line architecture descriptions, product configurations and expert knowledge. The documentation phase consists of the following four steps that are depicted in Figure 6.3:

- Step 1.1: **Identification of variability mechanisms**. During the first step of the documentation phase, the product line manager identifies the *variability mechanisms* [SGB01] that are used for the realization of variable features in the product line, e.g., software configuration management. This step is necessary because further steps for variability documentation and variability analysis depend on the used variability mechanisms. Furthermore, the methods for extraction and identification of the necessary information need to be tailored to the used variability mechanism by the platform developer.

- Step 1.2: **Identification of variable features**. The platform developer identifies the variable features that are offered by the software product line for configuration. Depending on the variability mechanism identified in the last step, there exist different representations of variable features that require different ways of identifying

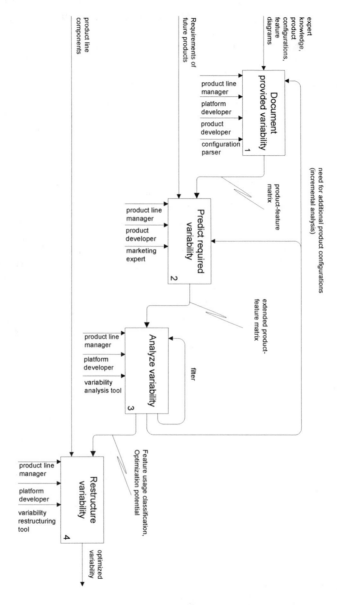

Figure 6.2: Process phases for variability optimization in IDEF0 notation [IDE93].

them. For example, if conditional compilation is used for variability realization, the identification of variable features requires to extract all preprocessor conditionals in the source code. However, if a SCM system is used for variability realization, the identification of variable features requires to extract configuration labels from the SCM system. In addition to the identification of variable features by looking at their realization, the platform developer may use other forms of explicit documentation such as existing component documentation or product line architecture descriptions to identify the set of variable features. Furthermore, he can interview other platform developers to specify the set of variable features for specific product line components.

- Step 1.3: **Selection of product configurations**. During the third step of variability documentation, the product line manager selects and obtains a set of product configurations from the product developers. Each product configuration specifies which of the features are included in a specific product and which features are not. Depending on the used variability mechanism these product configurations will have different forms, e.g., if conditional compilation is used as variability mechanism a product configuration consists of a simple file that defines the values for the preprocessor conditionals used in #ifdef statements. If a SCM system is used for variability realization, a product configuration contains configuration labels that define which variants of the versioned source code files are included in the product. The set of product configurations should contain the product configurations of all products that have already been derived from the product line. If this is not possible, the set of product configurations should at least contain a representative selection of product configurations, e.g., the set should contain at least one product configuration of each customer. This is very important because the selection of product configurations influences the accuracy of the results that are obtained during variability analysis.

- Step 1.4: **Construction of a product-feature matrix.** Based on the identified features and product configurations for the analysis, the product line manager constructs a product-feature matrix. Columns of the matrix hold the identified product configurations and rows of the matrix hold the identified variable features. For each feature f used in a product configuration p, the entry (p, f) in the matrix is marked with a cross. This tedious task can be fully automated with the help of a product configuration parser that automatically analyzes the product configurations and sets the crosses in the table accordingly.

6.2.2   Variability Prediction

During the second phase, the product line manager predicts the required variability for future products together with the marketing expert and product developer. The inputs to this process phase are the product-feature matrix that has been constructed during phase 1, future product requirements, and a market analysis that is performed by the marketing

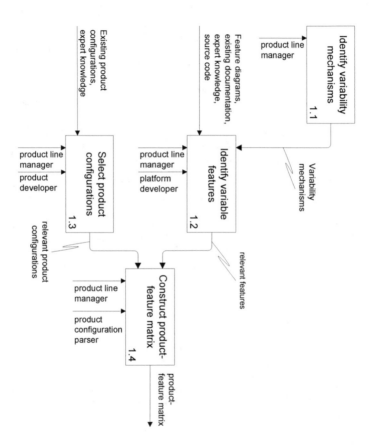

Figure 6.3: Process steps for variability documentation in IDEF0 notation [IDE93].

expert. The output of this process phase is a product-feature matrix that has been extended by preliminary product configurations and features that cover the required variability of the product line in the future.

The variability prediction phase consists of three individual steps which are depicted in Figure 6.4 and described in the following:

- Step 2.1: **Determination of future product portfolio.** The marketing expert performs a market analysis to determine the future product portfolio. The product line manager and product developer compile a list of future product configurations that should be derived from the product line and identify their requirements.

- Step 2.2: **Creation of product configurations.** During the next step the product line manager and the product developer classify the requirements of each future product into requirements that can be fulfilled by selecting existing features from the platform and into requirements that require the development of new features. For each product to be built, the product developer constructs a preliminary product configuration based on the set of required features.

- Step 2.3: **Extension of the product-feature matrix.** The product line manager adds the preliminary product configurations to the product-feature matrix. To distinguish these future product configurations from existing product configurations in the product feature matrix, they are marked with the suffix "PLANNED". In addition to adding product configurations to the product-feature matrix, the product line manager also adds new features which have not yet been developed to the product-feature matrix. To distinguish them from existing features they are also marked with the suffix "PLANNED".

6.2.3 Variability Analysis

The product-feature matrix that has been constructed during variability documentation (phase 1) and extended during variability prediction (phase 2) is analyzed using Formal Concept Analysis (FCA). The resulting concept lattice is interpreted to determine the usage of features in current and in future product configurations. Features are classified according to their usage, feature constraints are identified, and the optimization potential is calculated in the case that the provided variability of the software product line is higher than the variability required for current and future products.

The variability analysis phase consists of three individual steps depicted in Figure 6.5 and described in the following:

- Step 3.1: **Selection of features**. The product line manager selects a set of features from the product-feature matrix that is subject of the following analysis and interpretation. This set should be self-contained, e.g., the set should represent all features that are offered by a specific product line component that is to be analyzed. Of course it is also possible to analyze the whole product-feature matrix. However,

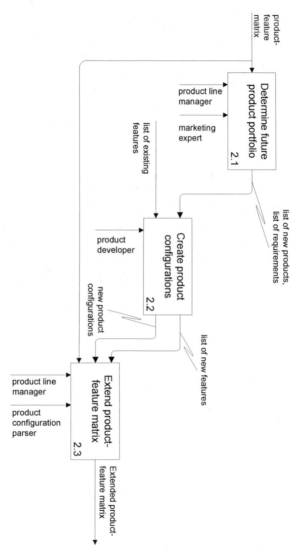

Figure 6.4: Process steps for variability prediction in IDEF0 notation [IDE93].

if the matrix is very large and cannot be analyzed in one step, feature selection provides a practical means to analyze the matrix step-by-step. In other words, this step is very similar to a pre-filtering mechanism to focus the analysis on specific parts of the product-feature matrix.

- Step 3.2: **Formal concept analysis**. The product line manager uses the variability analysis tool to perform a formal concept analysis on the selected parts of the product-feature matrix. The resulting concept lattice is visualized as a graph in the tool.

- Step 3.3: **Interpretation**. The product line manager interprets the concept lattice to classify the usage of features, to identify feature constraints, and to calculate the optimization potential as described in Chapter 4.

The output of this process phase is the feature usage classification and the optimization potential that are used as input for variability restructuring (phase 4). Furthermore, the variability analysis phase allows the derivation of useful information for product derivation such as feature constraints (see Section 4.2.7 for details). The interpretation of the concept lattice also allows the product line manager to determine whether additional product configurations, e.g., future product configurations, are necessary to be included in the analysis to improve the accuracy of the results. Depending on the size of the resulting concept lattice the product line manager can decide whether to repeat the analysis with a smaller set of features to reduce the effort that is needed for a manual interpretation of the concept lattice (see Section 6.2.5 and Section 4.3.2 for details).

6.2.4   Variability Restructuring

The results of variability analysis, i.e., the feature usage classification and the calculated optimization potential are used for restructuring and simplifying the provided variability without affecting the configurability of the software product line for current and future products. The output of the variability restructuring phase are restructured product line components and updated product configurations that reflect the performed changes.

The variability restructuring phase itself consists of the following four individual steps that are depicted in Figure 6.6:

- Step 4.1: **Derivation of restructuring decisions**. Based on the feature usage classification calculated during variability analysis and hypotheses about the intended usage of the features, decisions about which features should be restructured and which features should be left as is are derived.

- Step 4.2: **Validation of restructuring decisions**. As the hypotheses and the restructuring decisions are based only on the analyzed product configurations and strongly depend on the usage of features in these product configurations, they need to be validated by the platform developer and corrected if necessary before the restructuring is performed. This validation is done by comparing the classification of features, the derived hypotheses, and the necessity of the variability provided by

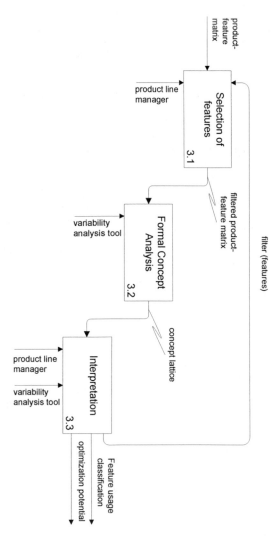

Figure 6.5: Process steps for variability analysis in IDEF0 notation [IDE93].

features with domain knowledge that has not been inferred by variability analysis. For example, explicit domain knowledge in the form of variability models, architecture descriptions, prescriptions for the configuration of products or implicit domain knowledge in the form of expert knowledge can be used for this comparison. Furthermore, additional knowledge about the future of the product portfolio that should be supported by the product line is very helpful in this comparison. For each feature that should be restructured according to the feature usage classification and the restructuring strategy, it is decided whether this restructuring should be performed or not. This decision is mainly based on domain knowledge about the correct usage of features and future requirements on the provided variability of the software product line that are already known by the platform developer. The variability analysis tool supports this step by allowing the platform developer to change the classification of features in the feature usage classification. For example, this allows the platform developer to exclude some features from being restructured.

- Step 4.3: **Analysis of feature implementation**. The platform developer analyzes the implementation of variable features to identify the mapping of features to mechanisms provided by the variability realization technique as described in Chapter 5. For example, if a software configuration management system is used for variability realization the configuration labels representing the variable features and its mapping on platform components and configuration items implementing these components need to be identified.

- Step 4.4: **Derivation of restructuring transformations**. Based on the analysis of the feature implementation and the variability realization technique, the platform developer derives concrete restructuring transformations. In a next step, the platform developer maps the restructuring transformations to the feature usage classes.

- Step 4.5: **Application of restructuring transformations**. In the last step, the platform developer applies the restructuring transformations on the implementation of the features that have been selected for restructuring as described in Chapter 5. Furthermore, the platform developer updates the variability description of platform components that are affected by the restructuring to reflect the performed changes.

6.2.5　Iterations

The variability optimization process contains several feedback loops for different purposes that require the iteration of a whole phase or the iteration of single steps within a phase. In the following we describe these feedback loops in detail:

- **Step 3.3 → Step 3.1 (Filtering).** In the case the resulting concept lattice is very large and difficult to interpret manually, it might be necessary to limit the features of the product-feature matrix for the analysis (step 3.1) and to repeat the concept analysis (step 3.2) and interpretation of the concept lattice (step 3.3).

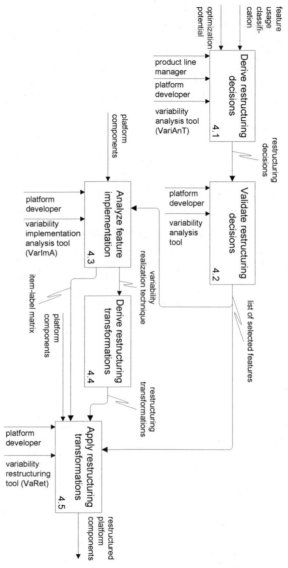

Figure 6.6: Process steps for variability restructuring in IDEF0 notation [IDE93].

- **Phase 3 → Phase 1, Phase 3 → Phase 2 (Additional product configurations).** During the interpretation of the concept lattice in Phase 3, it might turn out that product configurations are missing that are required for an accurate analysis the variability. These can either be existing product configurations that have not been considered during the selection of product configurations in the variability documentation phase (phase 1) or future product configurations that need to be created during the variability prediction phase (phase 2). In either case the product-feature matrix is extended with these product configurations and the variability analysis phase (phase 3) needs to be reiterated.

- **Phase 3 → Phase 2 (Feature usage classification).** Sometimes it might be necessary to have an overview of the existing product portfolio and the use of features in the existing product configurations before the required variability of the product line in the future can be predicted (phase 2). In this case, the feature usage classification obtained during variability analysis (phase 3) serves as an input for variability prediction (phase 2).

6.3   Tool Framework and Implementation

The variability optimization process that has been presented in the last sections is supported by tools that automate some tasks the participants have to execute in specific process steps. These tools are integrated in a tool framework that provides the basic architecture for the tools to exchange data. The tool framework for variability optimization can be adapted to multiple variability mechanisms by exchanging the tools that are tailored for specific variability mechanisms. In Section 6.3.1 we first present the general tool framework for variability analysis and optimization. The tools that support the participants in executing specific process steps are described in Section 6.3.2.

6.3.1   Framework Architecture

Our framework for variability analysis and optimization is structured similarly to a compiler, i.e., it consists of a front end, a middle end, and a back end. The division into these three parts like in a compiler architecture offers great flexibility of the framework with regard to the variability realization technique. Like in a compiler, the middle end is independent of the variability realization technique. By providing different front ends and back ends, the tool framework can be adapted to different variability realization techniques. Figure 6.7 illustrates this architecture. The individual parts are:

- **Front End: Variability Documentation and Prediction.** The front end is responsible for parsing the product configurations and constructing a product-feature matrix out of the features used in the product configurations. As the format of the product configurations depends on the used technique for variability realization, the front end is dependent on the used variability realization technique as well. However, multiple front ends can be provided for the variability realization techniques that should be supported by the tool framework.

Figure 6.7: Framework architecture for variability optimization.

- **Middle End: Variability Analysis.** The middle end uses Formal Concept Analysis (FCA) to transform the product-feature matrix into a graph that visualizes the relations between product configurations and features. Furthermore the middle end provides a classification of the feature usage, a list of possible feature constraints including feature implications and feature exclusions, and a table showing the optimization potential.

- **Back End: Variability Restructuring.** The back end does the restructuring of platform components according to the restructuring strategies that have been derived from the feature usage classification and according to the list of features that should be restructured. As the application of the restructuring strategies depends on the variability realization technique, the implementation of the back end depends on the variability realization technique as well. However, multiple back ends can be provided for the variability realization techniques that should be supported by the tool framework.

The front end and the back end can be implemented as automated tools. Only the middle end needs to be implemented as an interactive tool because the product line manager needs to interpret the information obtained by variability analysis.

6.3.2   Description of Tools

In the following we describe the tools that support the participants in executing specific process steps:

- **Identification of variable features (Step 1.2).**
  There exist a number of different tools that can be used for the identification of variable features. The tools that can be used depend on how the features have been implemented, i.e., which variability realization technique has been used for implementation. In our case the variability has been realized by a SCM system as described in Chapter 5 and Appendix A. Therefore, we use specific SCM scripts to obtain a list of all configuration labels. If the variability has been implemented using conditional compilation, we can use the standard unix tool **grep** to obtain a list of used preprocessor symbols in the code that represent implemented variable features.

- **Construction (Step 1.4) and Extension of the product-feature matrix (Step 2.3).**
  For the task of the initial construction of a product-feature matrix (Step 1.4) and its extension (Step 2.3), we developed a product configuration parser called **ClearCase-ConfigSpecParser (CCCSP)**. **CCCSP** obtains a list of provided variable features

and a list of product configurations that exist in the form of ClearCase configuration specifications [Leb94] which contain configuration labels (see Chapter A for details) by executing specific scripts on ClearCase. **CCCSP** analyzes the configuration files to obtain a list of features - represented by configuration labels - that are used in each product configuration. Based on this information, **CCCSP** constructs the initial product-feature matrix and outputs it as a file that can be directly read by our variability analysis tool **VariAnT**.

CCCSP can also be used for the extension of an already existing product-feature matrix with additional product configurations (Step 2.3). In this case, **CCCSP** analyzes the additional product configurations and extends the product-feature matrix accordingly. If the additional product configurations contain features that are not yet in the list of identified variable features, they are added automatically to the product-feature matrix.

- **Construction of new product configurations (Step 2.3).** ClearCase [Leb94] provides an integrated editor for configuration specifications that can be used to manually construct new product configurations. These product configurations can then be added to the product-feature matrix using our **ClearCaseConfigSpecParser (CCCSP)**.

- **Formal Concept Analysis (Step 3.2).**
  For the calculation of the concept lattice a formal concept analysis tool is required. The tool should support the import of formal contexts, the calculation of the concepts for a given formal context, and the visualization of the resulting concept lattice. Furthermore, the tool should support the calculation of implications between attributes for a given concept lattice.

  During the last years a number of different tools for formal concept analysis have been developed, e.g., **concepts** [Lin00], **ConImp** [Bur00], **ToscanaJ** [BHS02], and **ConExp** [Yev00]. **Concepts** is a text-based tool that only calculates a list of concepts for a given formal context. It does not provide any visualization capabilities. **ConImp** is also a text-based tool that has additional features for calculating implications between attributes but it also does not support the visualization of the concept lattice. **ToscanaJ** and **ConExp** are the only tools that provide a visual representation of the concept lattice.

  We use **ConExp** for formal concept analysis because it not only provides a graphical user interface for working on the formal context and for visualizing the concept lattice, but it also supports several other useful features to fine-tune the visualization of the concept lattice including different highlighting strategies for concepts, different labeling strategies for objects and attributes, and different layouts of the concept lattice. Furthermore, the concept lattice is interactive and the layout can be changed by the user. **ConExp** has been used as a formal concept analysis tool for a number of different purposes including mining association rules for databases.

- **Interpretation of the concept lattice (Step 3.3) and validation of restructuring decisions (Step 4.2).**
  In order to support the product line manager in interpreting the concept lattice during the variability analysis phase, we developed a variability analysis tool called **VariAnT** which is based on **ConExp**. Beyond the basic features provided by **ConExp**, **VariAnT** supports the following additional features that are specifically tailored for the purpose of variability analysis:

  - Coloring of specific nodes and edges of the concept lattice
  - Views on the concept lattice for better analyzing the usage of features in product configurations
  - Visualization of shared features for a set of product configurations
  - Visualization of distinct features for a set of product configurations
  - Calculation and visualization of mutually exclusive features
  - Visualization of the feature usage classification
  - Calculation of the optimization potential

  Besides support for the tasks that are performed during variability analysis, **VariAnT** also supports the validation of restructuring decisions (Step 4.2) by allowing the product line manager to change the feature usage classification that has been calculated in Step 3.3.

  Details of the implementation of **VariAnT** are described in Perunicic's master thesis [Per07].

- **Analysis of feature implementation (Step 4.3).**
  For the analysis of features that have been realized by a SCM system we developed a tool called **VarImA** that provides the following features:

  - Analysis of the mapping of features represented by configuration labels to configuration items implementing them
  - Analysis of the relationship between configuration labels
  - Analysis of branches and configuration items

  The tool receives a list of features whose implementation should be analyzed. As these features are represented by configuration labels in the SCM system, the tool extracts the configuration items and branches for this set of configuration labels from the SCM system. The tool uses this information to construct a formal context relating branches and configuration items. It then applies formal concept analysis on this context to calculate a concept lattice for the item-label relationship. The item-label relationship provides several hints about the implementation of features and serves as a basis for the restructuring of features in Step 4.4. Details of the **VarImA** tool are described in Li's master thesis [Li06].

- **Application of restructuring transformations (Step 4.5).**
  For the application of restructuring transformations on the implementation of the
  features that have been selected for restructuring in Step 4.2 we have developed
  a tool called **VarReT** (Variability Restructuring Tool). This tool uses the concept
  lattice that has been obtained by **VarImA** in order to apply restructuring transformations on configuration labels, branches, and configuration items in ClearCase.

6.3.3   Tool Chain

The individual tools described in the last subsection are chained together to form a *tool
chain* which follows the general framework architecture we described in Subsection 6.3.1.
Figure 6.8 shows the tool chain we used to implement the variability optimization process
for variability that has been realized using the SCM system ClearCase. The tool chain
shows the information flow between the individual tools as well as the partitioning of the
tools into front end, middle end, and back end.

The front end and back end tools (CCCSP, VarImA, and VarReT) directly operate on
the information stored in the SCM system ClearCase [Leb94]. CCCSP extracts configuration labels and configuration specifications out of ClearCase and constructs a product-
feature matrix relating configuration specifications representing product configurations
and configuration labels representing features. VariAnT transforms the product-feature
matrix that has been constructed by CCCSP into a concept lattice using formal concept
analysis. Furthermore, VariAnT classifies the features, derives feature constraints, and
calculates the optimization potential. The product line manager interprets the information
generated by VariAnT to identify a list of features that should be restructured. VarImA
analyzes the implementation of these features including their mapping to configuration
items and the branch structure of these configuration items. This feature implementation
structure is handed over to VarReT that receives the restructuring strategies and the list of
features that should be restructured from VariAnT. VarReT then applies specific restructuring transformations on these features that result in a changed branch structure in the
SCM system.

As one can see from Figure 6.8, the front end and back end are dependent on the used
SCM system, but the middle end is independent. Thus, the tool chain can be adapted to
different SCM systems or different variability mechanisms by exchanging the front end
and back end tools. The middle end does not need to be changed because it is independent
from the variability mechanism as long as the variability can be represented as a product-
feature matrix.

6.4   Summary

This chapter has shown how variability analysis and variability restructuring can be combined into a process that describes the necessary actions that need to be taken by different
persons in the organization in order to optimize the variability in their software product
lines. The overall process that has been described in this chapter consists of four phases,

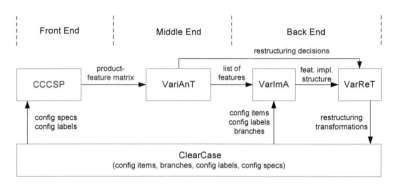

Figure 6.8: Tool chain for variability optimization.

namely, variability documentation, variability prediction, variability analysis, and variability restructuring. Each of the four phases has been described in detail in this Chapter using IDEF0 diagrams that depict the process steps and show which activities have to be performed by which participants in the process.

The variability optimization process that has been presented in this Chapter is supported by tools that automate a number of steps for variability documentation, variability analysis, and variability restructuring that otherwise would have to be performed manually by the participants. These tools have been organized into a generic tool framework that can be adapted to different variability realization techniques depending on the techniques used for implementing variability in the analyzed software product line. This tool framework considerably improves the acceptance of the process in industrial organizations that typically are not willing to spend much time for maintenance and evolution tasks because they are under a constant pressure to develop new products.

Chapter 7

Case Studies

Our method for variability analysis and optimization as well as the process and tools, i.e., the framework for systematic analysis, visualization and restructuring of variability, have been described in the previous chapters. In this chapter, we present two case studies which serve to evaluate the applicability, the appropriateness, and the utility of our method for the task of variability maintenance and optimization.

Overview. Section 7.1 gives an overview of the general objectives of the case studies and the approach we used to conduct the case studies. The individual objectives and the results of the case studies are described in Section 7.2 and Section 7.3. A summary of the results and lessons learned is presented in Section 7.4.

7.1 Overview

This section gives an overview of the case studies. It includes a description of the goals and objectives, the approach and process, the methodology for conducting the case studies, and a description of the tools that were applied in order to obtain the results.

7.1.1 Goals and Objectives

As stated in Chapter 1, the overall goal of the case studies is to evaluate the applicability, the appropriateness and the usability of our approach for the task of variability management during software product line evolution, i.e., variability maintenance. Thus, the first goal is to evaluate whether our approach can be applied to real-world software product lines. The second goal is to analyze the appropriateness of our approach, i.e., whether our approach provides the necessary means to optimize variability. The third goal is to evaluate how useful the information obtained by variability analysis is for variability management during software product line evolution.

These three abstract goals can be broken down into the following concrete research questions:

133

Applicability

1. Can the variability analysis and optimization approach be applied to subsystems of software product lines of industrial size?

2. Does highlighting and filtering support the understanding of the concept lattice during manual interpretation?

3. Is the runtime of formal concept analysis for large concept lattices low enough for our approach to be applicable?

Appropriateness

1. How good are the results obtained by variability analysis in comparison to existing domain knowledge?

2. Which improvements can be achieved by comparing the calculated classification with already existing domain knowledge?

3. Which influence does filtering of features have on the accuracy of the feature usage classification and the optimization potential?

4. How many of the identified potential feature constraints are valid feature constraints, i.e., what is the precision and recall?

Utility

1. How useful is the variability analysis approach for optimizing the existing variability of software product lines?

2. Does the variability analysis approach provide useful information for other variability management tasks during software product line evolution than optimization?

7.1.2   Approach and Process

In order to fulfill the objectives and to answer the research questions stated in the previous Section, we conducted two case studies. The software product lines that we analyzed in the case studies are taken from different domains and were developed by different developers in different business units with different organization structures. In order to obtain comparable results both case studies had similar objectives. In each case study, we first analyzed whole subsystems at once, i.e., the analysis included all provided features of a subsystem. The concept lattices for each subsystem were used to derive the feature usage classification and to calculate the optimization potential. As the resulting concept lattices were in all cases very large, we subsequently analyzed the provided variability of separate feature groups, i.e., groups of features that semantically belong together.

Figure 7.1 graphically depicts this process. Each subsystem is analyzed first before it is decomposed into feature groups. These feature groups are shown below the subsystems for each case study. The results obtained by separately analyzing these feature groups are summarized as indicated by the Y-junctions going from the feature groups to the result boxes. The results of the analysis are represented separately for each subsystem and are structured by different aspects of our variability analysis method, i.e., manual interpretation of the concept lattice, feature usage classification and optimization potential, comparison with domain knowledge, and derivation and analysis of feature constraints.

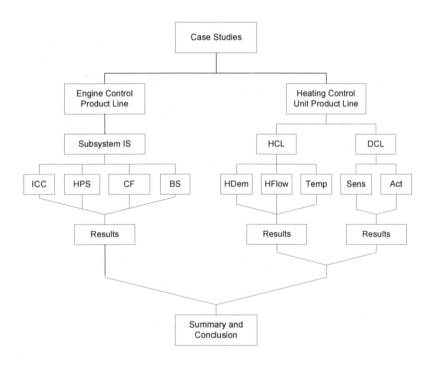

Figure 7.1: Case Studies - Approach and Process.

7.1.3   Methodology

When we conducted the case studies we followed the variability analysis and optimization process as described in Chapter 6. In order to obtain the set of product configurations that were to be analyzed in each case study, we queried a software product catalog or asked the product line manager. In either case, we paid attention that the list of product configurations contained all available product configurations in order to provide an accurate basis for variability analysis. For each case study, we obtained a list of offered features from existing documentation. In the next step, we constructed a product-feature matrix by analyzing the product configurations.

For formal concept analysis and visualization of the concept lattice we used our own tool *VariAnT* [Per07]. Besides basic functions for performing formal concept analysis and layouting concept lattices this tool supports the interpretation of the concept lattice with multiple views that use highlighting for making specific relationships between features and product configurations visible, and provides an automatic classification of the feature usage and a calculation of the optimization potential.

The resulting concept lattices, the derived feature usage classification, and the calculated optimization potential were then presented to the domain experts for validation. To make a clear distinction between these validating experts and the expert who assisted in the selection of product configurations, the former will be called *platform developers* and the latter *product line manager* in the following descriptions of the case studies.

The platform developers were familiar with the provided variability of the software product line but were not involved in the selection of product configurations that were analyzed. We explained to them the set of product configurations that were selected and the interpretation of the concept lattice as described in Chapter 4. We asked the platform developers to explain the usage of variable features in product configurations with the concept lattice and whether there were any surprises in the lattice. In the next step, we used our tool *VariAnT* to calculate the feature usage classification and the optimization potential. In order to validate this classification and the optimization potential, we used two independent oracles. As a first oracle, we asked a platform developer to classify the set of features into the classes I (always used), II (never used / obsolete), and IV (used separately / optional). For class III (used together), we asked the platform developer to identify groups of features that are always used together. As a second oracle, we used existing explicit domain knowledge in the form of variability models, architecture descriptions, and rules for the configuration of products. Whenever we identified a mismatch between the derived classification and the two oracles or between the two oracles, we made a decision which among the three was correct. In cases in which the existing domain knowledge was correct, the classification was changed as described in Chapter 5. After this validation which incorporated the changes made by the platform developers the resulting classification was used as a basis for restructuring the existing variability as described in Section 5.2.

In the following we describe the tools that were used for conducting the case studies and the hardware on which these tools were executed.

Tool Support

We used the following tools for case study A (Section 7.2):

- In order to obtain the product configurations for case study A we queried the **software catalog**, i.e., a web application that lists all platform and customer project deliveries. This catalog is sorted by customers, projects, and deliveries. For each delivery of a project its corresponding product configuration in the form of a ClearCase [Leb94] configuration specification can be obtained.

- The product-feature matrix was automatically constructed by our own parser for ClearCase configuration specifications (CCCSP). The list of features was obtained from existing documentation.

- For formal concept analysis and the visualization of the concept lattice we applied our own tool **VariAnT** [Per07]. Besides basic functions for performing formal concept analysis this tool provides several extensions that support the following process steps of the variability analysis and optimization process:

    - Interpretation of the concept lattice
    - Highlighting of specific relationships between features and product configurations
    - Filtering of large concept lattices
    - Feature Usage Classification
    - Comparison of variability analysis results with additional explicit and implicit domain knowledge
    - Derivation of potential feature constraints

For case study B (Section 7.3) we used the following tools:

- The product configurations for case study B were provided by the product developers in the form of simple text files. The list of features was obtained from existing documentation such as requirements documentation.

- We manually constructed the product-feature matrix from the product configurations and the list of features.

- For the analysis of the product-feature matrix and the visualization of the concept lattice we applied **VariAnT** [Per07] again.

Hardware We used a laptop with an Intel Pentium Centrino M 765 2,1 GHz processor with 1 MB Level2-Cache and 1024 MB RAM for both case studies. On this laptop Windows 2000 with Java Virtual Machine version 1.6.0-b105 was installed. The ClearCase repository for the case studies was located on a network server and was accessed using the Rational ClearCase Tools version 2003.06.10 which were installed locally on the laptop PC. The repository was accessed using dynamic views.

7.2 Case Study A

7.2.1 Context

In case study A we analyzed a subsystem of the electronic engine control software product line that is used to control engines of passenger cars and trucks [HBJ+03]. The software product line provides capabilities for reading and evaluating sensor values of several engine relevant sensors such as pressure sensors, temperature sensors, fill sensors, air mass sensors, and exhaust gas sensors. Furthermore, it provides functions that control different actuators that are engine relevant such as ignition actuators, injectors, and different valves [HBJ+03].

The architecture of the software product line is divided into several layers which are shown in Figure 7.2.

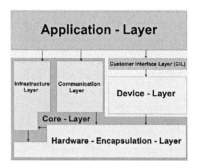

Figure 7.2: Engine control software architecture layers (taken from [HBJ+03]).

Each layer is itself divided into several subsystems which consist of components. Figure 7.3 shows the subsystems for each layer. For this case study, we focused on subsystem IS, a subsystem of the application layer.

The engine control software product line can be configured for different products by including or excluding features of each of the subsystems described above. Additionally for some features there exist multiple alternatives from which one can be selected for a particular configuration. The features of the engine control software product line evolved over several years. Today the engine control software product line provides more than 1.000 features [STB+04].

In order to derive a concrete product from the engine control software product line, the selection of features is mapped to a *selection of configuration labels*. These configuration labels are specified in a so called *configuration specification* which is interpreted by the software configuration management system ClearCase [Leb94]. ClearCase then retrieves specific versions of the actual source code files that match the selection of configuration labels. Details of this process are described in Appendix A. The selected source code files are then compiled and linked. In addition to mapping a selection of variable features to a selection of source code files, some variable features of the engine control software

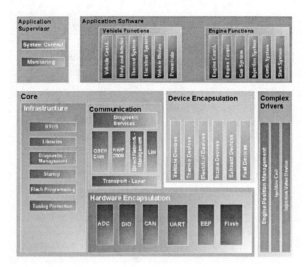

Figure 7.3: Subsystems of engine control software (taken from [HBJ$^+$03]).

product line are mapped to values of *preprocessor constants* that are used to fine-tune the behavior of the system. In this case study, we only analyzed the variability that was realized using configuration labels and did not take preprocessor constants into account.

7.2.2 Objectives

The case study described in this Section had the following goals:

1. To apply the variability analysis and optimization approach on a whole subsystem. Compared to the running example with 22 features and 11 product configurations which we used for illustrating our approach in Chapter 4 and Chapter 5, the formal context for the subsystem IS consists of 67 features and 47 product configurations. Thus, the goal of this case study was to show that the variability analysis and optimization approach can also be applied to larger systems of industrial size.

2. To compare the results obtained by variability analysis to existing domain knowledge in order to infer the appropriateness of our approach.

3. To show how the manual interpretation of large concept lattices is supported by providing visual aids such as highlighting (as described in Section 4.3.3).

4. To demonstrate how filtering of features in large concept lattices helps to improve the understanding of the concept lattice during manual interpretation.

5. To analyze which influence filtering of features has on the feature usage classification and on the recall of the optimization potential.

6. To analyze the detection quality of our approach for potential feature constraints in terms of precision and recall.

7. To show that the runtime of formal concept analysis is not significant for variability analysis even for large concept lattices.

7.2.3   Case Study Setup

For the analysis of the subsystem IS, we obtained a total of 47 product configurations from the software catalog that lists all platform and customer project deliveries. This catalog is sorted by customers, projects, and deliveries. For each delivery of a project the corresponding product configuration in the form of a ClearCase configuration specification can be downloaded. The analyzed product configurations cover the whole range of products that are derived from the engine control software product line including passenger car and truck projects 27 customers. At the time the case study was conducted this set covered all available product configurations that used versions 8.0.3 up to version 11.1.2 of the subsystem IS. The set of features provided by these versions of the subsystem IS is equivalent, i.e., only smaller bugfixes and changes have been performed on the source code files. Features have neither been added nor removed between version 8.0.3 and version 11.1.2.

Figure 7.4 graphically depicts the number of selected features for the subsystem IS per product configuration. As one can see from this Figure, for a typical product configuration, between 22 and 45 features of subsystem IS need to be selected.

We conducted two experiments. In the first experiment, we analyzed the variability of subsystem IS in total, i.e., we included all 67 features and 47 product configurations in the product-feature matrix. This analysis included a manual interpretation of the concept lattice, the derivation of the feature usage classification, the calculation of the optimization potential, and the derivation and validation of potential feature constraints. In order to validate the feature usage classification and the optimization potential we used two independent oracles. As a first oracle, we obtained a classification of the features into classes I-IV from the platform developers. They constructed this classification without looking at the feature usage classification we derived from the concept lattice. As a second oracle we used existing explicit domain knowledge in the form of variability models, architectural descriptions, and rules for the configuration of products. The goal of this validation was to show how the results obtained by automatic feature usage classification based on the information present in the product configurations compares to existing implicit and explicit domain knowledge.

As the manual interpretation of the concept lattice that we derived in the first experiment was rather complicated, we conducted a second experiment, in which we separately analyzed the variability of each feature group of subsystem IS. This experiment exemplified the process of filtering large concept lattices by constraining the analysis on subsets of features. In order to obtain meaningful subsets of features, we grouped the features with

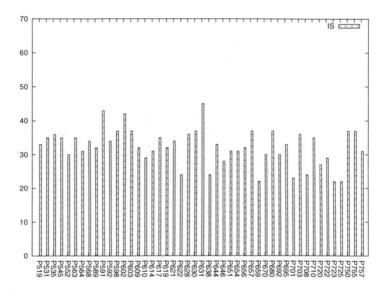

Figure 7.4: Number of selected features for each product configuration.

the help of platform developers. A feature group typically includes features that perform similar functions of subsystem IS. Usually these features have the same name prefix, e.g., all features start with the prefix H_. Some of the feature groups are directly represented by components in the architecture, e.g., the high pressure system, while other feature groups are not directly represented in the product line architecture. In the latter case, the features are distributed among several architectural components. Therefore, we decided not to use components for analyzing subsets of features. Instead of components we used the feature groups as describe above. Table 7.1 shows the analyzed features groups and the number of features for each feature group of subsystem IS.

Feature Group	Features
ICC	36
HPS	11
CF	5
BS	14
Total	67

Table 7.1: Analyzed feature groups of subsystem IS.

For each concept lattice we measured the execution time for computing the concepts and the time needed for layouting and drawing the concept lattice as a graph on the screen. In order to avoid biases in the execution times by external factors such as the just-in-time compilation of functions by the Java Virtual Machine, we repeated each measurement 10 times and calculated an average value from these 10 measurements.

7.2.4   Results

In this section, we present the results that we obtained by analyzing the existing variability of subsystem IS. The presentation of results is organized by the different aspects of our variability analysis method, i.e., manual interpretation of the concept lattice, feature usage classification and optimization potential, comparison with domain knowledge, and analysis of feature constraints. Furthermore, we measured the time that was needed to compute the concepts and to layout and draw the concept lattices on the screen.

Interpretation of the Concept Lattice

The resulting concept lattice for the analysis of subsystem IS is shown in Figure 7.5. It consists of 681 concepts and 2316 non-transitive subconcept relations. As shown in Figure 7.5, 34 of a total of 681 concepts introduce at least one new variable feature, i.e., to these nodes a variable feature is attached.

We manually inspected the lattice and used the documentation of subsystem IS to assign meaning to the features. Using the names of features helped to build groups of features that are likely to be related because of a common prefix in the name, e.g., A1_A is likely to be an alternative of A1_T.

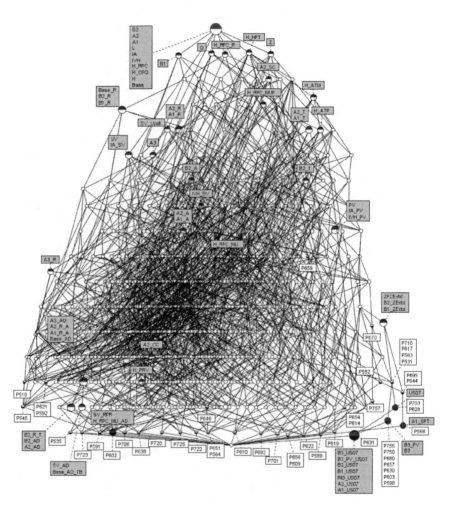

Figure 7.5: Concept lattice for subsystem IS.

Using the labeled boxes shown in Figure 7.5 we could infer groups of features that are used together in a number of product configurations. For example, we read off the following sets of features from the concept lattice:

- {A1_US07, A2_US07, A3_US07, B1_US07 B2_US07, B3_PV_US07, B3_US07}

- {A1_A, A2_A}

- {IA_PV, PV, IVH_PV}

- {ZFCExtd, B1_ZExtd, B2_ZExtd}

- {Base_R, B1_R, B2_R}

An interesting observation we made by looking at the names of the features in a feature set is that they often have the same suffix. A conclusion that can be drawn from this fact is that the features in a feature set are somehow related and probably have to be used together.

Another interesting fact we inferred from the concept lattice was that the following sets of product configurations have exactly the same configuration for subsystem IS:

- {P592, P621}

- {P651, P564}

- {P654, P614}

- {P656, P609}

- {P531, P563, P617, P710}

- {P644, P695}

- {P598, P603, P630, P657, P680, P750, P755}

By further inspecting these sets of product configurations we found out that most of the product configurations that belong to the same set are product configurations from a specific customer. A conclusion that can be drawn from this fact is that the configuration of subsystem IS is very similar for product configurations of the same customer but it is different for product configurations of different customers.

While the concept lattice shown in Figure 7.5 allowed us to easily derive sets of features and sets of product configurations, a detailed analysis of the usage of combinations of features that do not belong to the same feature set was not feasible due to the large number of concepts and edges in the lattice especially in the middle region where a large number of concepts and edges interfere.

In order to solve this problem, we used highlighting of specific parts of the lattice as provided by our analysis tool VariAnT [Per07]. The process of highlighting (coloring) is described in detail in Chapter 4. For example, we wanted to know in which product configurations the features A1_A, A2_A, and B2_T are used together. Using the concept lattice shown in Figure 7.5, we were not able to answer this question. However, by using highlighting this question could be easily answered as shown in Figure 7.6. In order to obtain this highlighting, we selected the features A1_A, A2_A and B2_T in the lattice. Our variability analysis tool VariAnT [Per07] then automatically computed the highlighted nodes and edges. As one can see from Figure 7.6, the features A1_A, A2_A, and B2_T and all product configurations using these three features are highlighted. Interestingly, there is only one product configuration, namely P701, in which the features A1_A, A2_A and B2_T are used together. This example shows that highlighting makes specific relationships between features and product configurations visible that are not visible in the original concept lattice shown in Figure 7.5 due to the large number of interfering edges. In other words, highlighting is a very useful feature to make concept lattices interpretable that appear to be unreadable and thus useless in the first place.

Although highlighting helps to overcome the limitations of large concept lattices to some extent, the interpretation of the relationships between features and product configurations is still time consuming and tedious especially if one is interested in specific subsets of the features, e.g., all features belonging to a specific feature group. For example, we wanted to know how the features belonging to the high pressure system feature group are used in the analyzed product configurations. In order to answer this question, we filtered the large concept lattice shown in Figure 7.5 by excluding all features that do not belong to the high pressure system feature group. The process of filtering was fully automated by using the filtering capabilities of VariAnT [Per07] (see Section 4.3 for details). The resulting concept lattice for the high pressure system features is shown in Figure 7.7.

Compared to the full lattice for subsystem IS shown in Figure 7.5, the concept lattice in Figure 7.7 is much smaller and thus easier to interpret manually. For example, we can directly infer from this lattice that a large number of product configurations (72%, 34 product configurations) has the same configuration of the high pressure system and that this configuration includes the features H_RPC_R, H_HPT, H_ATM, H_RPC_MUP, and H_ATP in addition to the high pressure system features that are included in every product configuration (shown at the top concept in Figure 7.7. This fact is much harder to read off the full concept lattice as one can see from Figure 7.8. Despite highlighting of the relevant features and product configurations in Figure 7.8, one still has to manually count the number of product configurations to obtain the same information which can be read off a single concept in Figure 7.7. Furthermore, the time needed to compute the highlighting shown in Figure 7.8 took more than 10 seconds, whereas the lattice shown in Figure 7.7 could be computed and drawn in less than 500 milliseconds.

As we were interested in a separate analysis of the provided variability of each feature group, we computed a concept lattice for each of the feature groups shown in Table 7.1. Together with the platform developer we manually inspected the resulting concept lattices for each feature group.

As an example, we describe the manual interpretation of the concept lattice for the feature group CF which is shown in Figure 7.9. When we showed the concept lattice to the platform developer, he immediately spotted an error in the configuration for the product configurations P545, P591, P591, P592, and P621. As one can see from Figure 7.9, these product configurations include the correction features IA_PV and IA_SV. However,

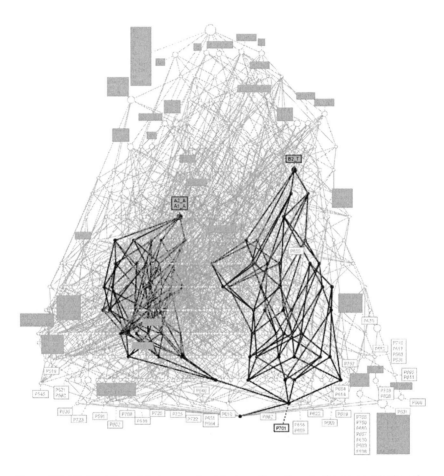

Figure 7.6: Highlighting of features and product configurations in the concept lattice of subsystem IS.

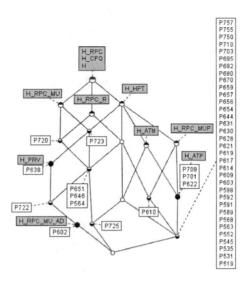

Figure 7.7: Concept lattice for feature group HPS.

according to the documentation and to the knowledge of the platform developer these features are mutually exclusively and should not be used together in any product configuration. Another interesting fact which can be derived from the concept lattice shown in Figure 7.9 is the usage of different features in the product configurations. For example, the feature Z is used in all product configurations except P535, P646, and P662. The feature Q is used in all product configurations except P535. Thus, we can draw the conclusion that these features are used in almost every product configuration. The platform developer explained us that these features were initially intended to be high-end features for a small percentage of product configurations but today have become commodity features that are used in almost every product configuration.

Feature Usage Classification and Optimization Potential

In order to derive quantitative data about the usage of features and the optimization potential, we analyzed the concept lattice of subsystem IS using our variability analysis tool VariAnT [Per07]. The tool automatically computed the feature usage classification and the optimization potential as described in Chapter 4. Table 7.2 shows a summary of the distribution of features on the feature usage classes I, II, III and IV, and the optimization potential. As one can see from Table 7.2, among the 67 features that are provided by subsystem IS, 10 features (15%) are used in all 47 product configurations (they appear at the top concept in Figure 7.5). These features are likely to be mandatory features. Out of the 67 features, each feature is selected at least in one product configuration, i.e., the bot-

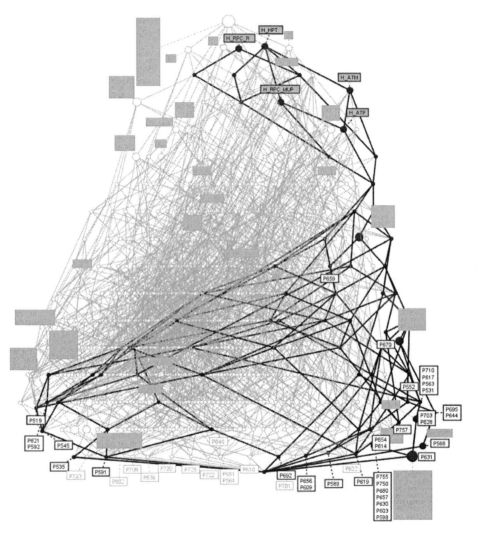

Figure 7.8: A common configuration of the feature group HPS highlighted in the full concept lattice.

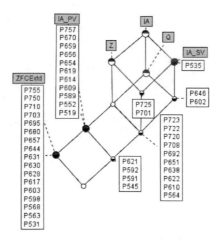

Figure 7.9: Concept lattice for feature group CF.

tom concept does not contain any features. Furthermore, 37 out of 67 features (55%) are always used together with other features. These features are likely features whose variability is not needed and can be reduced by combination. The last row of Table 7.2 shows that the current number of features for subsystem IS (67 features) is much higher than the required number of features (34) for deriving the 47 analyzed product configurations. Thus, the variability provided by subsystem IS shows a great potential for optimization.

Usage Class	Current		Optimized	
	# features	%	# features	% saved
Always used	10	15%	1	90%
Never used	0	0%	0	0%
Used together	37	55%	13	65%
Used singularly	20	30%	20	0%
Total	**67**	**100%**	**34**	**49%**

Table 7.2: Feature usage classification and optimization potential for subsystem IS.

We further analyzed the feature usage classification and the local optimization potential of each feature group. Table 7.3 shows these results for the feature groups of subsystem IS. Column FC shows the current number of features for each feature group. Columns I, II, III, IV show the distribution of features to the feature usage classes. Column FO shows the minimal number of variable features required for achieving the desired variability. Column OP shows the maximal percentage of savings (optimization potential) that can be achieved by optimizing the variability. The row *Summary* shows the aggregated results for the separated analysis of the feature groups. The row *InjSys* shows the results that have been directly obtained from analyzing the concept lattice for the whole subsystem IS shown in Figure 7.5.

	FC	I	II	III	IV	FO	OP
ICC	36	3	0	25	8	18	50%
HPS	11	3	0	0	8	9	18%
CF	6	1	0	0	5	6	0%
BS	14	3	0	4	7	10	29%
Summary	67	10	0	29	28	43	36%
IS	67	10	0	37	20	34	49%

Table 7.3: Feature usage classification and optimization potential for feature groups of subsystem IS.

By comparing the row *Summary* with the row *IS* one can see which influence the filtering of features has on the recall of the feature usage classification and the optimization potential. While the filtering does not change the results for feature classes I (always used), and feature classes II (never used), the results for feature classes III (used together) and IV (used separately) are influenced by filtering. This effect is rather obvious because features of different feature groups that are used together cannot be identified by separately analyzing the feature groups. This explains why the value for features that are used together in column III of the summary row is lower than the value in column III of the IS row. Consequently, the values in column IV are higher for the Summary row and lower for the IS row as more features appear to be used separately while in fact they are used together with features of other feature groups. Nevertheless, the summary row still shows an optimization potential of 36%. A conclusion we can draw from this observation is that the concept lattice for the whole subsystem IS shall be used when the focus of the analysis is on the identification of the optimization potential. If the purpose of variability analysis is to understand the existing variability and the usage of features of individual feature groups, the smaller concept lattices for each feature group are more suitable than the large concept lattice because the facts can be read off more easily.

As one can see from Table 7.3, the feature group ICC has a large number of features that are used together compared to the other feature groups that do not have features which are used together. This indicates that ICC offers more variability than actually required by the analyzed set of 57 product configurations. Another observation is, that the variability provided by the feature group CF is actually required by the analyzed product configurations because almost all features are used separately.

Furthermore, we can see from Table 7.3 that all feature groups except CF show an optimization potential of more than 15%. The relative optimization potential is particularly high for the feature group ICC. Thus, restructuring the provided variability of this feature group will have the greatest effect on the overall reduction of the provided variability of the subsystem IS.

Validation of Feature Usage Classification

As we have seen in the previous section, the analysis of the feature usage classification using our approach showed a great potential for optimizing the variability. However, the identified optimization potential is based solely on the information obtained from the analyzed product configurations. In order to validate the feature usage classification, we used two oracles. As a first oracle, we asked the platform developer to classify the set of features into the classes I-IV. As a second oracle, we used existing variability documentation in the form of configuration rules which included a rudimentary classification of features into mandatory, alternative and optional features. The comparison of the feature usage classification derived by our analysis and the two oracles is shown in Table 7.4. Due to space reasons Table 7.4 does not show the comparison for class II as there are no obsolete features for subsystem IS, i.e., neither the documentation nor the developer nor the feature usage classification classified any of the features as never used or obsolete. Furthermore, for class III only those groups of features are shown in the Table that were also identified by the platform developer.

As one can see from Table 7.4, the feature usage classification derived from the concept lattice is very precise with regard to feature usage classes I, II and IV. Interestingly enough, the classification in the documentation is incomplete. For example, the features A1_US07, A2_US07, A3_US07, B1_US07, B2_US07, B3_PV_US07, B3_US07 are not listed in the documentation. By inspecting the concept lattice shown in Figure 7.5, we found out that these features are currently only used in product configuration P631 (shown in the lower right corner of the lattice). The platform developer explained us that these features are currently prototyped and will be included in the documentation in the future.

Another interesting observation we made is that the documentation shows most of the features that are used together with other features as optional features, i.e., features that can be used separately although the clusterings have been confirmed by the platform developer. For example, the features A1_A and A2_A are shown as optional features in the documentation although the feature usage classification states that these features are always used together and the platform developer confirmed this.

The classification of the platform developer for classes I, II and IV is for most cases in accordance with the documentation. However, the platform developer seemed to have additional knowledge which was not present in the documentation. For example, the platform developer knew that the feature IVH_SV is optional while it was shown as mandatory in the documentation. Furthermore, he knew that the features A2_SC and A2_CC respectively the features B2_T and B2_A can only be used mutually exclusively.

By comparing the feature usage classification with the two oracles we found out that for class I there are only two mismatches, namely for the feature B2 (FCA: class I, developer and documentation: class IV) and for the feature IA (FCA: class I, developer: class I, documentation: class IV). Out of the 37 features that are used together in 13 different clusters according to the feature usage classification shown in Table 7.2, the platform developer confirmed 6 clusters (18 features in total).

As described in Chapter 5, our variability analysis approach allows us to change the automatically derived classification or the documentation in the case of mismatches. For

Formal Concept Analysis	Developer	Documentation
I: Always used / Mandatory		
A1	A1	A1
A2	A2	
B2		
Base	Base	Base
H	H	H
H_CPQ	H_CPQ	H_CPQ
H_RPC	H_RPC	H_RPC
IA	IA	
IVH	IVH	IVH
		IVH_SV
L	L	L
III: Used together		
{A1_US07, ..., B3_US07}	confirm	not listed
{A1_A, A2_A}	confirm	optional
{A1_T, A2_T}	confirm	optional
{A1_R, A2_R}	confirm	optional
{IA_SV, SV}	confirm	optional
{IA_PV, PV, IVH_PV}	confirm	optional
IV: Used singularly / Optional or Alternative (mut. ex.)		
A1_SPT	A1_SPT	not listed
A2_SC	mut. ex. A2_CC	A2_SC
A2_CC	mut. ex. A2_SC	A2_CC
A3	A3	A3
A3_R	A3_R	A3_R
B1	B1	B1
	B2	B2
B2_A	mut. ex. B2_T	B2_A
B2_T	mut. ex. B2_A	B2_T
H_ATM	not classified	H_ATM
H_ATP	not classified	H_ATP
H_HPT		H_HPT
H_PRV	H_PRV	H_PRV
H_RPC_MU	mut. ex. H_RPC_MUP	mut. ex. H_RPC_MU
H_RPC_MUP	mut. ex. H_RPC_MU	mut. ex. H_RPC_MUP
H_RPC_R	H_RPC_R	H_RPC_R
		IA
		IA_SV
IVH_SV	IVH_SV	
Q	Q	Q
SV_U	SV_U	SV_U
US07	US07	US07
Z	Z	Z

Table 7.4: Comparison of feature usage classification with oracles.

example, we decided to change the class of feature B2 from class I (mandatory) to class IV (used separately) because the platform developer and the documentation stated that this feature is optional, i.e., does not have to be used in every product configuration. For feature IA, we decided to change the classification of the feature from optional to mandatory in the documentation because both analysis of product configurations and the platform developer classified this feature as mandatory. For the remaining 19 features of class III which were not classified as being always used together by the platform developer, we changed their classification from class III to class IV.

Table 7.5 shows the resulting feature usage classification and the optimization potential after consolidation with the information obtained from the two oracles. Compared to the initial optimization potential (49,25% savings) the optimization potential is now lower (30% savings) but still high enough for a restructuring effort to pay off. Furthermore, we can now be sure that the variability restructuring will not destroy variability which is required for future product configurations as the classification incorporates the information about the required variability from the developer and the documentation.

Usage Class	Current		Optimized	
	# features	%	# features	% saved
Always used	9	13%	1	89%
Never used	0	0%	0	0%
Used together	18	27%	6	67%
Used singularly	40	60%	40	0%
Total	67	100%	47	30%

Table 7.5: Feature usage classification and optimization potential for subsystem IS after consolidation.

Analysis of Feature Constraints

In addition to the derivation of the feature usage classification and the calculation of the optimization potential, we also used the concept lattices to derive potential feature constraints. For the whole subsystem, we identified a total of 997 implications between features, i.e., implications of the form $a \rightarrow b$. These implications represent potential constraints of the form "feature a *requires* feature b". Furthermore, we identified 392 potential exclusion constraints between features, e.g., "feature m *excludes* feature n".

Table 7.6 shows a summary of the constraint analysis results for analyzed feature groups of subsystem IS. The row *Summary* shows the aggregated values for each column and the row *InjSys* shows the values that were directly obtained from the concept lattice shown in Figure 7.5. A comparison of the number of implications and potential exclusion constraints yields some interesting facts. First of all, all numbers shown in row *IS* are higher than the numbers shown in row *Summary*. This is due to the fact that the values in row *IS* were obtained from the complete concept lattice shown in Figure 7.5 which includes also implications and potential exclusion constraints that exist between different

	Implications	Exclusions
ICC	365	162
HPS	13	8
CF	5	1
BS	33	13
Summary	416	184
IS	997	392

Table 7.6: Constraint analysis results for subsystem IS.

feature groups. Thus, the advantage is that the number of constraints that need to be validated is considerably decreased. However, the disadvantage is that constraints between features of different feature groups cannot be identified if feature groups are analyzed separately.

Validation of Feature Constraints

As described in Chapter 4 the potential feature constraints need to be validated by an expert. Due to the large number of potential feature constraints and the limited time of experts, we decided not to validate the full list of potential feature constraints for subsystem IS. Instead, we asked the platform developers to separately validate the list of potential feature constraints for each feature group. The results of this validation are described in the following.

As an example, we describe the validation of feature constraints for the high pressure system feature group. Table 7.7 shows the implications between the HPS features that have been directly derived from the concept lattice shown in Figure 7.7. The platform developer confirmed that 6 out of the 13 implications shown in Table 7.7 represent valid feature constraints and need to be observed when a product is derived from the product line. For example, it is necessary that whenever the feature H_ATP is included the features H_ATM, H_HPT, and H_RPC_MUP have to be included as well. Furthermore, the platform developer decided that two implications are not valid as indicated by a N in column Valid in Table 7.7. For the other implications the platform developer was not sure whether they represent valid or invalid feature constraints. These implications are marked with a question mark in the column Valid.

Table 7.8 lists the potential exclusion constraints for the HPS features. Out of these 8 potential exclusion constraints, the platform developer confirmed 6 exclusion constraints as representing valid exclusion constraints between alternative features. The other 2 potential exclusion constraints were classified as invalid by the platform developer.

The potential feature constraints that we derived for the other feature groups shown in Table 7.1 were similarly validated by the platform developers. A feature constraint was marked with a Y in column Valid when the platform developer decided that it represents a valid feature constraint. It was marked with a N in column Valid when the platform developer was sure that the potential feature constraint did not represent a valid feature

Implications			PC	GS	LS	Valid
H_ATM	$\rightarrow$	H_HPT	38	81%	83%	Y
H_RPC_MUP	$\rightarrow$	H_HPT	38	81%	83%	Y
H_ATP	$\rightarrow$	H_ATM	37	79%	97%	Y
H_ATP	$\rightarrow$	H_HPT	37	79%	80%	Y
H_ATP	$\rightarrow$	H_RPC_MUP	37	79%	97%	Y
H_ATM $\wedge$ H_HPT $\wedge$ H_RPC_MUP	$\rightarrow$	H_ATP	37	79%	80%	?
H_PRV	$\rightarrow$	H_HPT	3	6%	7%	?
H_PRV	$\rightarrow$	H_RPC_MU	3	6%	33%	Y
H_ATM $\wedge$ H_HPT $\wedge$ H_RPC_MU	$\rightarrow$	H_RPC_R	1	2%	2%	N
H_RPC_MU_AD	$\rightarrow$	H_HPT	1	2%	2%	?
H_RPC_MU_AD	$\rightarrow$	H_PRV	1	2%	33%	?
H_RPC_MU_AD	$\rightarrow$	H_RPC_MU	1	2%	11%	Y
H_RPC_MU_AD	$\rightarrow$	H_RPC_R	1	2%	2%	N

Table 7.7: Implications between high HPS features. Column PC shows the number of product configurations satisfying the implication, column GS shows the global support, column LS shows the local support, and column Valid shows whether the implication is valid or not.

Exclusion Constraint			Valid
H_ATM	$\oplus$	H_PRV	N
H_ATM	$\oplus$	H_RPC_MU_AD	N
H_ATP	$\oplus$	H_PRV	Y
H_ATP	$\oplus$	H_RPC_MU	Y
H_ATP	$\oplus$	H_RPC_MU_AD	Y
H_PRV	$\oplus$	H_RPC_MUP	Y
H_RPC_MU	$\oplus$	H_RPC_MUP	Y
H_RPC_MUP	$\oplus$	H_RPC_MU_AD	Y

Table 7.8: Exclusion constraints between features of the high pressure system (HPSys).

constraint. Whenever the platform developer was not sure whether the constraint was valid or invalid it was marked with a question mark in column Valid.

In order to evaluate the detection quality of our approach for valid feature constraints, we calculated the following numbers for each feature group:

- **Number of true positives (TP)**: The number of feature constraints that have been found by our approach and have been classified as being valid by the expert.

- **Number of false positives (FP)**: The number of feature constraints that have been found by our approach and have been classified as being invalid by the expert.

- **Number of don't knows (DK)**: The number of feature constraints that have been found by our approach and can neither be classified as being valid nor as being invalid due to missing domain knowledge of the platform developer. If additional knowledge was available these feature constraints could be classified as being either valid or invalid.

- **Number of false negatives (FN)**: The number of feature constraints that have not been found by our approach but represent valid feature constraints.

Using these numbers we calculated the following values:

$$min\ precision = \frac{TP}{TP + (DK + FP)} \tag{7.1}$$

$$max\ precision = \frac{(TP + DK)}{(TP + DK) + FP} \tag{7.2}$$

$$recall = \frac{TP}{TP + FN} \tag{7.3}$$

The *minimum precision* represents the precision under the assumption that all *don't knows (DK)* are invalid feature constraints, i.e., are *false positives (FP)*. The *maximum precision* represents the precision under the assumption that all *don't knows (DK)* are valid feature constraints, i.e., are *true positives (TP)*. The real precision lies between the minimum and maximum precision. The distance between minimum and maximum precision represents the uncertainty about the precision due to missing knowledge of the platform developer. In order to obtain a reference value for the detection quality we calculated an average precision under the assumption that 50% of the don't knows are true positives and 50% are false positives.

Table 7.9 and Table 7.10 list the number of true positives (TP), the number of don't knows (DK), the number of false positives (FP), the number of false negatives (FN), the minimum and maximum precision, and the recall for the implications and potential exclusion constraints that we derived from the feature groups.

As one can see from Table 7.9 and Table 7.10, the average precision, i.e., the precision under the assumption that 50% of the don't knows are valid and 50% are false positives is in the range of 61% to 90% for the implications and in the range of 44% to 100% for the exclusions. The recall is 100% except for the exclusion constraints for feature group

	Implications	TP	DK	FP	FN	Precision (min-max/avg)	Recall
ICC	365	84	272	9	0	23-98/61%	100%
BS	33	16	13	4	0	48-88/68%	100%
HPS	13	7	4	2	0	54-85/70%	100%
CF	5	4	1	0	0	80-100/90%	100%

Table 7.9: Precision and recall for implications for the feature groups of subsystem IS.

	Exclusions	TP	DK	FP	FN	Precision (min-max/avg)	Recall
ICC	162	9	126	27	0	5-83/44%	100%
BS	13	4	9	0	0	31-100/66%	100%
HPS	8	6	0	2	0	80/80%	100%
CF	1	1	0	0	1	100/100%	50%

Table 7.10: Precision and recall for exclusion constraints for the feature groups of subsystem IS.

CF. The recall in this case is only 50% due to the erroneous product configurations that include both IA_SV and IA_PV although these features are mutually exclusive.

Another interesting fact that can be derived from Table 7.9 and Table 7.10 is that the distance between minimum and maximum precision gets smaller when the number of implications respectively the number of exclusions decreases. A conclusion that can be drawn from this fact is that obviously the smaller the concept lattice the more precisely can the feature constraints be classified as being valid or invalid by the platform developer.

Analysis of Execution Time

In theory, the time needed to compute a concept lattice can be exponential in the number of product configurations and features in the worst case. In order to show that our approach can also be applied to large concept lattices, we measured the time that was needed to calculate the concepts and to layout the concept lattices for the whole subsystem IS and each feature group. The results of this analysis are shown in Table 7.11. For each concept lattice we report the number of features (shown in column FC), the number of concepts (shown in Column C), the number of edges (shown in Column E), the time needed for calculation of the concepts (calculation time), and the time needed for layouting and drawing the lattice on the screen (layout time).

As one can see from Table 7.11, the time needed for the calculation of the concepts for each feature group took less than 500 ms on the Intel Pentium Centrino 2,1 GHz machine running Windows with 1024 MB, even for the analysis of the whole subsystem IS. This shows that the execution time to compute a concept lattice is not significant in our cases although in theory it can be exponential in the number of product configurations and features.

However, there seems to be a significant increase in the time needed for layouting and drawing large concept lattices as the number shown in the last column of Table 7.11 indicate. While the layouting and drawing of the concept lattices for individual feature

	C	E	FC	Calculation time [ms]	Layout time [ms]
ICC	53	101	36	120	450
HPS	19	32	11	100	400
CF	12	18	6	60	181
BS	23	39	14	70	270
Summary	107	190	67	350	1,301
IS	681	2316	67	480	139,000

Table 7.11: Execution time for calculation and layout of concept lattice.

groups in total only takes roughly 1300 ms, the layout and drawing of the concept lattice for subsystem IS takes more than a hundred times longer with 139,000 ms. This big increase in time is due to the fact that the layout algorithm tries to find a layout with a minimal intersection of edges. Unfortunately the complexity of this layout algorithm is exponential in the number of edges. This explains why it takes 139 seconds to layout and paint the lattice.

7.2.5 Summary

Section 7.2.2 listed the objectives of the case study on the engine control software product line. This section summarizes the main results of the case study and shows how these objectives have been met.

Objective 1: The variability analysis and optimization approach can be applied to whole subsystems: Our approach meets this objective very well. Indeed, the case study showed that the approach can be applied for the variability analysis of a whole subsystem. The only problem that we encountered during the case study was the large number of potential feature constraints that have been derived from the concept lattice. The high number makes the task of validating these potential constraints very time consuming.

Objective 2: The results of variability analysis should be compared to existing domain knowledge to determine the appropriateness of our approach: We validated the feature usage classification obtained during variability analysis by comparing it with two oracles. As a first oracle, we asked the platform developer to classify the features into the classes I-IV. As a second oracle, we used existing variability documentation. The results of this comparison are shown in Table 7.4. The results obtained from the concept lattice were very precise with regard to feature usage classes I, II, and IV. The comparison even revealed errors in the existing variability documentation.

Objective 3: It should be shown how the manual interpretation of large concept lattices can be supported by highlighting: In Figure 7.5 we presented the original concept lattice. Due to the large number of concepts and relations between these concepts, this lattice could not be easily interpreted. In order to support the manual interpretation we highlighted specific concepts and edges that are of interest for interpretation. Figure

7.6 shows the same concept lattice with highlighting. Obviously the required information can be read off much faster than in Figure 7.5.

Objective 4: It should be demonstrated how filtering of features in large concept lattices helps to improve the understanding of the concept lattice during manual interpretation: In Figure 7.8, the product configurations using specific features of the HPS feature group are highlighted. As one can see from this figure, it is still hard to count the number of product configurations that use these features. Using filtering, the same information can be read off a single concept as shown in Figure 7.7. This comparison demonstrates that the manual interpretation can be considerably improved by filtering. However, cross-feature group relationships between features cannot be found using filtering.

Objective 5: It should be analyzed which influence filtering of features has on the feature usage classification and the recall of the optimization potential: We conducted two experiments to analyze the influence of filtering on the feature usage classification and the recall of the optimization potential. In the first experiment, subsystem IS as a whole was analyzed. The feature usage classification and the optimization potential were calculated based on the full concept lattice shown in Figure 7.5. In the second experiment, subsystem IS was partitioned into feature groups and each feature group was analyzed separately, i.e., all features not belonging to the feature group under analysis were filtered. For each feature group, we calculated the feature usage classification and the optimization potential as shown in Table 7.3. We then compared these results to the results we obtained from the first experiment. While the decomposition did not influence the results for feature classes I (always used), and feature classes II (never used), the results for feature classes III (used together) and IV (used separately) were influenced by filtering. As a consequence, the optimization potential for the separate analysis of feature groups was lower (30%) as the optimization potential for the analysis of subsystem IS (49%) but still high enough for a restructuring effort to pay off.

Objective 6: The detection quality of our approach for feature constraints in terms of precision and recall should be analyzed: In order to evaluate the detection quality of our approach for feature constraints in terms of precision and recall we calculated the number of true positives (TP), the number of false positives (FP), the number of don't knows (DK), and the number of false negatives (FN). Feature constraints that were accepted by the platform developer during validation were counted as true positives, feature constraints that were rejected were counted as false positives. All other feature constraints that were derived from the concept lattice and neither counted as true positive or false negative were counted as don't know. Using these values we calculated a minimum precision value under the assumption that all don't knows represent false positives and a maximum precision value under the assumption that all don't knows represent true positives. The recall value was calculated by dividing the number of true positives by the number of true positives plus false negatives. The results showed that the average precision, i.e., the precision under the assumption that 50% of the don't knows are true positives and 50%

are false positives is in the range of 61% to 90% for the implications and in the range of 44% to 100% for the exclusions. The recall is 100% except for the exclusion constraints for feature group CF.

Objective 7: It should be shown that the runtime for formal concept analysis is not significant for variability analysis even for large concept lattices: We measured the execution time for formal concept analysis for subsystem IS as a whole and for each feature group. On our case study hardware the calculation of the concept lattice for subsystem IS with 47 product configurations and 67 features took only 480 milliseconds. Thus, the execution time for formal concept analysis is not significant.

7.3   Case Study B

7.3.1   Context

The heating control unit (HCU) is a software product line used to control various boilers for heating water in the household. It provides capabilities for reading and evaluating sensor values of the boiler, controlling different actuators of the system such as the central heating flame, multiple fans and pumps, handling the user interface, and multiple data interfaces for accessories such as room temperature control and diagnostic functions.

Figure 7.10: HCU feature layers.

The HCU software product line evolved over several years. Today, it roughly provides 300 features that can be classified into three different layers. Figure 7.10 shows these feature layers as described by one of the software architects, namely user interface layer (UI), heat system control layer (HCL), and device control layer (DCL). The device control layer (DCL) contains features for reading and evaluating sensor values and controlling the actuators of the system. Typically these features have a corresponding hardware device such as a sensor or actuator. The heat system control layer (HCL) contains features for controlling heat demands, combustion, venting, fans, pumps, and temperatures of the heating system. The user interface layer (UI) consists of features for controlling LEDs of the user interface, reading values from user interface knobs and driving 7-segment displays to display the temperature and error codes of the system.

The HCU software product line can be configured for different products by including or excluding features of each of the layers described above. Additionally for some features there exist multiple alternatives from which one can be selected for a particular configuration. In order to derive a concrete product from the HCU software product line, the selection of features is mapped to a *selection of software modules*. The selected software modules are then compiled and linked. The selection of software modules is realized using a SCM system. In addition to mapping a selection of variable features to a selection of software modules, some variable features of the HCU product line are mapped to values of *parameters* that are used to fine-tune the behavior of the system. In this case study, we only analyze the variability at the level of features and do not take the mapping of features to software modules or parameters into account.

7.3.2 Objectives

The case study described in this section had the following goals:

1. To show that our approach is applicable on a full software product line. Compared to the last case study in which we applied our approach on a subsystem including 67 features we now want to apply it to the whole product line containing 300 features.

2. To identify the optimization potential of the HCU software product line.

3. To analyze the detection quality of our approach for feature constraints in terms of precision and recall.

4. To show that the execution time of formal concept analysis is not significant even for concept lattices with more than 300 features.

7.3.3 Case Study Setup

The software architects of the HCU software product line provided us with 19 product configurations for the analysis. Table 7.12 shows the 19 product configurations that we analyzed in our case study. The analyzed product configurations cover the whole range of appliances using the HCU software product line for controlling sensors and actuators, including appliances for condensing boilers and non-condensing boilers. The table shows the number of selected features for each feature layer and product configuration as well as the total number of selected features for each configuration. Furthermore, the boiler type for each of the product configurations is shown.

We conducted three experiments. In the first experiment, we tried to analyze the variability of the HCU software product line at once, i.e., the formal context included all 300 features and 19 product configurations. The resulting concept lattice consisted over 1300 concepts. Although the worst case execution time to compute a concept lattice is exponential in the number of features and product configurations, the computation of the concept lattice for HCU software product line took only 1061 milliseconds on the Intel Pentium Centrino 2.1 GHz machine running Windows with 1024 MB. However, the layout and drawing of the lattice on the screen took more than 15 minutes. We soon realized that the resulting concept lattice was too big to be interpretable manually.

ID	DCL	HCL	UI	Total	C	NC
P1	25	51	42	118	x	
P2	36	61	43	140	x	
P3	36	61	43	140	x	
P4	27	51	41	119	x	
P5	21	46	38	105	x	
P6	36	60	42	138	x	
P7	31	57	42	130	x	
P8	37	59	40	136	x	
P9	19	37	28	84	x	
P10	29	46	41	116		x
P11	28	46	43	117		x
P12	28	46	43	117		x
P13	22	39	41	102		x
P14	18	34	30	82		x
P15	30	45	38	113		x
P16	26	48	40	114		x
P17	27	48	40	115		x
P18	25	44	40	109		x
P19	19	36	30	85		x

Table 7.12: Analyzed product configurations and number of selected features for each layer (columns DCL, HCL, and UI). Columns C and NC indicate the boiler type (condensing vs. non-condensing).

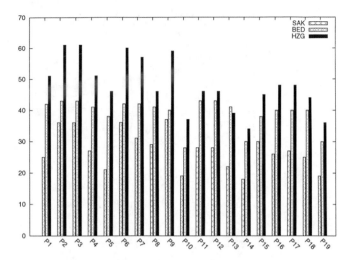

Figure 7.11: Number of selected features for each layer and product configuration.

Therefore, we decided to separately analyze the variability of each feature layer in the second experiment. This experiment included a manual interpretation of the concept lattice, the derivation of the feature usage classification, the calculation of the optimization potential, and the derivation of potential feature constraints for the heat system control layer (HCL) and the device control layer (DCL). We did not analyze the variability of the user interface layer (UI).

As the manual interpretation of the concept lattices for the heat system control layer (HCL) and the device control layer (DCL) was still rather complicated, we conducted a third experiment in which we analyzed the variability of each feature group inside both feature layers. This experiment exemplified the process of filtering large concept lattices by constraining the analysis on subsets of features. In order to obtain meaningful subsets of features, we grouped the features by feature groups according to their name prefixes, e.g., all features starting with the name HCL.HDem. We then applied formal concept analysis on each subcontext consisting of all product configurations and a subset of features belonging to a single feature group. Table 7.13 shows the analyzed feature groups for the heat system control layer (HCL) and Table 7.14 shows the feature groups for the device control layer (DCL).

7.3.4 Results for Heat System Control Layer

In this section, we present the results that have been obtained by analyzing the existing variability of the heat system control layer. The presentation of results is organized by

Feature Group	Features
HCL.Acc	6
HCL.CtlFunc.Burn	10
HCL.CtlFunc.Comb	5
HCL.CtlFunc.Hflow	11
HCL.CtlFunc.Temp	7
HCL.Eval/Efunc	7
HCL.FlueG	4
HCL.HDem	20
HCL.Misc	3
HCL.PuDem	5
HCL.Stop	18
Total	96

Table 7.13: Analyzed feature groups and number of features for heat system control layer.

Feature Group	Features
DCL.Sens	55
DCL.Act	34
Total	89

Table 7.14: Analyzed feature groups and number of features for device control layer.

the different aspects of our variability analysis method, i.e., interpretation of the concept lattice, feature usage classification and optimization potential, and analysis of feature constraints. Furthermore, we measured the execution time of formal concept analysis.

Interpretation of the Concept Lattice

The resulting concept lattice for the analysis of the usage of features for the heat system control layer is shown in Figure 7.12. It consists of 243 concepts and 678 non-transitive subconcept relations.

As shown in Figure 7.12, 65 of a total of 243 concepts introduce at least one new variable feature, i.e., to these nodes a variable feature is attached. 178 of the concepts do not introduce any new variable feature and merely combine variable features included in several product configurations. Among the 96 features that are provided by the heat system control layer, 17 features (18%) are used in all 19 product configurations (they appear at the top concept in Figure 7.12). These features are likely to be features that have to be always selected. Furthermore, 9 features of 96 (9%) are not selected in any of the product configurations, i.e., these features are likely to be obsolete (they appear at the bottom concept in Figure 7.12).

Among the 19 product configurations, we inferred from the concept lattice that the following pairs of product configurations have exactly the same configuration for the heat system control layer:

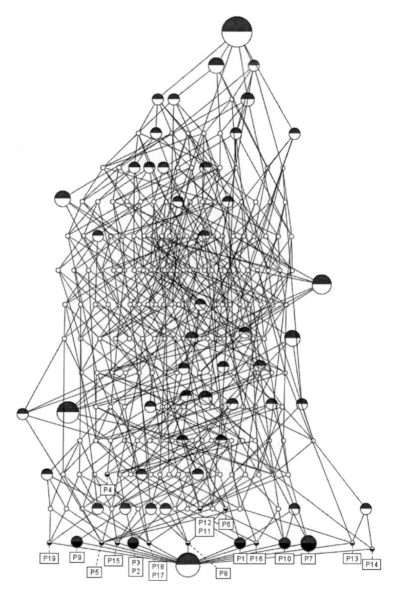

Figure 7.12: Concept lattice for heat system control layer.

- {P2, P3}

- {P11, P12}

- {P17, P18}

While the concept lattice shown in Figure 7.12 allowed us to easily derive groups of features and groups product configurations, a detailed analysis of the usage of features in product configurations was not feasible due to the large number of concepts and edges in the lattice especially in the middle region where a large number of concepts and edges interfere.

In order to solve this problem, we separately analyzed each feature group as shown in Table 7.13. In the following, we present some interesting facts that we observed while interpreting the resulting concept lattices for each feature group.

We first analyzed the heat demand features. The resulting concept lattice for this feature group is shown in Figure 7.13. It consists of 39 concepts and 76 non-transitive subconcept relations.

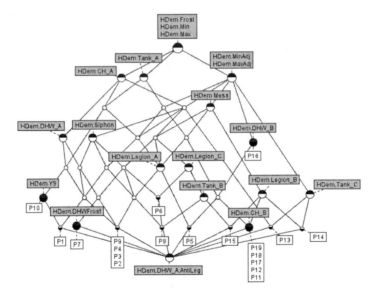

Figure 7.13: Concept lattice for heat demand features.

From the concept lattice in Figure 7.13, we inferred that HDem.Min, HDem.Max, and HDem.Frost are used in all 19 product configurations because they appear at the top concept. Furthermore, we can see from the lattice that HDem.MinAdj and HDem.MaxAdj are always used together because they appear at the same concept. From the high number of concepts in the concept lattice we can infer that there are many ways of combining the heat demand features. In total, there exist 11 different configurations of the heat demand features. Compared to the total number of 19 product configurations, this number is rather high which indicates that the required variability of the heat demand feature group is high or in other words a large number of products need a special combination of heat demand features.

After having analyzed the heat demand features, we manually inspected the concept lattice of the heat flow control features which is shown in Figure 7.14. It consists of 14 concepts and 20 non-transitive subconcept relations.

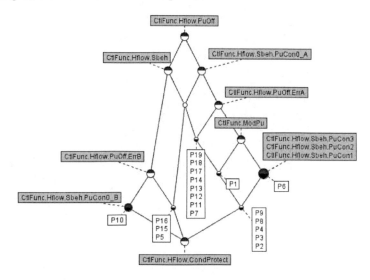

Figure 7.14: Concept lattice for heat flow control features.

As one can see from Figure 7.14, the feature *PuOff* is used in every product configuration because it appears at the top concept of the lattice and the feature *CondProtect* is never used in any product configuration because it appears at the bottom concept and the bottom concept does not contain a product configuration.

As a third example, we present the facts that we observed by manually inspecting the resulting concept lattice for the temperature control features which is shown in Figure 7.15. It consists of 25 concepts and 49 non-transitive subconcept relations. From the concept lattice shown in Figure 7.15, we inferred that the feature Temp.Pri is used in every product configuration as it appears at the top concept of the concept lattice and the feature Temp.Oshunt is used in all product configurations except P13 and P14. The high number of concepts indicates that the variability provided by the temperate control feature group is indeed needed by the analyzed product configurations or in other words each product needs a special combination of temperature control features.

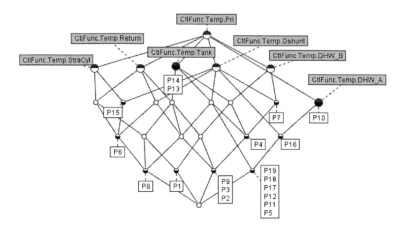

Figure 7.15: Concept lattice for temperature control features.

Feature Usage Classification and Optimization Potential

As in case study A we used our variability analysis tool VariAnT [Per07] to obtain the feature usage classification and the optimization potential for the heat system control layer. Table 7.15 shows a summary of the distribution of features on the feature usage classes I, II, III and IV, and the optimization potential. As one can see from Table 7.15, the current number of variable features for the heat system control layer (96 features) is much higher than the required number of variable features (50) for deriving the analyzed product configurations. Thus, the variability provided by the heat system control layer (HCL) shows a great potential for optimization. Interestingly, the optimization potential for the heat system control layer with 48% is similarly high as the optimization potential for case study A with 49%.

Table 7.16 shows a summary of the feature usage classification and the optimization potential for the feature groups of the heat system control layer. Column FC shows the number of features for each feature group. Columns I, II, III, IV show the distribution of features to the feature usage classes. Column FO shows the minimal number of features required for achieving the desired variability. Column OP shows the maximal percentage of savings (optimization potential) that can be achieved after optimizing the variability.

	Current		Optimized	
Usage Class	**# features**	**%**	**# features**	**% saved**
Always used	17	17%	1	92%
Never used	9	9%	0	100%
Used together	30	31%	9	70%
Used singularly	40	42%	40	0%
Total	**96**	**100%**	**50**	**48%**

Table 7.15: Optimization potential for heat system control layer (HCL).

The row *Summary* shows the summary for the feature groups and the row *HCL* shows the results that have been directly obtained from the concept lattice in Figure 7.12.

	FC	**I**	**II**	**III**	**IV**	**FO**	**OP**
HCL.Acc	6	0	2	0	4	4	33%
HCL.CtlFunc.Burn	10	4	0	0	6	7	33%
HCL.CtlFunc.Comb	5	0	0	2	3	4	10%
HCL.CtlFunc.HFlow	11	1	1	3	6	8	27%
HCL.CtlFunc.Temp	7	1	0	0	6	7	0%
HCL.FlueG	4	0	1	3	0	1	75%
HCL.Eval/Efunc	7	3	0	0	4	5	29%
HCL.HDem	20	3	1	2	14	16	20%
HCL.Misc	3	1	0	0	2	3	0%
HCL.PuDem	5	0	0	2	3	4	20%
HCL.Stop	18	4	4	2	8	9	50%
Summary	96	17	9	14	55	68	29%
HCL	96	17	9	30	40	50	48%

Table 7.16: Feature usage classification and optimization potential for heat system control layer feature groups.

As one can from Table 7.16, the feature group HCL.HDem has a large number of features that are only used separately which indicates that HCL.HDem has a high degree of variability that is required by the product configurations.

Furthermore, we can see from Table 7.16 that all feature groups except HCL.CtlFunc.-Temp show an optimization potential of more than 10%. The relative optimization potential is particularly high for the feature groups HCL.Acc, HCL.CtlFunc.Burn, HCL.FlueG, HCL.Eval/Efunc, and HCL.Stop. Thus, restructuring these feature groups will have the greatest effect on the overall restructuring of the provided variability of the heat system control layer.

Analysis of Feature Constraints

In total, we identified 1144 implications between features. These implications represent potential constraints of the form "features A *require* feature b". Furthermore, we identified 660 exclusion constraints between features, e.g., "feature m *excludes* feature n".

Table 7.17 shows a summary of the constraint analysis results for the heat system control layer feature groups. The first column shows the number of potential implications and the second column the number of potential exclusion constraints.

	Implications	Exclusions
HCL.Acc	3	3
HCL.CtlFunc.Burn	7	8
HCL.CtlFunc.Comb	7	4
HCL.CtlFunc.HFlow	21	11
HCL.CtlFunc.Temp	9	3
HCL.FlueG	6	1
HCL.Eval/Efunc	3	0
HCL.HDem	60	40
HCL.Misc	1	0
HCL.PuDem	7	4
HCL.Stop	27	15
Summary	151	89
HCL	1144	660

Table 7.17: Constraint analysis results for HCL feature groups.

The row *Summary* shows the aggregated values for each column and the row *HCL* shows the values that were directly obtained from the concept lattice shown in Figure 7.12. A comparison of the number of implications and exclusion constraints yields some interesting facts. First of all, all numbers shown in row *HCL* are higher than the numbers shown in row *Summary* because the values in row *HCL* were obtained from the complete concept lattice shown in Figure 7.12 which also includes potential implications and exclusions that exist between features of different feature groups. Thus, filtering the HCL lattice by feature group influences the results for the constraint analysis as potential constraints between features of different feature groups cannot be identified if we analyze each feature group separately. However, these constraints can be identified by analyzing the concept lattice shown in Figure 7.12. The large difference between the values in row *Summary* and in row *HCL* indicates that there exists a large number of potential feature constraints between features of different feature groups. However, we believe that the number of valid feature constraints does not differ much because a large number of these potential feature constraints is simply caused because the HCL lattice in Figure 7.12 is much more interconnected and this obviously increases the number of potential feature constraints. Therefore, it is not advisable to validate all potential feature constraints derived from the concept lattice shown in Figure 7.12. Instead, the potential feature constraints should be validated for each feature group separately.

For the feature groups HCL.HDem, HCL.CtlFunc.HFlow, and HCL.CtlFunc.Temp we calculated the number of true positives, the number of don't knows, and the number of false positives, i.e., the number of exclusion constraints that were derived from the concept lattice but rejected by the expert as being valid. Using these numbers we could calculate the minimum and maximum precision of our approach for the detection of valid exclusion constraints as well as the recall value. Table 7.18 lists the number of true positives (TP), the number of don't knows (DK), the number of false positives (FP), the number of false negatives (FN) the minimum and maximum precision, and the recall for the three feature groups that we analyzed in detail.

	Exclusions	TP	DK	FP	FN	Precision	Recall
HCL.HDem	40	7	30	3	0	18-93%	100%
HCL.CtlFunc.HFlow	11	7	3	0	0	63-100%	100%
HCL.CtlFunc.Temp	3	2	1	0	0	66-100%	100%

Table 7.18: Number of false positives and precision for exclusion constraints.

If we compare the results for precision with the results for precision obtained during case study A (see Table 7.10), we can confirm the hypothesis that with a decreasing number of potential exclusion constraints the percentage of don't knows is decreasing, i.e., the uncertainty of the platform developer about whether an exclusion constraint is valid or not decreases.

Analysis of Execution Time

Table 7.19 shows the results for the analysis of the execution time. As one can see from this Table, the results are comparable to the results we obtained when we analyzed the execution time for calculating the concepts and layouting the concept lattices for case study A (see Table 7.11 for comparison).

7.3.5 Results for Device Control Layer

In this section, we present the results that we obtained by analyzing the existing variability of the device control layer.

Interpretation of Concept Lattice

The resulting concept lattice for the analysis of the usage of features for the device control layer is shown in Figure 7.16. It consists of 212 concepts and 560 non-transitive subconcept relations. For reasons of clarity, the labels for features are omitted in Figure 7.16. However, the size of the nodes is proportional to the number of features attached to each node.

The resulting concept lattice shown in Figure 7.17 for the sensor features contains a total of 116 concepts and 272 subconcept relations. As shown in Figure 7.17, 65 of a total of 116 concepts introduce at least one new variable feature, i.e., to these nodes a variable

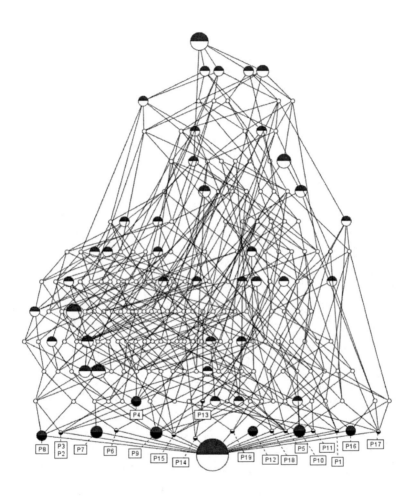

Figure 7.16: Concept lattice for device control layer (DCL).

	C	E	FC	Calculation time [ms]	Layout time [ms]
HCL.Acc	6	6	6	40	100
HCL.CtlFunc.Burn	6	6	10	39	98
HCL.CtlFunc.Comb	8	10	5	42	110
HCL.CtlFunc.HFlow	14	20	11	45	200
HCL.CtlFunc.Temp	25	49	7	50	211
HCL.FlueG	3	2	4	10	120
HCL.Eval/Efunc	8	10	7	30	191
HCL.HDem	39	76	20	70	230
HCL.Misc	3	2	3	10	130
HCL.PuDem	6	6	5	12	145
HCL.Stop	13	17	18	30	80
Summary	131	204	96	360	1,592
HCL	243	678	96	300	23,385

Table 7.19: Execution time for calculation of concepts and layout of concept lattice.

feature is attached. Concepts that introduce at least one variable feature are half-filled with gray in the lattice. 178 of the concepts do not introduce any new variable feature and merely combine variable features included in several product configurations (these concepts are shown in white in the lattice). Concepts are half-filled with black if to these nodes one or more product configurations are attached.

Among the 55 sensor features that are provided by the device control layer, 4 features (7%) are used in all 19 product configurations (they appear at the top concept in Figure 7.17). These features are likely to be features that have to be always selected. Furthermore, 14 features of 55 (25%) are not selected in any of the product configurations, i.e., these features are likely to be obsolete (they appear at the bottom concept in Figure 7.17).

The resulting concept lattice for the actuator features, as shown in Figure 7.18, contained a total of 31 concepts and 53 subconcept relations.

18 of a total of 31 concepts introduce at least one new variable feature, i.e., to these nodes a variable feature is attached. 13 of the concepts do not introduce any new variable feature and merely combine variable features included in several product configurations.

Feature Usage Classification and Optimization Potential

Table 7.20 shows the distribution of features on the feature usage classes I, II, III and IV, and the optimization potential. As one can see from Table 7.20, the current number of variable features for the device control layer (89 features) is much higher than the required number of variable features (45) for deriving the analyzed product configurations. Thus, the provided variability of the device control layer (DCL) offers a great potential for optimization.

Table 7.21 shows a summary of the feature usage classification and the optimization potential for each feature group of the device control layer.

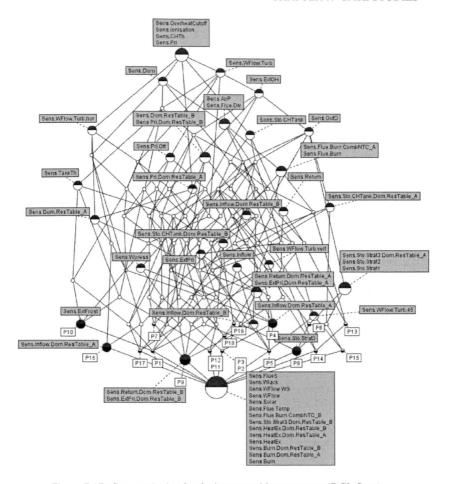

Figure 7.17: Concept lattice for device control layer sensors (DCL.Sens).

	Current		*Optimized*	
Usage Class	**# features**	**%**	**# features**	**% saved**
Always used	6	7%	1	83%
Never used	24	27%	0	100%
Used together	26	29%	11	58%
Used singularly	33	37%	33	0%
Total	**89**	**100%**	**45**	**50%**

Table 7.20: Optimization potential for device control layer (DCL).

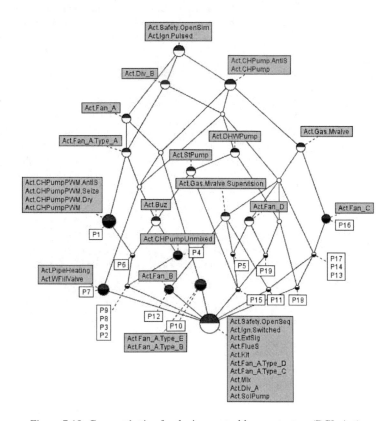

Figure 7.18: Concept lattice for device control layer actuators (DCL.Act).

	FC	I	II	III	IV	FO	OP
DCL.Sens	55	4	14	13	24	31	44%
DCL.Act	34	2	10	10	12	17	50%
Summary	89	6	24	23	36	48	46%
DCL	89	6	24	26	33	45	50%

Table 7.21: Feature usage classification and optimization potential device control layer feature groups.

Interestingly, 14 sensor features respectively 25% and 10 actuator features respectively 29% are not used in any of the product configurations. Thus, these features are very likely obsolete features that can be removed. Another 13 sensor features respectively 24% and 10 actuator features respectively 29% are always used together. By merging the features that are always used (class I) and used together (class III) and by removing the features that are never used (class II), we can reduce the number of sensor features by 24 respectively 44% and the number of actuator features by 17 respectively 50%.

Three interesting conclusions can be drawn from these results. First, obviously, the provided variability of the device control layer features is much higher than actually required for the analyzed product configurations. Second, many of the device control layer features are not used in any of the product configurations. Therefore, it should be checked whether these features are obsolete and if so they should be removed. Third, the provided variability of the device control layer offers an equally high optimization potential (50%) as the optimization potential of the heat system control layer (48%) and the optimization potential we obtained in case study A (49%).

Analysis of Feature Constraints

In total, we identified 882 potential implications between features and 518 potential exclusion constraints. Table 7.22 shows a summary of the constraint analysis results for the device control layer feature groups.

	Implications	Exclusions
DCL.Sens	371	177
DCL.Act	98	106
Summary	469	283
DCL	882	518

Table 7.22: Constraint analysis results for device control layer feature groups.

As the platform developers were particularly interested in the potential exclusion constraints of the actuator system we further analyzed these constraints. From these 106 potential exclusion constraints, 17 exclusion constraints between features, have been verified as valid exclusion constraints between alternative features by consulting the documentation and asking the platform developers of the HCU system. One exclusion constraint specified in the documentation, namely feature Act.CHPump XOR Act.CHPumpPWM has been identified as wrong because there are several product configurations that use both features, i.e., these features cannot be mutually exclusive.

We further analyzed the usage of some of these alternative features. The results of this analysis are shown in Table 7.23. From this table one can see, that Fan_A is the preferred alternative because it is used in 47,4% of all product configurations. Fan_C also has a reasonably high usage percentage (31,6%) whereas the alternatives Fan_B and Fan_D are used only in 5,3%, respectively 15,8% of all product configurations. This example shows that our approach can not only be used to identify exclusion constraints but also to evaluate the usage of alternative features. The information about the usage of different alternative features can be very helpful in deciding the future scope of the software product line. For example, the product line manager should decide whether the alternatives with a low usage, i.e., Fan_B and Fan_D should be supported in the future.

Alternatives	1st	2nd	3rd	4th	None
Act.Fan_A / _B / _C / _D	47,4%	5,3%	31,6%	15,8%	0%
Act.Div_A / _B	0%	94,7%	N/A	N/A	5,3%

Table 7.23: Usage of alternative features for DCL actuators.

Analysis of Execution Time

Table 7.24 shows the results for the analysis of the execution time. The results are comparable to the results we obtained from analyzing the heat system control layer.

	C	E	FC	Calculation time [ms]	Layout time [ms]
DCL.Sens	116	272	55	110	2,544
DCL.Act	31	53	34	40	221
Summary	147	325	89	160	2,765
DCL	212	560	89	260	36,274

Table 7.24: Execution time for calculation of concepts and layout of concept lattice.

7.3.6 Summary

Section 7.3.2 listed the objectives of the case study on the HCU product line. This section summarizes the main results of the case study and shows how these objectives have been met.

Objective 1: It should be shown that our variability analysis and optimization approach can be applied to a full product line: Our approach meets this objective to some extent. The execution time for formal concept analysis was not significant even when we analyzed the full product line including more than 300 features and 19 product configurations. However, we encountered the problem that the layout and drawing of the concept lattice for the full product line took more than 15 minutes and the resulting concept lattice was impracticable for human analysis. This long execution time was caused by the layout algorithm which tried to compute a minimal intersection of edges in the graph. As this algorithm is exponential in the number of edges it takes very long to compute a layout for a complex lattice containing several thousand edges. In order to solve the problem of manually analyzing very large concept lattices we successfully applied filtering to incrementally analyze two of three subsystems of the software product line.

Objective 2: The optimization potential of the HCU software product line should be identified: We calculated the optimization potential for the heat system control layer (HCL) and the device control layer (DCL). As shown in Table 7.15 and Table 7.20 each feature layer offers an optimization potential of approximately 50%. Interestingly, the optimization potential is similarly high as the optimization potential we obtained in case study A (49%). Furthermore, each separately analyzed feature group of the heat system control layer (HCL) as shown in Table 7.16 and the device control layer (DCL) as shown in Table 7.21 offers an optimization potential in the range from 10% up to 50%.

Objective 3: The detection quality of our approach for feature constraints in terms of precision and recall should be analyzed: In Table 7.18 we list the precision and recall for the detection of valid exclusion constraints for three feature groups of the heat system control layer (HCL). As one can see free from this Table, the average precision for the detection of valid exclusion constraints ranges from 57% to 83% under the assumption that 50% of the don't knows represent valid exclusion constraints and 50% represent invalid feature constraints. The recall is 100% for the analyzed feature groups under the assumption that the products were correctly configured.

Objective 4: It should be shown that the runtime of formal concept analysis is not significant for variability analysis even for large concept lattices with more than 300 features: We measured the execution time for formal concept analysis for the HCU software product line. On our case study hardware the calculation of the concept lattice for the HCU software product line with more than 300 features and 19 product configurations took only 1061 milliseconds. The resulting concept lattice consisted of more than 1300 concepts. This shows that the execution time for formal concept analysis is not significant even for large concept lattices with more than 300 features.

7.4 Summary and Discussion

7.4.1 Applicability

In this Chapter, we applied our variability analysis and optimization approach to two different case examples. The two case examples were taken from different domains and were developed in different business units. Furthermore, the two case examples differed in terms of the complexity of the analyzed product line, i.e., in the number of product configurations and the number of features. Despite these differences, we successfully applied our variability analysis and optimization approach in both case studies.

Both case studies showed that our approach can be applied to analyze subsystems of the product lines. Despite the exponential execution time for formal concept analysis, the time needed for the calculation of the concept lattice remained in all cases below one second on our case study hardware. In cases when the resulting concept lattices became complicated and hard to interpret manually due to the large number of product configurations and features, we successfully applied highlighting and filtering to make important information contained in the concept lattices visible. Using highlighting and filtering we were able to manually interpret even very complicated concept lattices as the one shown in Figure 7.5. Highlighting made relationships between features and product configurations visible that were invisible due to the large number of edges in complicated concept lattices. Filtering helped to improve the understanding of large concept lattices especially in cases when we were interested in a subset of the features and decreased the number of false positives during the analysis of feature constraints. The platform developer that had to manually inspect the concept lattices and explain them to us learned how to read the concept lattice surprisingly quickly. The use of our variability analysis tool VariAnT [Per07] considerably shortened the time needed for training before the platform developer could work with our method as the mathematical details of formal concept analysis did not have to be learned.

Both case studies demonstrated that our variability analysis and optimization approach can be successfully applied in order to automatically derive a classification of the usage of features in product configurations, to calculate the optimization potential and to derive potential feature constraints. Interestingly, the provided variability of each of the three subsystems that we analyzed was considerably higher than the variability that is actually required for the analyzed product configurations. The calculated optimization potential for the provided variability of the analyzed subsystems in both case studies was approximately 50% although the software product lines were taken from different domains and have been developed by independent business units.

7.4.2 Appropriateness and Usefulness

The validation of the feature usage classification and the calculated optimization potential by the platform developer and the documentation showed that our approach provides appropriate results. Furthermore, this comparison showed that the feature usage classification and the calculated optimization potential can further be improved if the different information sources, i.e., the feature usage classification derived from the concept lattice, the knowledge of the platform developer, and the existing domain knowledge in the documentation are integrated. Thus, the comparison step provided in our variability optimization process is appropriate and necessary in practice. The optimization potential after validation was still 30% which is still high enough for a restructuring effort to pay off.

The validation of the potential feature constraints that we derived from the concept lattices showed that the detection quality of our approach is quite good. The results showed that the average precision, i.e., the precision under the assumption that 50% of the don't knows are valid and 50% are invalid is in the range of 60% to 90% for the implications and in the range of 49% to 100% for the exclusions. The recall rate for our approach was 100% for all feature groups except one.

In addition to variability optimization we found out that the information that can be derived from the concept lattices can also be used for a number of other variability management related tasks such as product derivation as well as scoping and evolution tasks. Feature constraints that have been validated by the platform developer can be used to automatically check product configurations for consistency which helps to avoid integration errors during product derivation. Furthermore, the analysis of the usage of alternative features can be used to decide if it is worth maintaining certain alternative features for the future of the product line or if these features should be better discarded because they are only used by a small number of product configurations. Decisions like these are very common when the scope of the product line needs to be adjusted due to evolution. Thus, our approach also facilitates the decision making process for scope adjustments during the evolution of the product line by providing exact numbers of the usage of features in product configurations.

The visualization of variability using concept lattices was reported by the platform developer and product line manager to be very useful to build a mental model of the existing variability and to understand how the provided features of the software product lines are used in the analyzed product configurations. In addition to the classification of feature usage the derivation of potential feature constraints helped to understand why certain combinations of features appear very often in product configurations and other combinations do never appear. The analysis of the concept lattice even allowed us to identify configuration errors, e.g., in the cases when we found counterexamples that violated known and valid feature constraints.

7.4.3   Limitations

The following limitations restrict the internal and the external validity of the two case studies that we used to evaluate the applicability, the appropriateness, and the usefulness of our variability analysis and optimization approach.

Empirical Basis

Despite the successful application of our variability analysis and optimization approach in both case studies, there is no long-term experience with our approach. We only analyzed the software product lines at a specific point in time and did not compare analysis results taken at different points in the lifecycle of the software product lines. Consequently, we cannot make any conclusions regarding the long-term effects and regarding the applicability at different points in the lifecycle of the software product line.

Number of Experts

The feature usage classification and the calculated optimization potential as well as the potential feature constraints have only been validated by one expert for each case study. We did not ask multiple experts for validation and compared their results. However, the experts we used for validation in both case studies were responsible for the product line architecture and had a good implicit domain knowledge about the usage of features and dependencies that exist between them.

Complexity of Software Product Line

Complexity of the software product line in terms of the number of product configurations and the number of features may pose a challenge for our variability analysis and optimization approach. This is apparent when looking at both case studies. However, in both case studies that represent real-world software product lines of industrial size with up to 70 product configurations and more than 300 features, the amount of information was still manageable by using highlighting and filtering which reduce the information clutter of large concept lattices. In the case of even more complex software product lines, we believe that an incremental analysis of parts of the software product line will be still possible.

Variability Realization Technique

We applied our variability analysis and optimization approach on variability which has been realized by a software configuration management system. Although our approach in general is independent of the chosen variability realization technique, we did not evaluate it with other variability realization techniques. We believe that our approach is also applicable on variability that has been realized with other variability realization techniques. However, we except that our approach needs some adaption.

7.4.4 Range of Validity

Based on the limitation identified in the previous subsection, we now determine to what extent our variability analysis and optimization approach can be expanded to new case studies.

We applied our variability analysis and optimization approach in two different case studies. The two software product lines that we analyzed in the case studies differed in terms of their complexity (number of features and product configurations) and in their application area, i.e., engine control software product line and control system for boilers. Furthermore, these product lines were developed by two different business units with different developers and different tools. Despite these differences our variability analysis and optimization approach could be applied successfully in both case studies. Interestingly, even the results regarding the optimization potential were very similar for both case studies.

Therefore, we conclude that our approach will generally work for software product lines that offer a similar level of complexity, that use a similar variability realization technique, and that are developed by similar organizations and by using similar processes.

- *Complexity*: Our variability analysis and optimization approach has been shown to work with software product lines that offer a similar level of complexity as the HCU software product line. Complexity is defined here as number of product configurations and number of features. Based on the experiences from this case study, it is concluded that our approach will also work for software product lines with a lower to slightly higher complexity.

- *Variability realization technique*: We successfully applied our variability analysis and optimization approach on software product lines in which the variability has been realized using ClearCase [Leb94]. Although ClearCase is a specific software configuration management system we believe that our approach will also work for other SCM systems that allow the features to be implemented in a similar way, i.e., the SCM system needs to support revisions, branches, and labels or tags.

- *Organization and Process*: We applied our variability analysis and optimization approach on software product lines which are developed according to the general product line approach, i.e., the development is divided into a domain engineering team that produces generic reusable artifacts and several application engineering teams that reuse these artifacts to derive concrete products from the software product line. The results for the optimization potential in both case studies was very similar. Therefore, we hope that our approach will provide similar results when applied to software product lines that are developed by similar organizations and by using similar processes.

It remains to be discussed and to be evaluated to what extent our approach can be extended to software product lines that do not fulfill the properties described above. However, both case studies demonstrated that our approach is applicable, appropriate, and useful for the task of variability maintenance. Furthermore, our approach fulfills the research objectives stated in Chapter 1.

Chapter 8

Conclusions

This chapter summarizes the main contributions and conclusions of our work. Furthermore, we give an outlook on future research avenues in the field of variability management in software product lines.

Overview. In Section 8.1, we present a summary and the main contributions of our work. Section 8.2 gives an outlook on future research in the field of variability management in software product lines. We conclude this thesis with our final remarks in Section 8.3.

8.1 Summary and Contributions

The objective of this work was to develop a method that can be repeatedly applied to analyze and to optimize the provided variability of a software product line. The necessity for developing such a method was motivated by the fact that variability management during software product line evolution needs to be addressed and treated in a systematic way. Otherwise the software product line will loose its ability to effectively exploit the similarities of its products. Our observations in industry indicated that this is indeed a big problem because currently no suitable methods to analyze the provided variability exist, the amount of variability is constantly increasing, and the necessary information to take informed decisions regarding the maintenance and evolution of variability is often not available. Therefore, the goal of this work has been to develop a method that addresses the aforementioned challenges and provides an answer to them.

In Chapter 1, this goal was formulated as an academic and industrial research objective. These rather abstract research objectives were broken down into five concrete research objectives. In the following we show how these research objectives have been achieved.

The first research objective was fulfilled in Chapter 3. Variability maintenance and optimization was positioned in the context of software product line engineering in general and variability management in particular. In variability management, three fields were identified to be relevant for this work, i.e., variability management during domain engineering, variability management during application engineering, and variability maintenance and evolution. By analyzing the state of the art in variability management we made two interesting observations. First, the state of the art of variability management is mainly focused on domain engineering and application engineering. Second, the existing methods for variability maintenance and evolution, which have been described in Section 3.4, lack the necessary precision when it comes to actually providing decision support in determining the necessary changes to the existing variability. In order to close this research gap, we formulated the following research question:

> *What is an operational and structured method to analyze the provided variability and its use in actual products that allows the decision maker to make informed decisions regarding its maintenance and optimization?*

Our variability analysis approach, which answers the research question and fulfills the second research objective, was presented in Chapter 4. The method describes a way to analyze and a new way to optimize the provided variability of an evolving software product line by making use of the knowledge in existing product configurations. These product configurations are analyzed to construct a product-feature matrix that precisely documents the usage of variable features in product configurations. Using a mathematical method, called Formal Concept Analysis (FCA), a visual representation of the product-feature matrix in the form of a concept lattice is derived that factors out which features are used together in specific product configurations and which features not. This powerful visual representation can be used to analyze the variability, to automatically classify the usage of variable features in product configurations, and to calculate the optimization potential for the provided variability. Thus, our method provides the necessary decision support for the analyst in order to make informed decisions about the maintenance and evolution of the provided variability in a software product line.

In order to provide a concise and complete decision basis for variability optimization, the results obtained by variability analysis need to be validated. In Chapter 5, we described how the analyst can validate the results by comparing them with explicit and implicit domain knowledge. The next step is to improve the feature usage classification by taking into account the results of the comparison. Finally, this improved feature usage classification is used to derive strategies for restructuring, i.e., minimizing the provided variability of the software product line without affecting its configurability. We described how these strategies can be implemented by using ClearCase [Leb94] as an exemplary realization technique for variability.

In Chapter 6, we presented a general process for variability optimization that combined the individual parts of the method which have been described in Chapter 4 and Chapter 5. The description of the process also includes a detailed elaboration on the different process phases, the inputs and outputs, as well as the distribution of the process tasks on different roles which are needed to operate the process. Furthermore, we developed several tools that support the product line manager and the platform developers during the variability optimization. These tools also served to evaluate whether an implementation of the process is actually feasible.

In order to evaluate the applicability, the appropriateness, and the usefulness of our approach, we conducted two case studies which are presented in Chapter 7. In the first case study, we applied our approach on a software product line for electronic control units for diesel cars. In the second case study, we analyzed the variability of a software product line used for electronic control units for condensing and non-condensing boilers. From the results of both case studies, the following conclusions could be drawn:

- Both case studies demonstrated that our variability analysis and optimization approach can be successfully applied in order to automatically derive a classification of the usage of features in product configurations, to calculate the optimization potential and to derive potential feature constraints.

- The analysis of the provided variability in both software product lines revealed a great potential for optimization. In both cases, we found out that approximately 50% of the existing variability is not required for the analyzed products and can be removed by variability restructuring. A detailed analysis of the individual feature groups in both case studies showed that more than 80% of the feature groups offer an optimization potential which is greater than 30%.

- The validation of the feature usage classification with explicit and implicit domain knowledge showed that our approach provides appropriate results. In addition to validation this additional domain knowledge can be used for improving the feature usage classification.

8.2 Future Research

This section proposes future research directions based on the results of this thesis.

8.2.1 Empirical Evaluation

We applied our variability analysis and optimization approach in two case studies. Although the two software product lines we analyzed were very different, it would be interesting to see how our approach performs in different companies and industries with different products. Since both software product lines were taken from the embedded system domain, it would be particularly valuable to apply the method to other types of systems such as information systems. It would be interesting to see whether variability management in these systems poses similar problems and whether these systems offer a similar potential for variability optimization.

Furthermore, it would be very useful to observe the long-term impact of variability optimization on the evolution of a software product line. In particular, it would be interesting to analyze whether the changes made during variability restructuring have a positive or negative effect on variability management.

8.2.2 Research Directions Concerning the Method

Although our variability analysis approach can in general be applied to different variability realization techniques, we focused in this thesis on variability which is realized using software configuration management techniques. Our approach could be further improved by making it applicable to other variability realization techniques. In order to achieve that only the variability documentation and the variability restructuring have to be adapted. As we abstracted the analysis from the implementation of variability, the variability analysis part of our method does not need to be changed.

Although our approach can be used to derive potential feature constraints, the evaluation has shown that the number of potential feature constraints that are derived from the concept lattices can get quite high for large concept lattices. Furthermore, the validation of the potential feature constraints revealed that for large concept lattices the number of implications or exclusions which cannot be validated due to missing knowledge of the expert is high. Two conclusions can be drawn from this observation with regard to the research directions concerning the method. First, it would be helpful to investigate means that help in reducing the overall number of potential feature constraints that need to be validated. Second, it would helpful to reduce the number of don't knows by incorporating other heuristics that help the expert to decide whether a potential feature constraint is valid or not.

8.2.3   Further Applications of Variability Analysis

The future research directions proposed above are aiming at variability analysis and optimization as such. However, we believe that variability analysis in general and the powerful visual representation in the form of concept lattices in particular can be used for a large number of tasks that are related to software product line variability. In the following we present some of these further applications:

Determination of the Future Scope

As we have found out during our case studies, the information provided by the concept lattices can also be used for determining the future scope of the software product line. The usage of features which can be easily obtained from the concept lattice provides a good starting point for planning the future scope of the software product line. For example, this information can be used to make the decision to remove features from the software product line which are only used in a small percentage of products. Furthermore, we could use variability analysis to evaluate different scenarios of preliminary or future product configurations with regard to the usage of features. This information is especially helpful for planning the roadmap of the software product line.

Testing of Software Product Lines

Managing variability, particularly limiting the amount of variability, is not only necessary for development. It is also essential to testing because the combinatorial explosion which is imposed by the provided variability of software product lines makes it impossible to test every variant which can in theory be configured out of the software product line. Our observations in industry indicate that software product line testing is currently not addressed from a strategic point of view. Very often test cases are randomly selected and the product line assets are not tested in a systematic way. In order to improve the test effectiveness, the test cases should be selected in such a way that the currently existing and future product variants are covered by the test cases. Our method for variability analysis and optimization could be adapted to provide the necessary information for selecting those test cases that are relevant for the current and future product configurations. If the test cases contain variation points the information contained in the concept lattice could be used to optimize the test suite, i.e., obsolete variation points in the test cases could be removed.

Furthermore, the concept lattices provide an ideal means to support incremental testing of products. Assume we have test cases and their results for a number of different products. To support regression testing we could apply formal concept analysis on these product configurations in order to see which combinations of features we have already tested. If new product configurations need to be tested we could simply add them to the formal context and repeat concept analysis to see how the configurations of these new products differ. For regression testing we then simply needed to exercise those tests that exhibit the features in which the new product configurations differ from the already tested product configurations.

Marketing and Pricing of Features

Another useful application area of variability is marketing and pricing of features. For example, it might be interesting to evaluate whether the information provided by variability analysis can be used as an input for marketing and pricing of features. For example, it might be possible to make use of the feature usage classification to charge lower prices for features which are used in almost every product and to charge higher prices for features which are only used in a small subset of products.

8.3 Final Remarks

This thesis has contributed to variability management in software product lines by providing a semi-automatic method for variability analysis, visualization, restructuring, and optimization. The methods and techniques described in this thesis are helpful for a large number of tasks that are related to variability management and product derivation. This thesis is a stepping stone toward variability maintenance and evolution. The need for variability maintenance and evolution will increase as the size and complexity of software product lines increase. However, the summit is not yet reached. As this chapter has discussed there is still a lot of work to do in variability maintenance and management for software product lines in general.

Appendix A

Software Configuration Management

In this Appendix, we describe software configuration management (SCM) systems. We first provide an overview of the general concepts and elements used in SCM systems and then explain the concepts of ClearCase, a specific software configuration management system that can be used to realize variability in software product lines that is modeled in the form of features.

A.1 General Concepts

A.1.1 Product and Version Space

In general, a SCM system allows to version so called *configuration items*, i.e., file-based software entities such as source code, documents, or test cases. Typically, a central repository, shared among developers, holds all versions of the configuration items as they are created. Versions are accessed by copying versions of configuration items from the repository to a private space (check out) and copy them back into the repository (check in). This is the simplest and oldest SCM model and is called Checkin/Checkout model. It is widely used, e.g., in SCCS [Roc75], RCS [Tic85], CVS [Gru86], Subversion [CSFP04], and ClearCase [Leb94].

According to [CW98] we generally have to distinguish between the *product space* and the *version space* in a SCM system. The *product space* describes the structure of the software product without taking versioning into account and the *version space* describes the different versions of the configuration items. SCM systems can differ in the way the product and version space are organized and how they interact. For example, some SCM systems only allow versioning at the file-level, while others also allow to version directories independently from files. In theory, the version space itself may be organized in many different ways. However, in practice there only exists a small number of different organizations of the version space in the SCM systems that are widely used. In its most simplest form, e.g., in SCCS [Roc75], the version space is one-dimensional and consists of *revisions* that are linked by a *successor relationship*. In RCS [Tic85], CVS [Gru86], and ClearCase [Leb94] the version space is two-dimensional and consists of *revisions, temporary, and permanent branches*.

189

In addition to the different possible ways to organize the version space, SCM systems also differ in the way the product space and version space interplay or interact. The interplay of product space and version space in different SCM systems can be classified according to the *selection order* during the configuration process as described in [CW98]:

- **Product first.** The product structure is selected first and then versions of configuration items are selected. For example, SCCS [Roc75] and RCS [Tic85] follow this approach. This approach suffers from the problem that the structure of the product is the same for all configurations.

- **Version first.** The product version is selected first and uniquely determines the versions of configuration items. Thus, different product versions may be structured in different ways. Examples of SCM systems using this organization are PCTE [OBG+89] and Subversion [CSFP04].

- **Intertwined.** In this organization the product structure and the versions of configuration items are selected in alternating order. This kind of organization is for example used in ClearCase [Leb94] which supports the versioning of files and directories.

For an in depth discussion of the different forms of interplay between product and version space we refer the interested reader to [CW98].

A.1.2   Versioning Dimensions and Version Graph

Depending on the intentions of the creator, the versions of software configuration items can be divided into the following three orthogonal *versioning dimensions* [EC95].

Historical versioning. Versions are created to *supersede* a specific version, e.g., for maintenance purposes. These superseding versions are called *revisions*. When a new revision is created, the evolution of the original version is phased out in favor of the new revision. In practice, new revisions of software configuration items are usually created by modifying a copy of the most recent revision. The old revisions are permanently stored for maintenance and documenting purposes. They form the *version history* of the software configuration item.

Logical versioning. In contrast to *revisions*, a *variant* is created as an *alternative* to a specific version. These variants are created in *branches*, i.e., parallel development threads that coexist at the same time unless they are merged. *Permanent variants* are created to adapt the product to different environments. This variance may arise due to different customer requirements or due to different system platforms that need to be supported. Especially in software product lines permanent variants of configuration items need to be supported because different customers may require alternative implementations of the same configuration item.

Cooperative versioning. In cooperative versioning, *temporary variants* are created, i.e., variants that will later be integrated (or merged) with another variant. Temporary variants are required, e.g., to change old revisions while the new revision is already under development, or to try out new functionality without disturbing the development on the main branch.

Figure A.1 depicts the differences between the three versioning dimensions. The boxes denote various versions as they are created. An arrow from version A to version B indicates that version B was created based on version A. The entire graph represents the *version graph* of the configuration item and shows how each version was created.

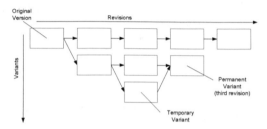

Figure A.1: Versioning dimensions.

In most SCM systems and tools, the different versioning dimensions are represented by different concepts. For example, early versioning systems like SCCS [Roc75] only support historical versioning using revisions, i.e., the version graph is a simple list of revisions that are linked by a successor relationship. As SCCS does not support logical versioning, variance has to be managed externally, e.g., by using the C preprocessor (CPP) [KR78]. RCS [Tic85], the successor of SCCS, supports historical versioning using revisions and logical versioning using branches.

More advanced SCM systems, like ClearCase [Leb94] support three-dimensional versioning, i.e., historical versioning using revisions, logical versioning using permanent named branches and cooperative versioning using temporary named branches that are at some point merged with other branches.

Recently, new SCM systems such as Perforce [Sei96] and Subversion [CSFP04] have emerged that use a different way to organize the version space which is called *inter-file branching* [Sei96]. The name inter-file branching comes from the fact that it creates branched configuration items as peers instead of versions of their predecessors, and tracks branching and merging as events that occur between configuration items instead of between versions of a configuration item. In this kind of organization *branches* are separated from configuration items and can be accessed like directories. The version graph of each configuration item is a simple list consisting of revisions that are linked by a successor relationship like in the SCCS system [Roc75]. When a new branch is created, the files are "copied" to the new branch. Internally, this copy operation is realized by linking the old and new files together and preserving the history for both.

A.1.3   Version Identification and Selection

In order to retrieve software configuration items in their specific versions, SCM systems provide a mechanism called *version selection* that relies on *extensional versioning, intensional versioning*, or a combination of *extensional* and *intensional versioning* to retrieve the versions from the version repository.

Extensional versioning means that the set of versions V of a configuration item c is defined by enumerating its members [CW98]:

$$V = \{v_1, \ldots, v_n\} \qquad (A.1)$$

Extensional versioning supports the selection of versions by explicitly specifying the version number to be selected. Most SCM systems use different identification schemes for the explicit identification of *revisions, permanent* and *temporary variants*.

Revisions are usually identified by *revision numbers* which reflect their creation date. Generally, the most recent revision is the one with the highest revision number. The revision number can either be a single integer, e.g., the first revision is named 1, the second named 2, and so on, like in ClearCase [Leb94], or a pair of integers as in SCCS [Roc75] and RCS [Tic85], e.g., the first revision is named 1.1, the second is named 1.2, and so on. If a pair is used the first number usually indicates the release number and the second number indicates the level number.

Permanent and temporary variants are usually identified using names not numbers, since they are not ordered. For example, ClearCase [Leb94] uses *named branches* in order to identify permanent and temporary variants of a configuration item. These named branches represent edges in the version graph. Figure A.2 shows an example of a configuration item's version graph in ClearCase with three named branches, namely, `main`, `basis`, `var_A`, and `var_B`.

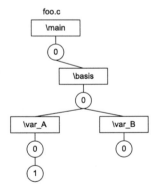

Figure A.2: Representation of permanent variants in ClearCase [Leb94].

As one can see from Figure A.2, the branches are organized hierarchically, i.e., the `basis` branch appears below the `main` branch, and the `var_A` and `var_B` branches appear below the `basis` branch. In order to identify a variant in ClearCase, one has to specify the name of the configuration item followed by the path of branch names, e.g., in our case `foo.c@@\main\basis\var_A\1` would select revision 1 of the `var_A` variant, of the `basis` variant, of the `main` variant. ClearCase does not distinguish between permanent and temporary variants, i.e., both version kinds are represented by named branches and identified by their branch names. Therefore, a temporary variant can only be distinguished from a permanent variant by looking at the version graph of the configuration item. If there is a merge link from a revision in a named branch to a revision in another named branch it is likely that the first named branch is a temporary variant.

In SCCS [Roc75] and RCS [Tic85] permanent and temporary variants are identified by additional numbering levels that are added to the revision numbers. For example, a variant of the original revision 2.1 is named 2.1.1.1, with subsequent revisions 2.1.1.2, 2.1.1.3, and so on.

In addition to *extensional versioning*, i.e., by explicitly specifying the revisions, permanent and temporary variants of a configuration item, most SCM systems, e.g., RCS [Tic85], CVS [Gru86], and ClearCase [Leb94], also support *intensional versioning*.

In contrast to extensional versioning, *intensional versioning* means that instead of enumerating the set of versions of a configuration item c, the version set is defined by a predicate p [CW98]:

$$V = \{v | p(v)\} \tag{A.2}$$

In this case, versions are implicit, and an arbitrary number of new sets of versions can be constructed on demand. The predicate p defines the *constraints* which have to be satisfied by all versions belonging to V. Usually, intensional versioning is applied when flexible, automatic construction of sets of consistent versions in a large version space needs to be supported. An important difference to extensional versioning is that intensional versioning allows the set V to contain versions, permanent, and temporary variants of multiple configuration items at the same time. A specific version v is described intensionally by its properties, e.g., the version supporting the operating system `Unix`. A specific set of versions stored in the version repository can be selected by executing a *query* against the version repository which consists of a set of *configuration rules*, each being composed of a *product part* and a *version part* [CW98]. The product part specifies on which configuration items the configuration rule is applied, and the version part specifies the predicate p that the versions need to fulfill to be selected by the configuration rule. For example, such a configuration rule would be "retrieve all revisions of all configuration items which were created after 2007-10-10". In this case, the predicate of this rule is $p(v) = d > 2007 - 10 - 10$ in which d represents the creation date of a revision. As a result of the execution of a query containing this configuration rule all revisions that were created after 2007-10-10 of all configuration items will be retrieved from the version repository.

Besides specifying configuration rules containing predicates for pre-defined attributes of revisions, e.g., the creation date, many SCM systems allow the specification of configuration rules with predicates for *user-defined attributes*. Typically, these *user-defined attributes* are arbitrary strings which are called *tags* or *labels* and can be attached to revisions in the version repository. To allow to retrieve more than one revision at the same time by specifying a label in a configuration rule, a label can be attached to revisions of multiple configuration items. However, it is not possible to attach the same label to multiple revisions belonging to a single configuration item as this would make the version selection indeterminable.

User-defined attributes such as *tags* or *labels* which can be attached to revisions are supported by many SCM systems. For example, RCS [Tic85] supports so called *branch tags* and *release tags* that can be attached to revisions, and ClearCase [Leb94] supports so called *labels* that can be attached to revisions. Figure A.3 shows the representation of labels in ClearCase [Leb94].

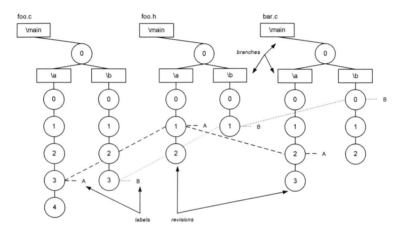

Figure A.3: Representation of labels in ClearCase [Leb94].

The figure shows the version graphs of three configuration items, namely foo.c, foo.h, and bar.c including their *branches* and *labels* that are attached to the revisions. As you can see from this figure, there are two labels, namely label A and B that are attached to multiple revisions in multiple branches of multiple configuration items. It is important to note that in theory the labels can be attached arbitrarily to any revision in any branch of any configuration item. In this particular example, the labels are attached in such a way that the set of revisions that will be selected by using each label in a configuration rule forms a set of consistent versions that represent a specific variant, namely variant A or variant B of the three configuration items foo.c, foo.h, and bar.c. In other words, the branches a and b hold the permanent variants of each configuration items, the revisions in each branch represent the chronological development of the permanent variants of each configuration item, and the labels A and B represent a consistent selection of permanent variants of the three configuration items. Another interesting observation you can make by looking at Figure A.3 is that the number of revisions in each branch may differ. Thus, the number of revisions in a branch only depends on how often a permanent variant of a configuration item, i.e., either variant a or variant b, have been modified.

A.1.4 Product Configurations

During product derivation the labels that represent feature versions are used to build so called *product configurations*. A *product configuration* consists of a simple list of configuration rules that itself contain labels. For example, such a rule would be *"select all versions of all configuration items that have the label A attached"*. ClearCase [Leb94] evaluates these configuration rules and copies the specified versions from the version repository into the private space. For example, a ClearCase product configuration could contain the following rules:

```
element \base\..   A
element \base\foo\..   B
element \base\bar\..    C
element \base\foobar\.. D
```

The first part `element` describes that we want to retrieve configuration elements, i.e., configuration items. The second part, e.g., `\base\foo\..`, specifies the directory, and the third part, e.g., A, specifies the configuration label. Thus, the configuration rule:

```
element \base\foo\.. A
```

means "Retrieve all revisions of configuration items in directory `\base\foo\..` that have the configuration label A attached".

If this *configuration specification* is used, ClearCase [Leb94] will evaluate the configuration rules and retrieve the revisions that fulfill the rules, i.e., that have the labels attached that are contained in the rules. These revisions are then copied from the version repository into the private workspace.

A.2 Summary

This appendix explained the general concepts of software configuration management including versioning dimensions, version identification, and version selection. The similarities and differences in the implementation of these general concepts in different commercial and open source SCM systems were presented. Throughout this presentation we elaborated on the specific versioning concepts provided by the SCM system ClearCase [Leb94] which can be used as a variability realization technique for variability that is modeled using feature diagrams.

Appendix B

Publications

B.1 Variability Analysis & Restructuring

A formal Method to Identify Variation Points in Software Product Line Assets [Loe06]

Abstract: Analyzing the provided variability in an evolving product line is necessary to determine if new products can be derived by configuration of existing product line assets. To analyze the provided variability, we need to identify the variation points, the variants, and its constraints. In this paper, we show how formal concept analysis can be used to derive this information.

Published: Workshop Software Reengineering (WSR'06), May 2006, Bad Honnef, Germany.

Restructuring Variability in Software Product Lines using Concept Analysis of Product Configurations [LP07b]

Abstract: The management of variability plays an important role in successful software product line engineering. As the set of products that is derived from the product line and their requirements are constantly changing, the variability in the product line needs to evolve as well. A typical problem in such an evolution scenario is that the number of variable features and variants will explode, and thus become unmanageable. One of the reasons for this explosion is that obsolete variable features are not removed. In order to address this problem, we present a new method for restructuring and simplifying the provided variability in a software product line. Our method is based on concept analysis. It analyzes the realized variability in a software product line, and constructs a lattice that provides a classification of the usage of variable features in real products derived from the product line. We show how this classification can be used to derive restructuring strategies for variability that solve the problem of variability explosion. The effectiveness of our method is demonstrated by presenting a case study of restructuring the variability in a large industrial software product line.

Published: In Proceedings of 11th European Conference on Software Maintenance and Reengineering (CSMR'07), March 21-23, 2007, Amsterdam, Netherlands, IEEE Computer Society Press.

B.2   Variability Optimization

Variability Optimization in Software Product Lines [Loe07]

Abstract: The widespread use of the product line approach allows companies to realize significant improvements in time-to-market, cost, productivity, and quality. However, these companies very often face the challenge of increasing degrees of complexity caused by the variability that needs to be provided by their product lines. To address this problem, we have developed a method to optimize, i.e., to document, to analyze, and to simplify the provided variability of software product lines without affecting the configurability of the software product line for existing and future products.

Published: In Proceedings of Bosch Conference on Systems and Software Engineering, March 26-28, 2007, Ludwigsburg, Germany.

Optimization of Variability in Software Product Lines [LP07a]

Abstract: The widespread use of the product line approach allows companies to realize significant improvements in time-to-market, cost, productivity, and quality. However, a fundamental problem in software product line engineering is that a product line of industrial size can easily incorporate several thousand variable features. The complexity caused by this amount of variability makes variability management and product derivation tasks extremely difficult. To address this problem, we present a new method to optimize the variability provided in a software product line. Our method constructs a visualization that provides a classification of the usage of variable features in real products derived from the product line. We show how this classification can be used to derive restructuring strategies for simplifying the variability. The effectiveness of our work is demonstrated by presenting a case study of optimizing the variability in a large industrial software product line.

Published: In Proceedings of 11th International Software Product Line Conference (SPLC'07), September 10-14, 2007, Kyoto, Japan, IEEE Computer Society Press.

B.3   Tool Support

Entwicklung eines Tools zur Extraktion und Analyse von Variationspunkten und Varianten in Software-Produktlinien [Li06]

Author: Sa Li, Diplomarbeit, Lehrstuhl für Programmiersprachen und Übersetzer, Universität Tübingen.

Development of a Tool for Variability Optimization in Software Product Lines [Per07]

Author: Jelena Perunicic, Master Thesis, University of Applied Sciences Stuttgart.

Bibliography

[AG01]   Michalis Anastasopoulos and Cristina Gacek. Implementing product line
              variabilities. In *Proceedings of the 2001 Symposium on Software Reusabil-
              ity (SSR'01)*, pages 109–117, New York, NY, USA, 2001. ACM Press.

[ALRS05]   Sven Apel, Thomas Leich, Marko Rosenmüller, and Gunter Saake. Fea-
              tureC++: On the symbiosis of feature-oriented and aspect-oriented pro-
              gramming. In *Proceedings of the 4th International Conference on Gen-
              erative Programming and Component Engineering (GPCE'05)*, Tallinn,
              Estonia, 2005.

[AMS06]   Timo Asikainen, Tomi Mannisto, and Timo Soininen. A unified conceptual
              foundation for feature modelling. In *Proceedings of the 10th International
              on Software Product Line Conference (SPLC'06)*, pages 31–40, Washing-
              ton, DC, USA, 2006. IEEE Computer Society.

[AMS07]   Timo Asikainen, Tomi Männistö, and Timo Soininen. Kumbang: A do-
              main ontology for modelling variability in software product families. *Adv.
              Eng. Inform.*, 21(1):23–40, 2007.

[AS94]   Rakesh Agrawal and Ramakrishnan Srikant. Fast algorithms for mining
              association rules. In Jorge B. Bocca, Matthias Jarke, and Carlo Zaniolo,
              editors, *Proceedings of the 20th International Conference on Very Large
              Data Bases (VLDB'94)*, pages 487–499. Morgan Kaufmann, 12–15 1994.

[Asi04]   T. Asikainen. Modelling methods for managing variability of configurable
              software product families. Master's thesis, Helsinki University of Tech-
              nology, 2004.

[ASM04]   T. Asikainen, T. Soininen, and T. Männistö. A Koala-based approach for
              modelling and deploying configurable software product families. In *Pro-
              ceedings of the 5th Workshop on Product Family Engineering (PFE-5)*,
              number LNCS 3014 in 1, pages 225–249. Springer Verlag Lecture Notes
              on Computer Science, May 2004.

[Bas96]   Paul G. Bassett. *Framing Software Reuse: Lessons from the real world*.
              Prentice Hall Inc., 1996.

[Bat03]   Don Batory. A tutorial on feature oriented programming and product-lines. In *Proceedings of the 25th International Conference on Software Engineering (ICSE'03)*, pages 753–754, Washington, DC, USA, 2003. IEEE Computer Society.

[BCM+04]   Günter Böckle, Paul Clements, John D. McGregor, Dirk Muthig, and Klaus Schmid. Calculating ROI for software product lines. *IEEE Software*, 21(3):23–31, 2004.

[BD99]   Bernd Bruegge and Allen A. Dutoit. *Object-Oriented Software Engineering; Conquering Complex and Changing Systems*. Prentice Hall PTR, Upper Saddle River, NJ, USA, 1999.

[Bec03]   M. Becker. Mapping variabilities onto product family assets. In *Proceedings of the International Colloquium of the Sonderforschungsbereich 501*. University of Kaiserslautern, March 2003.

[Beu03]   Danilo Beuche. *Composition and Construction of Embedded Software Families*. PhD thesis, Otto-von-Guericke-Universität Magdeburg, 2003.

[BFG+01]   J. Bosch, G. Florijn, D. Greefhorst, J. Kuusela, and H. Obbink. Variability issues in software product lines. In *Proceedings of the Fourth International Workshop on Product Family Engineering (PFE-4)*, pages 11–19, 2001.

[BFK+99]   Joachim Bayer, Oliver Flege, Peter Knauber, Roland Laqua, Dirk Muthig, Klaus Schmid, Tanya Widen, and Jean-Marc DeBaud. PuLSE: a methodology to develop software product lines. In *Proceedings of the 5th ACM SIGSOFT Symposium on Software Reusability (SSR'99)*, pages 122–131, New York, NY, USA, 1999. ACM Press.

[BGGB01]   M. Becker, L. Geyer, A. Gilbert, and K. Becker. Comprehensive variability modelling to facilitate efficient variability treatment. In *Fourth International Workshop on Product Family Engineering (PFE-4)*, Bilbao, Spain, 2001.

[BGL+04]   F. Bachmann, M. Goedicke, J. Leite, R. Nord, K. Pohl, B. Rames, and A. Vilbig. Managing variability in product family development. In *Proceedings of the 5th Workshop on Product Family Engineering (PFE-5)*, May 2004.

[BGW+99]   Joachim Bayer, Jean-François Girard, Martin Würthner, Jean-Marc DeBaud, and Martin Apel. Transitioning legacy assets to a product line architecture. *SIGSOFT Softw. Eng. Notes*, 24(6):446–463, 1999.

[BHS02]   Peter Becker, Joachim Hereth, and Gerd Stumme. ToscanaJ: An open source tool for qualitative data analysis. In V. Duquenne, B. Ganter, M. Liquiere, E. M. Nguifo, and G. Stumme, editors, *Proceedings of the*

FCAKDD Workshop colocated with the 15th European Conference on Artificial Intelligence (ECAI 2002), July 23 2002.

[Bir79]   Garrett Birkhoff. *Lattice Theory*. American Mathematical Society, Providence, RI, 1979.

[BM01]   Ira D. Baxter and Michael Mehlich. Preprocessor conditional removal by simple partial evaluation. In *Proceedings of the 8th Working Conference on Reverse Engineering (WCRE'01)*, page 281, Washington, DC, USA, 2001. IEEE Computer Society.

[Boe88]   Barry W. Boehm. A spiral model of software development and enhancement. *IEEE Computer*, 21(5)(5):61–72, 1988.

[Bos00]   Jan Bosch. *Design and use of software architectures: adopting and evolving a product-line approach*. ACM Press/Addison-Wesley Publishing Co., New York, NY, USA, 2000.

[BST⁺94]   Don S. Batory, Vivek Singhal, Jeff Thomas, Sankar Dasari, Bart J. Geraci, and Marty Sirkin. The genvoca model of software-system generators. *IEEE Software*, 11(5):89–94, 1994.

[Bur00]   Peter Burmeister. ConImp: Ein Programm zur Formalen Begriffsanalyse. In Gerd Stumme and Rudolf Wille, editors, *Begriffliche Wissensverarbeitung: Methoden und Anwendungen*, pages 25–56, Heidelberg, 2000. Springer.

[CE00]   Krzysztof Czarnecki and Ulrich W. Eisenecker. *Generative Programming: Methods, Tools, and Applications*. Addisson Wesley, 2000.

[CHW98]   James Coplien, Daniel Hoffman, and David Weiss. Commonality and variability in software engineering. *IEEE Software*, 15(6):37–45, 1998.

[CK05]   Krzysztof Czarnecki and Chang Hwan Peter Kim. Cardinality-based feature modeling and constraints: A progress report. In *Proceedings of the International Workshop on Software Factories At OOPSLA 2005*, 2005.

[CMC05]   Paul C. Clements, John D. McGregor, and S. G. Cohen. The structured intuitive model for product line economics (simple). Technical report, Carnegie Mellon University, Software Engineering Institute, 2005.

[CN01]   Paul Clements and Linda Northrop. *Software Product Lines: Practices and Patterns*. Addison-Wesley, 2001.

[Coh99]   Sholom Cohen. From product-line architectures to products. In *Proceedings of the ECOOP'99 Workshop on Object-Oriented Technology*, pages 198–199, London, UK, 1999. Springer-Verlag.

[Coh03] S. G. Cohen. Predicting when product line investment pays. Technical Report CMU/SEI-2003-TN-017, Carnegie Mellon University, Software Engineering Institute, 2003.

[CSFP04] Ben Collins-Sussman, Brian W. Fitzpatrick, and C. Michael Pilato. *Version Control With Subversion*. O'Reilly & Associates, Inc., Sebastopol, CA, USA, 2004.

[CW85] Luca Cardelli and Peter Wegner. On understanding types, data abstraction, and polymorphism. *ACM Comput. Surv.*, 17(4):471–523, 1985.

[CW98] Reidar Conradi and Bernhard Westfechtel. Version models for software configuration management. In *ACM Comput. Surv.*, volume 30, pages 232–282. ACM Press, 1998.

[DdHT01] Eric M. Dashofy, André Van der Hoek, and Richard N. Taylor. A highly-extensible, xml-based architecture description language. In *Proceedings of the Working IEEE/IFIP Conference on Software Architecture (WICSA'01)*, page 103, Washington, DC, USA, 2001. IEEE Computer Society.

[DGR07] D. Dhungana, P. Gruenbacher, and R. Rabiser. DecisionKing: A flexible and extensible tool for integrated variability modeling. In *Proceedings of the First International Workshop on Variability Modeling of Software-Intensive Systems (VaMoS'07)*, 2007.

[Dhu06] Deepak Dhungana. Integrated variability modeling of features and architecture in software product line engineering. In *Proceedings of the 21st IEEE International Conference on Automated Software Engineering (ASE'06)*, pages 327–330, Washington, DC, USA, 2006. IEEE Computer Society.

[DRG+06] Deepak Dhungana, Rick Rabiser, Paul Grunbacher, Herbert Prahofer, Christian Federspiel, and Klaus Lehner. Architectural knowledge in product line engineering: An industrial case study. In *Proceedings of the 32nd EUROMICRO Conference on Software Engineering and Advanced Applications (EUROMICRO'06)*, pages 186–197, Washington, DC, USA, 2006. IEEE Computer Society.

[DRG07] Deepak Dhungana, Rick Rabiser, and Paul Grünbacher. Decision-oriented modeling of product line architectures. In *Proceedings of Sixth Working IEEE / IFIP Conference on Software Architecture (WICSA'07)*, page 22, Mumbai, Maharashtra, India, January 2007.

[DS99] Jean-Marc DeBaud and Klaus Schmid. A systematic approach to derive the scope of software product lines. In *Proceedings of the 21st international conference on Software engineering (ICSE'99)*, pages 34–43, Los Alamitos, CA, USA, 1999. IEEE Computer Society Press.

[DSB04]   Sybren Deelstra, Marco Sinnema, and Jan Bosch. Experiences in soft-
             ware product families: Problems and issues during product derivation. In
             *Proceedings of the Third International Software Product Line Conference
             (SPLC'04)*, pages 165–182, Boston, MA, USA, August 30-September 2
             2004.

[DSB05]   Sybren Deelstra, Marco Sinnema, and Jan Bosch. Product derivation in
             software product families: a case study. *Journal of Systems and Software*,
             74(2):173–194, 2005.

[DSNB04]   S. Deelstra, M. Sinnema, J. Nijhuis, and J. Bosch. COSVAM: A technique
             for assessing software variability in software product families. In *Proceed-
             ings of the 20th IEEE International Conference on Software Maintenance
             (ICSM'04)*, pages 458–462, September 2004.

[DvdHT02]   Eric M. Dashofy, André van der Hoek, and Richard N. Taylor. An infras-
             tructure for the rapid development of XML-based architecture description
             languages. In *Proceedings of the 24th International Conference on Soft-
             ware Engineering (ICSE'02)*, pages 266–276, New York, NY, USA, 2002.
             ACM Press.

[EC95]   Jacky Estublier and Rubby Casallas. Three dimensional versioning. In
             *Selected papers from the ICSE SCM-4 and SCM-5 Workshops, on Software
             Configuration Management*, pages 118–135, London, UK, 1995. Springer-
             Verlag.

[EKS01]   T. Eisenbarth, R. Koschke, and D. Simon. Feature-driven program under-
             standing using concept analysis of execution traces. In *Proceedings of the
             9th International Workshop on Program Comprehension (IWPC'01)*, page
             300, Washington, DC, USA, 2001. IEEE Computer Society.

[EKS02]   Thomas Eisenbarth, Rainer Koschke, and Daniel Simon. A formal method
             for the analysis of product maps. In *International Workshop on Require-
             ments Engineering for Product Lines (REPL'02)*, Essen, September 9
             2002.

[EKS03]   Thomas Eisenbarth, Rainer Koschke, and Daniel Simon. Locating features
             in source code. *IEEE Transactions on Software Engineering*, 29(3):210–
             224, 2003.

[ES01a]   T. Eisenbarth and D. Simon. Aiding program comprehension by static
             and dynamic feature analysis. In *Proceedings of the IEEE International
             Conference on Software Maintenance (ICSM'01)*, page 602, Washington,
             DC, USA, 2001. IEEE Computer Society.

[ES01b]   Thomas Eisenbarth and Daniel Simon. Guiding feature asset mining for
             software product line development. In *Proceedings of the International*

Workshop on Product Line Engineering - The Early Steps: Planning, Modeling, and Managing (PLEES'01), 2001.

[FFB02]   Dániel Fey, Róbert Fajta, and András Boros. Feature modeling: A meta-model to enhance usability and usefulness. In *Proceedings of the Second International Conference on Software Product Lines (SPLC'02)*, pages 198–216, London, UK, 2002. Springer-Verlag.

[FKBA07]   Pierre Frenzel, Rainer Koschke, Andreas Breu, and Karsten Angstmann. Extending the reflection method for consolidating software variants into product lines. In *Proc. of 14th Working Conference on Reverse Engineering*, pages 160–169, Vancouver, British Columbia, Canada, October 29–31 2007. IEEE Computer Society.

[FV03]   D. Faust and C. Verhoef. Software product line migration and deployment. *Software: Practice & Experience*, 33:933–955, 2003.

[GB02]   L. Geyer and M. Becker. On the influence of variabilities on the application engineering process of a product family. In *Proceedings of the 2nd International Conference on Software Product Lines (SPLC'02)*, San Diego, USA, 2002.

[GFd98]   M. Griss, J. Favaro, and M. d'Alessandro. Integrating feature modeling with the RSEB. In *Proceedings of the 5th International Conference on Software Reuse (ICSR'98)*, pages 76–85, Vancouver, BC, Canada, 1998.

[Gru86]   Dick Grune. Concurrent versions system, a method for independent cooperation. Technical Report IR 113, Vrije Universiteit, Amsterdam, 1986.

[GS02]   Hassan Gomaa and Michael Eonsuk Shin. Multiple-view meta-modeling of software product lines. In *Proceedings of the Eighth International Conference on Engineering of Complex Computer Systems (ICECCS '02)*, page 238, Washington, DC, USA, 2002. IEEE Computer Society.

[GW96]   Bernhard Ganter and Rudolf Wille. *Formal Concept Analysis - Mathematical Foundations*. Springer Verlag, 1996.

[GW04]   Hassan Gomaa and Diana L. Webber. Modeling adaptive and evolvable software product lines using the variation point model. In *Proceedings of the Proceedings of the 37th Annual Hawaii International Conference on System Sciences (HICSS'04)*, pages 10–20, Washington, DC, USA, 2004. IEEE Computer Society.

[HBJ+03]   Christof Hammel, Birgit Boss, Holger Jessen, Andreas Traub, Christian Tischer, and Harald Hönninger. A common software architecture for diesel and gasoline engine control systems of the new generation EDC/MED17. In *World Congress & Exhibition of Automotive Engineers (SAE 2003)*, number 2003-01-1048 in SAE Technical Papers, Detroit, MI, USA, March 2003.

[Hei99]   Juergen Heina. *Variantenmanagement: Kosten-Nutzen Bewertung zur Optimierung der Variantenvielfalt.* PhD thesis, Brandenburgische Technische Universitaet, Cottbus, 1999.

[HK03]   L. Hotz and T. Krebs. Supporting the product derivation process with a knowledge-based approach. In *Proceedings of Software Variability Management Workshop at ICSE 2003.*, Portland, Oregon, 2003.

[HKW+06]   L. Hotz, T. Krebs, K. Wolter, J. Nijhuis, S. Deelstra, M. Sinnema, and J. MacGregor. *Configuration in Industrial Product Families - The ConIPF Methodology.* IOS Press, 2006.

[HPR89]   Susan Horwitz, Jan Prins, and Thomas Reps. Integrating noninterfering versions of programs. *ACM Transactions on Programming Language Systems*, 11(3):345–387, 1989.

[IDE93]   IDEF0. http://www.idef.com/idef0.html, December 1993.

[JBR99]   Ivar Jacobson, Grady Booch, and James Rumbaugh. *The unified software development process.* Addison-Wesley Longman Publishing Co., Inc., Boston, MA, USA, 1999.

[JGJ97]   I. Jacobson, M. Griss, and P. Jonsson. *Software Reuse: Architecture, Process and Organization for Business Sucess.* Addison-Wesley, Reading, MA, 1997.

[JRvdL00]   Mehdi Jazayeri, Alexander Ran, and Frank van der Linden. *Software architecture for product families: principles and practice.* Addison-Wesley Longman Publishing Co., Inc., Boston, MA, USA, 2000.

[KCH+90]   K. C. Kang, S. G. Cohen, J. A. Hess, W. E. Novak, and A. S. Peterson. Feature-oriented domain analysis (FODA) feasibility study. Technical Report CMU/SEI-90-TR-21, SEI, 1990.

[KKL+98]   Kyo C. Kang, Sajoong Kim, Jaejoon Lee, Kijoo Kim, Euiseob Shin, and Moonhang Huh. FORM: A feature-oriented reuse method with domain-specific reference architectures. *Annual Software Engineering*, 5:143–168, 1998.

[KLD02]   Kyo C. Kang, Jaejoon Lee, and Patrick Donohoe. Feature-oriented product line engineering. *IEEE Software*, 19(4):58–65, 2002.

[KLM+97]   Gregor Kiczales, John Lamping, Anurag Mendhekar, Chris Maeda, Cristina Videira Lopes, Jean-Marc Loingtier, and John Irwin. Aspect-oriented programming. In *Proceedings of the 11th European Conference on Object-Oriented Programming (ECOOP'97)*, pages 220–242,

Jyväskylä, Finland, June 1997. Springer Verlag, Berlin and Heidelberg, Germany, 1997.

[KMB⁺02]   Peter Knauber, Jesus Bermejo Munoz, Günter Böckle, Julio Cesar Sampaio do Prado Leite, Frank van der Linden, Linda M. Northrop, Michael Stark, and David M. Weiss. Quantifying product line benefits. In *Proceedings of the 4th International Workshop on Software Product-Family Engineering (PFE '01)*, pages 155–163, London, UK, 2002. Springer-Verlag.

[KMPY05]   Ronny Kolb, Dirk Muthig, Thomas Patzke, and Kazuyuki Yamauchi. A case study in refactoring a legacy component for reuse in a product line. In *Proceedings of the 21st IEEE International Conference on Software Maintenance (ICSM'05)*, pages 369–378, Washington, DC, USA, 2005. IEEE Computer Society.

[KMPY06]   Ronny Kolb, Dirk Muthig, Thomas Patzke, and Kazuyuki Yamauchi. Refactoring a legacy component for reuse in a software product line: a case study: Practice articles. *J. Softw. Maint. Evol.*, 18(2):109–132, 2006.

[KR78]   B. W. Kernighan and D. M. Ritchie. *The C Programming Language*. Prentice-Hall, Englewood Cliffs, New Jersey, 1978.

[Kru95]   Philippe Kruchten. The 4+1 view model of architecture. *IEEE Software*, 12(6):42–50, 1995.

[Kru02]   Charles W. Krueger. Variation management for software production lines. In *Proceedings of the Second International Software Product Line Conference, SPLC 2, San Diego, CA, USA, August 19-22, 2002*, volume 2379 of *Lecture Notes in Computer Science*, pages 37–48. Springer, 2002.

[KS94]   Maren Krone and Gregor Snelting. On the inference of configuration structures from source code. In *Proceedings of the 16th International Conference on Software Engineering (ICSE'94)*, pages 49–57, Los Alamitos, CA, USA, 1994.

[KS03]   Rainer Koschke and Daniel Simon. Hierarchical reflexion models. In *Proceedings of the 10th Working Conference on Reverse Engineering (WCRE '03)*, page 36, Washington, DC, USA, 2003. IEEE Computer Society.

[Leb94]   David B. Leblang. The CM challenge: Configuration management that works. *Trends in Software*, pages 1–37, 1994.

[Li06]   Sa Li. Entwicklung eines Tools zur Extraktion und Analyse von Variationspunkten und Varianten in Software Produktlinien. Master's thesis, University of Tuebingen, 2006.

[Lin00]   Christian Lindig. Fast concept analysis. In *Working with Conceptual Struc-tures - Contributions to ICCS 2000*, pages 152–161. Shaker Verlag, August 2000.

[LJG05]   Sana Ben Abdallah Ben Lamine, Lamia Labed Jilani, and Henda Haj-jami Ben Ghezala. Cost estimation for product line engineering using cots components. In *Proceedings of the 9th International Software Product Line Conference (SPLC 2005)*, 2005.

[LLM99]   Karl Lieberherr, David Lorenz, and Mira Mezini. Programming with as-pectual components. Technical Report NU-CCS-99-01, College of Com-puter Science, Northeastern University, Boston, MA, March 1999.

[Loe06]   Felix Loesch. A formal method to identify variation points in product line assets. In *Workshop Software-Reengineering (WSR'06)*, Bad Honnef, Germany, May 2006.

[Loe07]   Felix Loesch. Variability optimization in software product lines. In *Pro-ceedings of 2nd Bosch Conference on Software and Systems Engineering (BOCSE'07)*, page 19, Ludwigsburg, March 26-28 2007. Robert Bosch GmbH.

[LP07a]   Felix Loesch and Erhard Ploedereder. Optimization of variability in soft-ware product lines. In *Proceedings of the 11th International Software Product Line Conference (SPLC 2007)*, pages 151–162, Kyoto, Japan, Sept 10-14, 2007. IEEE Computer Society.

[LP07b]   Felix Loesch and Erhard Ploedereder. Restructuring variability in soft-ware product lines using concept analysis of product configurations. In *Proceedings of the 11th European Conference on Software Maintenance and Reengineering (CSMR'07)*, pages 159–168, Amsterdam, Netherlands, March 21-23, 2007.

[MA96]   Boris Magnusson and Ulf Asklund. Fine grained version control of config-urations in coop/orm. In *Proceedings of the SCM-6 Workshop on System Configuration Management (ICSE'96)*, pages 31–48, London, UK, 1996. Springer-Verlag.

[MBKM08] T. Mende, F. Beckwermert, R. Koschke, and G. Meier. Supporting the grow-and-prune model in software product lines evolution using clone de-tection. In *Proceedings of 12th European Conference on Software Main-tenance and Reengineering (CSMR 2008)*, pages 163–172, April 2008.

[McI68]   M.D. McIlroy. Mass produced software components. In *Proceedings of the NATO Software Engineering Conference*, pages 138–155, Garmisch, Germany, 1968.

[MD94]   Jonathan P. Munson and Prasun Dewan. A flexible object merging framework. In *Proceedings of the 1994 ACM Conference on Computer Supported Cooperative Work (CSCW '94)*, pages 231–242, New York, NY, USA, 1994. ACM.

[Men02]   T. Mens. A state-of-the-art survey on software merging. *IEEE Transactions on Software Engineering*, 28(5):449–462, 2002.

[Nei80]   James Milne Neighbors. *Software construction using components*. PhD thesis, University of California, Irvine, 1980.

[NI01]   Eila Niemelä and Tuomas Ihme. Product line software engineering of embedded systems. *SIGSOFT Software Engineering Notes*, 26(3):118–125, 2001.

[OBG+89]   Flávio Oquendo, Karima Berrada, Ferdinando Gallo, Régis Minot, and Ian Thomas. Version management in the pact integrated software engineering environment. In *Proceedings of the 2nd European Software Engineering Conference (ESEC '89)*, pages 222–242, London, UK, 1989. Springer-Verlag.

[OMG03]   OMG. UML 2.0 OCL Specification. http://www.omg.org/docs/ptc/03-10-14.pdf, 2003.

[Par76]   David L. Parnas. On the design and development of program families. *IEEE Transactions on Software Engineering*, 2(1):1–9, 1976.

[PBvdL05]   Klaus Pohl, Günter Böckle, and Frank van der Linden. *Software Product Line Engineering : Foundations, Principles and Techniques*. Springer, September 2005.

[Per07]   Jelena Perunicic. Development of a tool for variability analysis and optimization in software product lines. Master's thesis, University of Applied Sciences Stuttgart, 2007.

[PS03]   Pure-Systems. Variability management with pure::variants. http://www.pure-systems.com, 2003.

[PSV98]   Dewayne E. Perry, Harvey P. Siy, and Lawrence G. Votta. Parallel changes in large scale software development: An observational case study. In *Proceedings of the 20th International Conference on Software Engineering (ICSE'98)*, pages 251–260, 1998.

[Rat03]   Rational Software Corporation. *Rational ClearCase Command Reference*, 2003.06.00 edition, 2003.

[RDG06] Rick Rabiser, Deepak Dhungana, and Paul Gruenbacher. Integrating knowledge-based product configuration and product line engineering: An industrial example. In *Workshop on Configuration, collocated with 17th European Conference on Artifical Intelligence (ECAI'06)*, 2006.

[RDG07] R. Rabiser, D. Dhungana, and P. Gruenbacher. Tool support for product derivation in large-scale product lines: A wizard-based approach. In *1st International Workshop on Visualisation in Software Product Line Engineering (ViSPLE 2007), held in conjunction with SPLC 2007*, 2007.

[RGD07] Rick Rabiser, Paul Gruenbacher, and Deepak Dhungana. Supporting product derivation by adapting and augmenting variability models. In *Proceedings of the 11th International Software Product Line Conference (SPLC 2007)*, pages 141–150, Washington, DC, USA, 2007. IEEE Computer Society.

[Roc75] M. J. Rochkind. The source code control system. *IEEE Transactions on Software Engineering*, 1(4):364–370, 1975.

[Roy70] Winston W. Royce. Managing the development of large software systems: Concepts and techniques. In *Technical Papers of Western Electronic Show and Convention (WesCon)*, Los Angeles, USA, August 25-28 1970.

[RR03] Claudio Riva and Christian Del Rosso. Experiences with software product family evolution. In *Proceedings of the 6th International Workshop on Principles of Software Evolution (IWPSE'03)*, page 161, Washington, DC, USA, 2003. IEEE Computer Society.

[RU98] D. Robertson and K. Ulrich. Planning for product platforms. In *Sloan Management Review*, volume 39, pages 19–31, 1998.

[SB98] Yannis Smaragdakis and Don Batory. Implementing layered designs with mixin layers. In *Proceedings of the European Conference on Object-Oriented Programming (ECOOP'98)*, pages 550–570. Springer-Verlag LNCS 1445, 1998.

[SB02] Yannis Smaragdakis and Don Batory. Mixin layers: an object-oriented implementation technique for refinements and collaboration-based designs. *ACM Transactions on Software Engineering Methodologies*, 11(2):215–255, 2002.

[SCK+96] M. Simos, D. Creps, C. Klinger, L. Levine, and D. Allemang. Software technology for adaptable reliable systems (STARS) organization domain modeling (ODM) guidebook version 2.0. Technical Report STARS-VC-A025/001/00, Lockheed Martin Tactical Defense Systems, Manassas, VA, USA, 1996.

[SD07] Marco Sinnema and Sybren Deelstra. Classifying variability modeling techniques. *Information and Software Technology*, 49(7):717–739, 2007.

[SDNB04a] M. Sinnema, S. Deelstra, J. Nijhuis, and J. Bosch. Managing variability in software product families. In *Proceedings of the 2nd Groningen Workshop on Software Variability Management*, 2004.

[SDNB04b] Marco Sinnema, Sybren Deelstra, Jan Nijhuis, and Jan Bosch. COVA-MOF: A framework for modeling variability in software product families. In *Proceedings of the Third International Conference on Software Product Lines (SPLC'04)*, pages 197–213, Boston, MA, USA, August 30-September 2 2004.

[SE02] Daniel Simon and Thomas Eisenbarth. Evolutionary introduction of software product lines. In *Proceedings of the Second International Software Product Line Conference (SPLC'02)*, pages 272–283, San Diego, CA, USA, August 2002.

[SEI] SEI. A framework for product line practice. http://www.sei.cmu.edu/plp.

[Sei96] Christopher Seiwald. Inter-file branching - a practical method for representing variants. In *Proceedings of the SCM-6 Workshop on System Configuration Management (ICSE'96)*, pages 67–75, London, UK, 1996. Springer-Verlag.

[SGB01] M. Svahnberg, J. van Gurp, and J. Bosch. A taxonomy of variability realization techniques. Technical report, University of Groningen, 2001.

[Sim05] Daniel Simon. *Lokalisierung von Merkmalen in Softwaresystemen*. PhD thesis, University of Stuttgart, 2005.

[SJ04] Klaus Schmid and Isabel John. A customizable approach to full lifecycle variability management. *Science of Computer Programming*, 53(3):259–284, 2004.

[Sne96] Gregor Snelting. Reengineering of configurations based on mathematical concept analysis. *ACM Transactions on Software Engineering and Methodology*, 5(2):146–189, 1996.

[STB+04] Mirjam Steger, Christian Tischer, Birgit Boss, Andreas Müller, Oliver Pertler, Wolfgang Stolz, and Stefan Ferber. Introducing PLA at Bosch Gasoline Systems: Experiences and Practices. In *Proceedings of the Third International Conference on Software Product Lines (SPLC'04)*, pages 34–50, Boston, MA, USA, 2004.

[Str67]   Christopher Strachey. Fundamental concepts in programming languages. Lecture Notes, International Summer School in Computer Programming, Copenhagen, August 1967. Reprinted in *Higher-Order and Symbolic Computation*, 13(1/2), pp. 1–49, 2000.

[Str86]   Bjarne Stroustrup. *The C++ Programming Language, First Edition*. Addison-Wesley, 1986.

[Swa76]   E. Burton Swanson. The dimensions of maintenance. In *Proceedings of the 2nd International Conference on Software Engineering (ICSE'76)*, pages 492–497, Los Alamitos, CA, USA, 1976. IEEE Computer Society Press.

[TH02a]   Steffen Thiel and Andreas Hein. Modeling and using product line variability in automotive systems. *IEEE Software*, 19(4):66–72, 2002.

[TH02b]   Steffen Thiel and Andreas Hein. Systematic integration of variability into product line architecture design. In *Proceedings of the Second International Conference on Software Product Lines (SPLC'02)*, pages 130–153, London, UK, 2002. Springer-Verlag.

[Tic85]   Walter F. Tichy. RCS — a system for version control. *Software — Practice and Experience*, 15(7):637–654, 1985.

[TMKG07]   Christian Tischer, Andreas Mueller, Markus Ketterer, and Lars Geyer. Why does it take that long? Establishing product lines in the automotive domain. In *Proceedings of the 11th International Software Product Line Conference (SPLC 2007)*, pages 269–274, Washington, DC, USA, 2007. IEEE Computer Society.

[TOHS99]   Peri Tarr, Harold Ossher, William Harrison, and Stanley M. Sutton, Jr. N degrees of separation: Multi-dimensional separation of concerns. In *Proceedings of the 21st International Conference on Software Engineering (ICSE'99)*, pages 107–119, New York, May 1999.

[vdH04]   André van der Hoek. Design-time product line architectures for any-time variability. *Sci. Comput. Program.*, 53(3):285–304, 2004.

[vdL02]   Frank van der Linden. Software Product Families in Europe: The Esaps & Café Projects. *IEEE Software*, 19(4):41–49, 2002.

[vOvdKM00] Rob van Ommering, Frank van der Linden, Jeff Kramer, and Jeff Magee. The koala component model for consumer electronics software. *IEEE Computer*, 33(3):78–85, 2000.

[W3C05]   W3C. XML Path Language (XPath) 2.0. http://www.w3.org/TR/xpath20/, 2005.

[WL99]   David M. Weiss and Chi Tau Robert Lai. *Software product-line engineer-ing: a family-based software development process*. Addison-Wesley Long-man Publishing Co., Inc., Boston, MA, USA, 1999.

[Yev00]   Serhiy A. Yevtushenko.   System of data analysis "concept explorer". In *Proceedings of the 7th National Conference on Artifcial Intelligence*, pages 127–134, Russia, 2000.

Curriculum Vitae

Personal Information

Name	Felix Lösch
Date of Birth	April 14th, 1980
Place of Birth	Stuttgart, Germany
Nationality	German

Education

Dr. rer. nat. (2008)
Institution: University of Stuttgart, Germany, Institute for Software Technology. *Supervisors:* Prof. Dr. E. Plödereder and Prof. Dr. R. Koschke (University of Bremen). *Dissertation (Dr. rer. nat.):* "Optimization of Variability in Software Product Lines".

Dipl.-Inf. (2005)
Institution: University of Stuttgart, Germany, Institute for Software Technology. *Supervisors:* Prof. Dr. J. Ludewig and Prof. Dr. E. Plödereder. *Diploma Thesis:* "Analysis of Control Flow in Java".

M.Sc. (2004)
Institution: Georgia Institute of Technology, Atlanta, USA. *Supervisors:* Prof. M.-J. Harrold and Prof. A. Orso. *Thesis Project:* "Tool for the Analysis and Visualization of Implicit Control Flow in Java".

Work Experience

2005-2008
Employer: Robert Bosch GmbH, Corporate Sector Research and Advance Engineering, Systems Engineering (CR/AEY), Schwieberdingen, Germany. *Function:* Doctoral researcher.

2000-2001
Employer: IBM Deutschland Entwicklung GmbH, Böblingen, Germany. *Function:* Werkstudent. *Tasks:* Development of tools for automated document transformation.

Work Address
Robert Bosch GmbH
Felix Lösch (CR/AEY1)
Postfach 30 02 40
70442 Stuttgart
felix.loesch@bosch.com